THE LOST *HISTORY* OF PETER THE PATRICIAN

The Lost History *of Peter the Patrician* is an annotated translation from the Greek of the fragments of Peter's *History*, including additional fragments which are now more often considered the work of the Roman historian Cassius Dio's so-called Anonymous Continuer. Banchich's annotation helps clarify the relationship of Peter's work to that of Cassius Dio. Focusing on the historical and historiographical rather than philological, he provides a strong framework for the understanding of this increasingly important source for the third and fourth centuries A.D.

With an introduction on Peter himself – a distinguished administrator and diplomat at the court of Justinian – assessing his literary output, the relationship of the fragments of Peter's *History* to the fragments of the Anonymous Continuer, and the contentious issue of the place of this evidence within the framework of late antique historiography, *The Lost* History *of Peter the Patrician* will be an invaluable resource for those interested in the history of the Roman world in general and of the third and fourth centuries A.D. in particular.

Thomas M. Banchich is Professor of Classics and History at Canisius College, Buffalo, New York. His research interests include ancient philosophy, history, and historiography. He is the author of *The* History *of Zonaras* (Routledge, 2009).

Routledge Classical Translations

Also available from Routledge:

Ctesias' 'History of Persia': Tales of the Orient
Lloyd Llewellyn-Jones and James Robson

The History *of Zonaras: From Alexander Severus to the Death of Theodosius the Great*
Trans. By Thomas M. Banchich and Eugene N. Lane
Introduction and commentary by Thomas M. Banchich

Greek and Roman Military Writers: Selected Readings
Brian Campbell

Ancient Greek Literary Letters: Selections in Translation
Patricia A. Rosenmeyer

Coming soon:

Byzantine Readings of Ancient Historians
Anthony Kaldellis

THE LOST *HISTORY* OF PETER THE PATRICIAN

An Account of Rome's Imperial Past from the Age of Justinian

Thomas M. Banchich

Routledge
Taylor & Francis Group
LONDON AND NEW YORK

First published 2015
by Routledge
2 Park Square, Milton Park, Abingdon, Oxon OX14 4RN

and by Routledge
605 Third Avenue, New York, NY 10017

Routledge is an imprint of the Taylor & Francis Group, an informa business

British Library Cataloguing-in-Publication Data
A catalogue record for this book is available from the British Library

Library of Congress Cataloging-in-Publication Data
A catalog record has been requested for this book

ISBN: 978-0-415-51663-1 (hbk)
ISBN: 978-1-315-71458-5 (ebk)

Typeset in Garamond
by HWA Text and Data Management, London

AN HOMAGE TO

URSULUS BOISSEVAIN (1855–1930)

AND CARL DE BOOR (1848–1923)

CONTENTS

ACKNOWLEDGMENTS

In April of 2011, Anthony Kaldellis raised with me the possibility of preparing for Routledge a translation of and commentary on the fragments of the lost *History* of Peter the Patrician. I duly submitted a prospectus, which was accepted.

The project at that time seemed relatively simple. Peter's *History* had first captured my attention as a result of my interest in Julian the Apostate, then again within the context of my research on the remains of Eunapius' *History*, and most recently in conjunction with my work on Books XII–XIII of John Zonaras' *Epitome of Histories*. Along the way, I had read with a particularly precocious student, David Goehrig, the anonymous historian whose fifteen fragments followed those of Peter's eighteen in Carl Müller's *FHG* and which were sometimes assigned to Peter. Now, over three years after Professor Kaldellis' query, it is obvious that my optimism was unfounded. Diversions, duties, and demands – some pleasant, others hardly so – combined to compromise my scholarly agenda, and Müller's eighteen fragments – or, counting those of his *Anonymus*, thirty-three – have mushroomed to 215. The nature of the translation and the scope, purpose, and presentation of the commentary, too, changed.

Of singular importance was when I learned that Andrea Martolini planned to edit, translate, and comment on what survived of Peter's *History*. My knowledge of Martolini's publications convinced me that he would produce a work of very high quality. Late in October of 2011, by which time I had completed an initial version of my translations of Peter and of a broad range of parallel texts, I informed Dr. Martolini about my own project and proposed that I set it aside. It was with mixed feelings that I learned from him that his own research had reached an impasse. He then very graciously supplied me with a copy of his dissertation, thereby making my own task easier and, in retrospect, more intellectually stimulating. It is to him that I dedicate this work, for the shortcomings of which he is in no way culpable.

I am deeply appreciative of the real or feigned interest in Peter's fragments expressed by several colleagues, friends, and students. Most prominent among them are Patrick Clancy, Mark Collins, Bruce Dierenfield, Steve Maddox, Matthew Mitchell, Matthew Riley, Stephen Russell, Brian Serwicki, Sam Stahl, Kathryn Williams, and Walter Winkler. Christos Bakoyannis and Massimiliano Vitiello alerted me to some modern scholarship I might otherwise have overlooked and Laura Mecella surprised with me a copy of her exemplary book on Dexippus. Two students, Patrick McMahon and Arrianna Hart, and Joseph McLaughlin, Administrative Associate for the Canisius College Departments of Classics and History, helped in many ways. Barbara Boehnke and the rest of the staff of Canisius' Andrew L. Bouwhuis Library – Jessica Blum, Matt Kochan, and Lori Miller, in particular – consistently went above and beyond what I could reasonably have expected of them. Finally, thanks are due to Lola Harre, John Hodgson, Holly Knapp, and to the rest of those at Routledge who transformed my manuscript into a book.

ABBREVIATIONS

For the few abbreviations not listed below, see *OCD*[3], pp. xxix–liv.

ACC	*The Acts of the Council of Constantinople of 553*
Amm. Marc.	Ammianus Marcellinus
Anon. Cont.	Anonymous Continuer of Cassius Dio
Blockley, *Men.*	Blockley, *Menander the Guardsman*
BNJ	*Brill's New Jacoby*
BNP	*Brill's New Pauly*
CAH	*Cambridge Ancient History*
CAH[2]	*Cambridge Ancient History*, 2nd edition
Ced.	Cedrenus
CFHB	*Corpus Fontium Historiae Byzantinae*
CHI	*Cambridge History of Iran*
CSHB	*Corpus Scriptorum Historiae Byzantinae*
EBH	Treadgold, *The Early Byzantine Historians*
EH	*Excerpta Historica Iussu Imperatoris Constantini Porphyrogeniti Confecta*
EI	*Excertpa de Insidiis*
ELGR	*Excerpta de Legationibus Gentium ad Romanos*
ELRG	*Excerpta de Legationibus Romanorum ad Gentes*
Epit. de Caes.	*Epitome de Caesaribus*
ES	*Excerpta de Sententiis*
Eun. *Hist.*	Eunapius' *History*
EV	*Excerpta de Virtutibus et Vitiis*
F	Fragment
FCH	Blockley, *The Fragmentary Classicising Historians of the Later Roman Empire*
FgrH	*Die Fragmente der griechischen Historiker*
FHG	*Fragmenta Historicorum Graecorum*
HE	*Historia Ecclesiastica*

Krumbacher	Krumbacher, *Geschichte der byzantinischen Litteratur*
Lactant. *De Mort. Pers.*	Lactantius *De Mortibus Persecutorum*
Mai	*Scriptorum veterum nova collectio*
Malal.	John Malalas
Mariev	*Ioannis Antiocheni, Fragmenta Quae Supersunt Omnia*
MBH	Treadgold, *The Middle Byzantine Historians*
Men.	Menander Protector
MGH	*Monumenta Germaniae Historica*
Niebuhr	*Dexippi, Eunapii, Petri Patricii, Prisci, Malchi, Menandri Historiarum Quae Supersunt*
OCD[3]	*Oxford Classical Dictionary*, 3rd edition
ODB	*Oxford Dictionary of Byzantium*
Orig. Const.	*Excerpta Valesiana*
PIR	*Prosopographia Imperii Romani*
PLRE	*Prosopography of the Later Roman Empire*
Plut.	Plutarch
Roberto	*Ioannis Antiocheni, Ioannis Antiocheni Fragmenta ex Historia Chronica*
SHA	*Scriptores Historiae Augustae*
Soz.	Sozomenus
Sym.	Symeon Magister
T	Testimony
TTH	*Translated Texts for Historians*
Vat. Gr. 73	*Codex Vaticanus Graecus* 73
Xiphil.	John Xiphilinus
Zonar.	Zonaras *Epitome of Histories*
Zos.	Zosimus *Historia Nova*

INTRODUCTION

Peter, *Patricius* and *Magister*

Peter was born in Thessalonica (T 2).[1] In his youth, he studied law, his knowledge of which was remarkable. With this he combined impressive skills as a speaker, a pleasing personal manner (T 1, 2, and 6), an estimable work ethic, and – at least in the eyes of his close personal acquaintance John Lydus but in contrast to the estimation of another contemporary, Procopius (T 4) – an uncompromising rectitude (cf. T 1 and 11). On top of this, John relates (T 1), Peter was devoted to learning, including the study of the past, and relished opportunities to demonstrate his knowledge of recondite subjects, sometimes to a degree that made even John uncomfortable. He was a Christian, perhaps a Monophysite.[2]

The Latin Peter must have mastered in the course of his legal studies, along with most of the qualities and qualifications noted above, helps to explain his first known imperial appointment in 534 as Justinian's envoy to the court of the Ostrogothic king Athalaric (b. 516 or 518, r. 526–534) and his regent and mother Amalasuntha in Ravenna. Before Peter's arrival, Athalaric had died and Theodahad, a cousin of Amalasuntha, had occupied the throne at the expense of Amalasuntha.[3] Peter subsequently shuttled between Constantinople and Italy at least two more times before being detained by Theodahad and held for three years (536–539). A swap for Gothic envoys, seized as collateral by Justinian's general Belisarius, eventually secured his freedom and return to Constantinople (T 3). There Justinian rewarded his service by making Peter *magister officiorum*, an honor he would hold until 565 (T 3–5). Perhaps on that occasion Peter also obtained the rank *patricius* and an honorary consulship.[4] Between 551–553, he was active in his official capacity in the run-up to the Council of Constantinople and was present for at least some of its proceedings.[5] Wealth, choice property (T 16), charges of corruption, and suspicion of having arranged – allegedly on Theodora's orders – Amalasuntha's murder (T 4–5) were by-products of Peter's position, prestige, and influence.

John Lydus' *De Magistratibus* of 554 or possibly 552 furnishes a *terminus ante quem* for Peter's earliest known literary work in its claim that: "to those longing not to be ignorant of the succession of *magistri* up to our day, Peter, the consummately great intellect and trusty teacher of general history suffices for instruction through the things which he composed about what is referred to as the *magisterium*."[6] John's reference is to Peter's "treatise on the ceremony of the palace" (T 21 and 22), titled Περὶ πολιτικῆς καταστάσεως or *About State Protocol* (T 6), substantial extracts of which survive in Constantine Prophyrogenitus' *De Cerimoniis*.[7] These confirm that Peter possessed the obsessive degree of attention to detail required of a *magister officiorum*. At the same time they reveal Peter's interest in the historical dimension of his subject – a feature which would have struck a responsive chord in John and which doubtless prompted his praise of Peter as a "trusty teacher of general history ... through the things which he composed about what is referred to as the *magisterium*." Indeed, it is difficult to imagine that Peter – just as is the case with most authors of highly specialized studies – wrote *About State Protocol* for anybody other than people like himself (and like John), men whose dress, gestures, words, and daily routines were scripted by the rules and rituals of the court and culture of Justinian's age.[8] Peter's "authorial voice" is that of a *magister officiorum*; it is all but inconceivable that the requisite research for *About State Protocol* could have been conducted anywhere other than in Constantinople.[9] That the book survives only in *De Cerimoniis*, the quintessential Byzantine compendium on the same subject, is hardly coincidental.

Evidently, Justinian's admiration for Peter was long-term, for between 550–562 the emperor entrusted to Peter a series of ambassadorial missions that involved issues of crucial importance to Rome and Persia. Menander the Guardsman's account of one of these – negotiations held in 561 concerning a peace treaty between the superpowers – draws directly on Peter's own dossier of what transpired.[10] Menander's notice that he rephrased the Greek of the speeches he found therein to make it "more Attic" implies that what Menander read was a record – sometimes, he thought, self-promoting on Peter's part – rather than a polished, literary production. It is not necessarily an indictment of Peter as incapable of composing speeches in a classicizing style nor is it a clue to the character of the Greek of Peter's *History*.[11] Menander also omitted material in this "immense tome" (τεῦχος μέγιστον), as his injunction to anyone interested in assessing the accounts seriatim to "read these from the collection of Peter himself" (ἀναλεξάσθω ταῦτα ἐκ τῆς αὐτοῦ Πέτρου συναγωγῆς) demonstrates.[12] Since, as the principal Roman participant in the negotiations, Peter himself could not have recorded the details of the proceedings as they unfolded, his "collection" must have comprised a combination of documents produced by his staff and augmented with his own notes and observations.[13] Not surprisingly, there were two features of these documents that Menander thought unsuitable for him as a writer of history: wordiness and excessive attention to minutiae.[14] "Indeed, if, I suppose, I had written up everything reported throughout that very parchment," he says, "the epic recitation of the treaty would have sufficed for me for a basis of an immense history."[15]

Menander places Peter's death soon after the latter's return to Constantinople in 562, around July. However, *Novella* 137 (Schoell p. 695.5) demonstrates he was still alive on March 26, 565. By 566 there was a new *magister officiorum*, a Theodorus, almost certainly Peter's son.[16] Besides his papers, his *About State Protocol*, and Theodorus, Peter left behind him, too, as the *Suda* testifies, a second published work – his *History* (T 6).

THE *EXCERPTA HISTORICA*, PETER'S *HISTORY*, AND THE *ANONYMUS POST DIONEM*

Peter's *History* survives thanks mainly to the efforts of the compilers of the so-called *Excerpta Historica* (*EH*), who worked at the behest of Constantine VII Porphyrogenitus (r. 908–959, sole emperor 945–959). Of the original fifty-three thematically organized volumes of the *EH*, just four have survived – *On Plots* or *On Ambushes* (*de Insidiis* = *EI*), the pre-imperial Rome section of *On Virtues and Vices* (*de Virtutibus et Vitiis* = *EV*), *On Maxims* (*de Sententiis*), and *On Embassies*, one portion of which was devoted to embassies of various peoples to Rome (*de Legationibus Gentium ad Romanos* = *ELGR*), another to embassies of Rome to various peoples (*de Legationibus Romanorum ad Gentes* = *ELRG*) – and, of these as they now stand, excerpts from the *History* appear only in the *ELGR*, *ELRG*, and, almost certainly, the *ES*. The standard modern edition of the *EH* stands as a monument to the philological virtuosity of its editors, Ursulus Boissevain, Carl de Boor, Theodor Büttner-Wobst, and Anton Roos.[17] Aside from the *EH*, the grammatical treatise *On Syntax* yields two brief but important quotations from the *History* (F 2 and 5, below).[18]

In Western Europe, the reputation of Peter himself had preceded the first printed editions of these texts, let alone their culling for excerpts and quotations of the *History* to be printed separately as fragments. Since the twelfth century, students of Roman law had encountered Peter's name.[19] Far earlier, Peter would have been known through his role in the prelude to and as a result of his presence at the Council of Constantinople.[20] By the mid-1500s, Procopius' *Gothic War* was available in Latin, Italian, and French translations, while 1533 saw the first printed edition of Cassiodorus' *Variae*.[21] Both of these works furnished glimpses of the impression Peter made on his contemporaries and of his role as Justinian's ambassador to Gothic Italy (cf. T 2–3 and 11–15 below). In contrast, 1603 marked the *editiones principes* of the *ELGR* and *ELRG*, 1827 that of the *ES*, recovered from a palimpsest manuscript by the famed Vatican librarian Angelo Mai.[22]

The manuscript – *Codex Vaticanus Graecus* 73 – contained Aristides' orations and Plato's *Gorgias*. However, Mai recognized that they had been copied sometime during the fourteenth century onto pages which already bore text he eventually dated to the tenth or eleventh century. To reach this conclusion, Mai had disassembled the codex and, in an attempt to make the palimpsest easier to read, treated its vellum pages with a chemical solution. Though this eventually did lasting damage to the pages, in the short run it enabled Mai to make far better sense of what he had discovered.[23]

What remained of the content of the original codex were 177 disordered folios – folded sheets – , each half of a sheet bearing the recto and verso of a page, the total pages being 354. Whoever had produced the palimpsest had gathered these folios four at a time into quaternions. In the process of assembling these quaternions, some had been reversed, with the result that what originally had been rectos became versos in the new codex. Less often, folios had been inverted before being grouped into quaternions, the top of a folio in the original now becoming the bottom of a folio.[24] With the sole exception of Eunapius of Sardis' *History*, no folios in the new codex bore the names of the authors or works included in its lower text.[25]

On the basis of his reordering of the surviving folios, Mai recognized that the palimpsest preserved portions of the *ES*, and, by comparison of the *ES* excerpts with texts preserved in other manuscript traditions, he sought to determine the authorship of each series of excerpts.[26] One portion of the *ES* material posed several problems. The bulk of these excerpts so closely paralleled Dio's *Roman History* that Mai thought they derived from it and, consequently, when he ordered the loose folios, he arranged them on the basis of the chronological order of their contents, which extended from Dio's proem through the death of Elagabalus.[27] The remainder, which treated events later than the terminus of Dio – specifically from *c*. 238 into the reign of Constantine the Great (Boissevain's *ES* 156–91) – he suspected had been drawn by the Constantinian excerptors from the lost *Chronica* of John of Antioch, noting in support of this that an excerpt about Diocletian betrayed its author's Christianity.[28] Though there was no indication in the palimpsest of any shift in sources at this point, Mai's *Scriptorum veterum nova collectio* distinguished these excerpts by beginning them on a new page under the heading: *Post Dio Excerpts to Constantine* (ΜΕΤΑ ΔΙΟΝΑ ΕΚΛΟΓΑΙ ΕΩΣ ΚΩΝΣΤΑΝΤΙΝΟΥ) or *Post Dio Excerpts from an Anonymous as far as to Constantine* (POST DIONEM EXCERPTA EX ANONYMO USQUE AD CONSTANTINUM).[29] Mai was careful to note the absence from the palimpsest of several pages he thought had borne material drawn from his *Anonymus*' treatment of Constantius and suggested that an awareness that Eunapius' *History* would offer abundant material from Julian's reign had caused the Constantinian excerptors to set the *Anonymus* aside at that point.[30] It must be stressed, then, that Mai, who had read the extracts from Peter's *History* in the *ELGR* and *ELRG*, made no connection whatsoever between

Peter and any of the historical excerpts in *Vat. Graec.* 73, which nowhere mentions Peter's name.

Only in 1829 did Barthold Niebuhr present the pair of quotations from *On Syntax* (F 2 and 5 below) and the *ELGR* and *ELRG* excerpts of Peter as fragments of the *History*.[31] In addition, he employed texts published after 1603 – mainly Procopius' *Anecdota* and John Lydus' *de Magistratibus* – and information about Peter preserved in the fragments of Menander the Guardsman to construct an account of Peter that, in most respects, remains accurate.[32]

Niebuhr recognized that the evidence from *On Syntax* both pushed the beginning of events treated in the *History* back from Tiberius, the earliest emperor mentioned in the excerpts on embassies, at least to Augustus and demonstrated that Peter had organized his content by emperor rather than by years or book divisions. As for the terminus of the *History*, Niebuhr followed Mai in thinking that Eunapius' emphasis on Julian was a key factor behind the Constantinian excerptor's decision in the *ELGR* to turn away from Peter's *History* at the point he did, i.e., during Julian's tenure as a Caesar (cf. below, F 215).[33] Finally, he was confident that "Peter had produced nothing more than a breviary of Dio as far as [Dio's] history allowed" and that Mai's *Anonymus* was Peter rather than John of Antioch.[34] Nonetheless, Niebuhr did not include the post-Dio excerpts from the *ES* as fragments of Peter's *History*. Of the *ES* excerpts which preceded those of Mai's *Anonymus* in *Vat. Graec.* 73 and which Mai had assigned to Dio, Niebuhr made no mention.

Carl Müller's *FHG* IV of 1851 remains today the most commonly consulted collection of testimony and fragments of the *History*. In most respects, it simply reproduces Niebuhr. This is true, too, of Ludwig Dindorf's edition of 1870.[35] Two things distinguish Müller's role in the history of the study of Peter's fragments. One was his decision to follow Mai's lead and to print under the heading "An Anonymous Who Continued the *Histories* of Dio Cassius" the thirty-five excerpts in the *ES* which Mai assigned to John of Antioch but which Niebuhr had attributed to Peter.[36] This firmly established in the minds of most scholars the unquestioned existence of the *Anonymus* and, for those who did not read Müller's introductory comments with care, divorced the study of the post-Dio excerpts in the *ES* from the *ES* excerpts thought by Mai to have come from Dio's treatment of imperial Rome.

Müller's second distinctive contribution was to champion the *Anonymus* as the adaptor of the Dio-inspired Augustus-to-Elagabalus excerpts which immediately preceded the following sequence of excerpts which Mai had assigned to Dio. To make his case, Müller first adduced a series of objections against Mai's association of the post-Dio excerpts with John and against Niebuhr's proposal of Peter as their author. With regard to John's *Chronica*, he thought it remarkable that the excerptors would begin their selections from a text which took Adam as its starting point with Alexander Severus. Likewise, why, he wondered, would they turn away from John in Constantine's reign when the *Chronica's* contents extended far beyond that point, especially since the excerpts from John in the *EV* and *EI* did not observe these limits? Müller called attention, too, to the contrast between the general succinctness of John – a trait he shared with George the Monk, Malalas, and Syncellus, no excerpts from any of whom appeared in the *ES* – and Dio's penchant for detail and to John's abridgement of Herodian for his account of the period from Commodus to the Gordians as opposed to the *Anonymus'* reliance on a different source in his handling of that era. Moreover, since it was not the practice of the compilers of the *ES* to link different historical works into a continuous text, Müller thought it unlikely that in this instance they would have joined excerpts from Peter's *History* or, in fact, anyone's *History*, to those taken from the end of Dio's; rather, the work of the nameless author of the post-Dio material must also be the source of the excerpts on imperial history judged by Mai to be from Dio and by Niebuhr from Peter. He also reasoned that the Constantinian excerptors themselves were ignorant of his identity. If they had known his name, why would they not have included it? They must, then, have employed an unattributed text which contained the mystery author's adaptation of Dio from Augustus through Elagabalus, continued by that same *Anonymus* – for Müller a Christian, as Mai and Niebuhr had recognized – to the reign of Constantine (F 212, below).[37]

Though advocates of a link between the excerpts to John of Antioch remained – Theodor Mommsen the most prominent among them[38] – , by the end of the nineteenth century, Georgios Sotiriadis had adduced so many divergences between John and the contested excerpts in the *ES* that the case for him was abandoned.[39] Indeed, with one inconsequential exception, there is not a single reference to the *ES* in recent editions of John.[40]

Prior to Sotiriadis and far less comprehensively, Boissevain, too, had made the case against John of Antioch.[41] However, Boissevain had also championed Niebuhr's view that the Augustus-to-Constantine excerpts of the *ES* had been drawn from Peter's *History*. Both Peter and the *Anonymus* were Christians; both of their works extended from Augustus to the dynasty of Constantine; neither Peter's Greek nor that of the unattributed excerpts was of high quality; entries explicitly taken from Peter in the excerpts on embassies and on *On Syntax* shared the unambiguous affinities with Dio's *History* evident in the *ES* entries which dealt with imperial Rome through the reign of Elagabalus; and Peter was a figure whose prominence would have attracted a readership in spite of his *History's* literary shortcomings and derivative character.[42]

Sotiriadis was not convinced, while Carl de Boor, who found Boissevain's specific points in favor of Peter less than compelling, soon adduced what he thought were far better arguments for the recognition of Peter's *History* as the source of the entire string of excerpts from Augustus to Constantine.[43] There had been, he maintained, no need to assume the existence of an *Anonymus* in the first place. His name, just as the names of all the authors of the *ES* entries save Eunapius, had been lost in the course of preparation of the palimpsest when scribes had discarded those folios whose lettering and decoration had made their texts too difficult to expunge.[44] He thought it unlikely, too, that there would have existed in the collection of the Imperial Library in Constantinople a work of unknown authorship whose chronological limits, reliance on Dio, and style (or lack of it) matched Peter's *History*.[45] Furthermore – and John of Antioch aside – , of the authors *known to have been included* in the *EH*, de Boor noted, Peter alone had covered Roman history from Augustus to Constantius. He further observed that the compilers of the *Suda* had drawn many of its historical entries from the still-extant volume of the *EV*, the content of which had been limited to material prior to the imperial era of Roman history. Since no entries from Peter appeared in the *Suda*, excerpts from his *History*, *if the EV had included them in the first place*, would have been in the no-longer-extant volume of the *EV* devoted to the imperial era. On this reckoning, the fragments of the *History* preserved in *On Syntax* and which treated the triumvirate of Lepidus, Antony, and Octavian would be precisely the starting point to be expected of a history of Rome commencing with Augustus.[46] Finally, de Boor took a close correspondence between a passage in Peter's *History* (F 213 = *ELGR* 14, p. 395.1–32) and John Zonaras' *Epitome of Histories* XIII.7.15–28 (III, pp. 37.5–39.4) as clear evidence of Zonaras' use of Peter.[47] Consequently, there was no need, then, to posit a shift in sources on Zonaras' part when it came to several close parallels between the *Epitome* and some of the post-Dio *ES* excerpts thought by Niebuhr and Boissevain to have been drawn from Peter.[48] Here de Boor (pp. 22–23) focused on comments of Ludwig Mendelssohn with respect to the relationship of these passages of Peter and Zonaras to Zosimus' *Historia Nova* I.36.1–2.[49] Though he recognized that the nature of the evidence precluded certainty, de Boor was confident that he had strengthened Niebuhr's and Boissevain's arguments to so high a degree that Peter's authorship was now difficult to deny on the basis of that same evidence. At the same time, with respect to Franz Görres and Sotiriadis, whose opposition to Peter rested on marked differences between the concerns and character of the Constantinian excerpts on embassies explicitly taken from Peter and those of the anonymous excerpts of the *ES*, he rightly objected that both scholars had ignored the obvious divergences anyone would reasonably expect between excerpts concerned with embassies in contrast to excerpts devoted to maxims.[50]

Boissevain's reordering of the folios of *Vat. Gr.* 73 in the course of his preparation of what remains to date the only critical edition of the *ES* provided an additional reason to dispense with the *Anonymus*. He pointed out that the discarded folio which had borne the name of the author and title of the Augustus-to-Constantine excerpts had also contained excerpts from the work which had preceded them in the *ES* and that this had been the *Babylonica* of Iamblichus rather than, as Mai had thought, the Republican portion of Dio's *History*.[51] Codicological evidence further revealed that, beginning with the excerpts from Dexippus through Dio, the relative order of the authors in the *ES* was Dexippus, Iamblichus, the contested Augustus-to-Constantine excerpts, Diodorus Siculus, and Dio. To this Boissevain compared the relative order of the excerpts from authors preserved in the *ELGR* from Dexippus through Dio: Dexippus, Socrates Scholasticus, *Peter the Patrician*, Diodorus, and Dio. Thus, the unassigned fragments of the *ES*, many features of which corresponded so closely with what was known of Peter's *History*, fell in the sequence of authors in the *ES* exactly where Peter's *History* fell in the sequence of authors in the *ELGR*.[52]

Boissevain's edition revealed something else: there was no lacuna, as one would expect there to have been in consequence of the jettisoning of folios bearing authors' names, between the last *ES* excerpt before the post-Dio string. Indeed, not only did Boissevain's *ES* 156 and 157 occupy the same page in *Vat. Gr.* 73 but the end of one and the beginning of the other actually shared the same line.[53] Müller, it appeared, had been right to posit a single text, produced by a Christian, as the source of the excerpts from Augustus through Constantine. His mistake had been to reject Peter as its author.

Most subsequent objections to the de Boor/Boissevain position have either repeated the methodological error of Görres and Sotiriadis – Panagiotis Antonopoulos provides an example – or, as in the cases of Santo Mazzarino and David Potter, have relied respectively on perceived contradictions between the *ES* and John Zonaras with respect to the capture of Valerian or the death of Odenathus.[54] But whatever significance these alleged differences may have for the debate about Peter and the *Anonymus* depends to a substantial degree on circular reasoning about Zonaras' handling of his sources and on the extent of his debt to Peter, provided that he used him at all. Given the absence of good critical editions of George Cedrenus and of the so-called *Synopsis Sathas* (now attributed to Theodore Scutariotes) and time for reflection on the nexus of sources behind the *Syntomos Historia* associated with Michael Psellus, a reliable *Quellenkritik* of Zonaras is also premature. After all, the method is, at its best, only as good the editions of the texts to which it is applied.[55] On the plus side, Umberto Roberto and Sergei Mariev have produced the first scholarly editions of John of Antioch. Stephan Wahlgren's edition of the *Chronicon* of Symeon Magister has revealed the inadequacies of Immanuel Bekker's Bonn Leo Grammaticus, and there is now an English translation of and commentary on Books XII.15–XIII.19 of Zonaras' *Epitome of Histories*.[56] We have François Paschoud's Budé Zosimus and Roger Blockley's Eunapius.[57]

Stephanie Brecht has rendered an invaluable service in assembling a carefully annotated collection of Byzantine literary sources for the Roman *Reichskrise* and, in a series of formidable, provocative, and controversial studies, Bruno Bleckmann has helped to redefine the parameters of scholarship on the historiography of the third and fourth centuries A.D. and the place of particular authors and texts within those parameters.[58] András Németh's dissertation is part of a broader reassessment of the *EH* and of Byzantine "encyclopedism" and Warren Treadgold has produced a much-needed overview of the Byzantine historians, all of whose works are now searchable in seconds thanks to the *Thesaurus Linguae Graecae*.[59] Alan Cameron has, it seems, laid the ghost – perhaps better, *phantasma* – of Nicomachus Flavianus, whose *Annales* have haunted the study of late antique historiography.[60] The *Anonymus post Dionem*, too, has departed. Peter's *History* remains, extending from the rise of Augustus at least to the reign of Constantius. In this new form, it will figure in future debates about Roman history and historiography as they can be reconstructed from Byzantine authors and in the study of Byzantine historiography itself.

PETER'S *HISTORY*

The headings of the excerpts from Peter's *History* in the *ELGR* and *ELRG* (= T 18–20) refer to him as *patricius* and *magister*. If this accurately reproduces what excerptors found in their exemplar of the *History* and if the titles given Peter were not anachronistically added by a copyist, owner, or librarian, *patricius* and *magister* together would set *c*. 539–542 as the *terminus post quem* for the *History*. For it was then, after his return to Constantinople from his third ambassadorial mission to Italy and detention there on the orders of Theodahad (536–539), that Justinian appointed him *magister officiorum*. While it is impossible to tell from this precisely where the *History* began, because *On Syntax* (= F 2) demonstrates that Peter's *History* included events as early as 36 B.C., it seems reasonable to set the rise of Octavian in the aftermath of Julius Caesar's murder as Peter's starting point.

The end of Peter's *History* is more difficult to determine. The safest guide to the latest event is an excerpt explicitly assigned to Peter – the embassy dispatched in 358 by the Chamavi to negotiate with Julian while he was Caesar of the Augustus Constantius (F 125 = *ELGR* 16) – , which demonstrates that Peter dealt at least with the bulk of Constantius' reign (September 9, 337–November 3, 361), much too long after Constantine the Great's death to maintain that the *History* culminated with the first Christian emperor and treated his heirs only as afterthoughts.

PRESENTATION AND PRINCIPLES OF TRANSLATION

Testimonia (= T) include passages which tell us something about the *History* itself or about facets of Peter's life, career, and character in so far as they have some direct bearing on him as a historian. The relative order of the fragments as they appear *within* the *ELGR*, *ELRG*, and *ES* has been retained irrespective of the date of the events each excerpt describes. This allows for the possibility that Peter may not always have dealt with events in strict chronological sequence or that an excerpt may reflect someone's description of an event from the past and seems the safest way to arrange the 215 fragments in a relative order that stands the best chance of reflecting their sequence in Peter's *History*. Conversely, with respect to the arrangement of the composite order of all the fragments, chronology has been the decisive factor. Where it has been possible to date the contents of a fragment, that date, within parentheses, follows the fragment number.

Though some fragments of the *History* stand alone, most align closely with other texts, especially with passages from Dio's *Roman History* or John Xiphilinus' *Epitome* of Dio. In such cases, the texts in question are presented below in parallel columns, with the earlier or earliest author in the left column. Dio, whether preserved in a manuscript of the *Roman History* or in the *EH*, is treated as prior to Peter and cited to the left of Peter. On the other hand, Dio as abbreviated by Xiphilinus or incorporated into John Zonaras' *Epitome of Histories* is treated as posterior to Peter and so stands on Peter's right. Xiphilinus and Zonaras do, after all, postdate Peter by about half a millennium. In every instance where Boissevain has incorporated passages of Peter, Xiphilinus, Zonaras, or any other author into his reconstructed text of Dio, their place in his edition appears after their actual provenance.

Because so much of what Dio treated in Books LXI–LXXX of his *History* has had to be reconstructed from the *EH*, Xiphilinus, Zonaras, and other witnesses, the precise termini of individual books are often unclear. Consequently, two of Dio's modern editors, Johannes Löwenklau – latinized as Leunclavius – and Boissevain, disagreed about where certain books began and ended. Both of their book divisions appear in Boissevain's edition, his own book numbers at the top of pages on the left of the opened text, Leunclavius' at the top of pages to the right and in the margins of those on the left. Because Earnest Cary's Loeb, by far the most accessible edition of Dio, uses Leunclavius' numbers and because Boissevain included them, citations of Dio here employ Leunclavius' book numbers followed in parentheses by the volume, page, and line numbers of Boissevain's edition.[61] Citations of Xiphilinus supply the page number in Ludwig Dindorf's edition of Dio,[62] followed in parentheses by Boissevain's volume and page numbers for Xiphilinus and then, after a = , the place(s) of the passage in the reconstructed text of Dio. Every citation of a passage from the *EH* includes the author's name, the abbreviated title of the relevant volume of the *EH*, the excerpt number, and page and line numbers along with the location of the fragment in one or more of the standard corpora of fragmentary authors. Though this is a cumbersome method, a simpler one would obscure the true provenances of passages, their own nature, and the nature of their relationship to one another. Those who wish to move from the *EH*, Müller's *FHG*, or Blockley's *FCH* to the fragments of Peter as numbered here should consult the tables of correlations between Müller's numeration of the fragments of Peter and of his *Anonymus* and the fragment numbers employed here and the "Index of Passages Cited" (pp.163–71).

TRANSLATION AND COMMENTARY

Many of the fragments of Peter's *History* and many of the other texts dealt with below have long been available in English. To offer one instance, Cary's Dio contains much from Peter, Xiphilinus, and Zonaras, though always and understandably for the purpose of the reconstitution of Dio's *Roman History*. Because the translations presented here serve other ends, they often differ from those earlier versions. To translate away truncated Greek, to revise a long period into shorter sentences, or to alter word order for the sake of clarity – important though it is for the production of highly readable, literary translations – could, in the case of remains of Peter's *History*, result in several degrees of distortion and give a false impression of the nature of the evidence. For example, passages from the *History* sometimes reflect Peter's own compression or, less often, expansion of his sources. At other times such features appear to be consequences of the process of excerption for incorporation into the *EH* or of the vicissitudes of textual transmission. Thus, only rarely has sentence structure been sacrificed for readability. In case of parallels between Peter and other authors, any translation risks obscuring distinctions or agreements in vocabulary and syntax evident in Greek. Consequently, whenever parallel translations appear below, the same words are translated in the same way and different words differently and care has been taken to preserve as much as possible the syntax and diction of the authors in question. Proper names in the translations are those which appear in the texts themselves. Only in the commentary are variant spellings regularized or misnomers corrected. Except for the most familiar – e.g., Trajan and Constantine – , proper names are latinized. The references to the *PIR*, *PLRE*, or *BNP* regularly included in the commentary and, when possible, after the names of individuals in the "Index of People, Gods, and Places" (below, pp. 171–85) secure their identity. In the case of individuals mentioned in the Introduction, the same index regularly contains abbreviated references to entries in the *OCD*[3], *ODB*, and *BNP*. Such entries do not appear in the bibliography.

The primary purpose of the commentary is to elucidate the content of fragments of the *History*. To that end, it offers historical context, identifies people, places, and the sources of quotations, and sometimes discusses words or phrases. Purely literary parallels – a subject handled well by Martolini – receive scant attention. With a few important exceptions, bibliographic references generally point readers toward one or two works – most often in English – which furnish additional background with regard to the content of a specific fragment. Such references most often appear in shortened form and sometimes refer to titles of book or journals by abbreviations. In the case of the former, the bibliography supplies what has been omitted; the list of abbreviations (above, pp. xi–xii) explains the latter. The "Index of People, Gods and Places" (below, pp. 171–85) includes those modern scholars who have figured most prominently in the study of Peter's *History* and then only with regard to discussion of their specific contributions to that study.

Since the *ES* preserves so much of the *History* in the form of memorable remarks of emperors, modern imperial biographies dominate such citations. Apart from texts presented in parallel to Peter, the commentary includes notices of ancient authors – Tacitus and Suetonius, for instance – whose content coincides with or sometimes contradicts the *History* but of whom there is no reason to suspect that Peter himself had direct knowledge. Where such points of contact exist, commentaries devoted to those authors often afford highly detailed analyses and far fuller references to modern scholarship than are warranted in a commentary on Peter, whom there is usually no reason to suspect knew more about what he was describing than what his immediate source told him, and these the commentary regularly notes. Only in a few instances – in part because of the nature of information in the fragments themselves – has the commentary ventured to use the fragments as the basis of a new evaluation of the historical events or personages they describe.

Another goal of the commentary – and, indeed, of the translation and the presentation of texts in parallel columns – is to set what we can know of Peter's *History* on a firmer footing as a necessary precondition to the study of Roman imperial and of late antique historiography proper. This investigation involves more than *Quellenforschung*. Important, too, is an appreciation of qualities and characteristics peculiar to specific authors, of the ways in which they employed their sources, and – especially in the case of texts incorporated into the *EH* – of adaptations of form and content they imposed on them. The commentary is, in varying degrees, concerned with all of these.

NOTES

1 The precise date of Peter's birth is uncertain, though it must have been *c.* 500. Whitby and Whitby, *The* History *of Theophylact Simocatta*, p. 37, n. 10, correctly warn against the association of the young Peter with Solachon, situated in Mesopotamia. For Peter's career, see *PLRE* III, pp. 994–98, *s.v.* Petrus 6; for his life and works, Krumbacher, Vol. I, pp. 237–40, Hunger, *Die Hochsprachliche Profane Literatur,* Vol. I, pp. 300–3, and Treadgold, *EBH*, pp. 264–69. Antonopoulos' Πέτρος Πατρίκιος, is the sole monograph devoted to Peter.

2 Peter's possible Monophysitism is a matter of inference. See, for example, Threadgold, *EBH*, pp. 264–65 and 267.

3 On Athalaric, Amalasuntha, and Theodahad, see *PLRE* II, pp. 175–76, *s.v.* Athalaricus; p. 65, *s.v.* Amalasuntha; pp. 1067–68, *s.v.* Theodahadus; and pp. 1330–31, Stemmata 37 and 38.

4 The earliest attestation of Peter as *patricius* is December 18, 542, and then only in one manuscript – *Codex Berolinensis* 269 – of Julianus' Latin epitome of Justinian's *Novella*, where it is coupled with *magister officiorum*. Cf. the *apparatus criticus* to *Novella* 117, ed. Schoell, p. 551. Peter as *ex consule* first appears in Vigilius' encyclical letter *Dum in Sancta Euphemia* of January 28, 552, *Epistula* 1, ed. Schwartz, p. 1.7–8 = *ACC,* Vol. I, p. 170.

5 Cf., for example, Vigilius *Epistula* 1, ed. Schwartz, p. 1.7–8 = *ACC,* Vol. I, p. 170, and *Acta Conciliorum Oecumenicorum*, Vol. 4.1, ed. Schwartz, pp. 27.8 and 18–19, 28.26, and 186.28–29 = *ACC*, Vols. I, pp. 213–15, and II, p. 78.

6 *De Magistratibus* II.25, ed. Wünsch, p. 80.19–24 = the opening of T 1. For the dates, see *De Magistratibus* I.2, ed. Wünsch, pp. 8.17–9.5, together with Treadgold, *EBH*, p. 262, and Wallinga, "The Date of Joannes Lydus' *De magistratibus*," pp. 359–80.

7 Constantine Porphyrogenitus, *De Cerimoniis* I.84–95, ed. Vol. I, pp. 386.23–433.23, = *The Book of Ceremonies*, trans. Moffatt and Tall, Vol. I, pp. 386–433, for example, largely and explicitly reproduce Peter's book. Angelo Mai's proposal that an unattributed and untitled dialogue on political science in *Vat. Gr.* 1298 is Peter's Περὶ πολιτικῆς καταστάσεως/*About State Protocol* – *Scriptorum veterum nova collectio,* Vol. II, pp. 571–609 – has been universally rejected. For a translation, see *Dialogue on Political Science*, trans. Bell, *Three Political Voices from the Age of Justinian*, pp. 123–88, and Bell's comments at pp. 9–13.

8 For *mise-en-scène*, see McCormick, "Emperor and Court," *CAH*², Vol. XIV, pp. 135–63.

9 See Rapp's evocative "Literary Culture under Justinian," pp. 376–97, on the combination of factors which made this so, and Treadgold, *EBH*, pp. 354–56, with his map on pp. 380–81, for historical writers from or drawn to Constantinople.

10 See *PLRE* III, p. 997, for particulars on the embassies. For a different view on Menander's source or sources than that advanced here, see, Blockley *Men.* p. 260, notes 84–85, who posits a distinction between the records Menander consulted and what Menander calls Peter's "collection" (συναγωγή).

11 Menander *ES* 11, p. 19.16–20 = Müller F 12 *FHG* IV, p. 217 = Blockley *Men.* F 6.2.4, pp. 86–88.

12 Menander *ES* 11, p. 20.7 = Müller F 12 *FHG* IV, p. 218 = Blockley *Men.* F 6.2.22, p. 88, and *ES* 11, p. 19.26–27 = F 12 Müller *FHG* IV, p. 217 = Blockley *Men.* F 6.2.13–14, p. 88.

13 On the paperwork and procedure of negotiation, see Lee, "Treaty-making in Late Antiquity," pp. 107–19, especially pp. 108–10. For the production of transcripts and translations of negotiations, see Menander Protector *ELRG* 3, pp. 179.30–180.5 = Müller F 11 *FHG* IV, pp. 211–12 = Blockley *Men.* F 6.1.304–313, p. 70, and *ELRG* 3, pp. 182.29–183.9 = Müller F 11 *FHG* IV, pp. 213–14 = Blockley *Men.* F 6.1.408–423, p. 76, and the commentary on Peter F 202 below.

14 *ES* 11, p, 20.12–14 = F 12 Müller *FHG* IV, p. 218 = Blockley *Men.* F 6.2.28–30, p. 88.

15 *ES* 11, p, 20.14–17 = F 12 Müller *FHG* IV, p. 218 = Blockley *Men.* F 6.2.30–32, p. 88.

16 Theodorus 34, *PLRE* III, pp. 1255–56, served as *magister* until before 576. Antonopoulos, Πέτρος Πατρίκιος, pp. 28–38 (English summary, pp. 229–30), advances a series of arguments in favor of Peter Barsymes (Petrus *qui et* Barsymes 9, *PLRE* III, pp. 999–1002) as Theodorus' father. If Antonopoulos is correct, a key piece of evidence in support of the identification of Peter the Patrician as a Monophysite vanishes.

17 *Excerpta Historica Iussu Imperatoris Constantini Porphyrogeniti Confecta*, 4 vols. (Berlin: Weidmann 1903–1910). Németh's *Imperial Systematization of the Past* has raised the study of the *EH* to a new level. Treadgold, *MBH*, pp. 153–65, provides a good overview of the *EH* and of recent scholarship devoted to it.

18 *On Syntax* (Περὶ Συντάξεως) survives as one of the treatises included in the *Lexica Segueriana*, for which see Krumbacher, Vol. I, pp. 571–73.

19 See under Πέτρος, ἀπὸ ὑπάτων καὶ πατρίκιος and Πέτρος ἐνδοξότατος μάγιστρος in the prosopographic index to Schoell and Kroll's edition of the *Novellae*, p. 812.

20 See Antonopoulos, pp. 237–39.

21 For the bibliographic particulars on Procopius' *Gothic War*, see Krumbacher, Vol. I, pp. 234–35. The *editio princeps* of Cassiodorus is Accursius' *Variarum libri XII* (Augsburg: Heinrich Steiner, 1533).

22 Krumbacher, Vol. I, p. 260, on the *ELGR* and *ELRG*; Mai, pp. 1–464.

23 *Cf.* Mai, pp. xxxi–xxxiii, and Németh, *Imperial Systematization of the Past,* pp. 127–29, who translates some of Mai's Latin description of the process.

24 See the diagrams of Boissevain, *ES*, pp. x–xvii, and Németh, *Imperial Systematization of the Past,* pp. 130–34, for the relationship of the order of folios in the palimpsest to the order of folios in the reconstructed *ES*.

25 *Cf.* Mai, p. 247, and Boissevain, *ES*, p. 71.1–2.

26 Apart from Eunapius, authors included in the *ES* are Agathias, Appian, Arrian, Cassius Dio, Dexippus, Diodorus Siculus, Iamblichus of Syria, Menander Protector, Polybius, Procopius, Theophylact of Simocatta, and Xenophon. Where it is possible to do so, Boissevain, *ES*, pp. 453–71, collates the excerpts with corresponding passages in those authors whose works exist independently of the *ES*.

27 Mai, pp. 135–233 = Boissevain, *ES*, pp. 241–64 and 408–52.

28 Cf. Mai, p. 234, n. 1, and F 199, below.

29 Mai, p. 234.

30 Ibid., p. 246, n. 8.

31 Niebuhr, pp. 121–36.

32 The *editio princeps* of Procopius' *Anecdota* appeared in 1623 (Krumbacher, Vol. I, pp. 234–35), Jean Dominique Fuss's of Lydus' *de Magistratibus* in 1812.

33 Niebuhr, pp. xxiii–xxiv.

34 Ibid., p. xxiv.

35 Cf. *FHG* IV, pp. 181–91, and Dindorf, *Historici Graeci Minores*, Vol. 1, pp. 425–37.
36 *FHG* IV, p. 191.
37 Ibid., pp. 191–92, and, on the Christianity of the *Anonymus*, p. 198, on Müller's F 13.1.
38 "Ueber die dem Cassius Dio beigelegten Theile der Planudischen und der Constantinischen Excerpte."
39 "Zur Kritik des Johannes von Antiochia."
40 See Roberto's apparatus to his F 162.2.4–7, p. 286, comparing it to the passages from Dio and the *ES* printed below in F 32. Mariev, p. 597, excludes the passage as spurious.
41 *De Excerptis Planudeis et Constantinianis ab Angelo Maio editis quae vulgo Cassio Dioni attribuuntur*, pp. 9–11. The citations below use the numbers of the consecutive pagination of Boissevain's contribution within the *Programma voor den Cursus 1884/1885*.
42 Ibid., p. 12.
43 Sotiriadis, "Zur Kritik des Johannes von Antiochia," pp. 29–36, where, with explicit reference to Boissevain, Sotiriadis dismisses the possibility that Peter is behind the unattributed *ES* entries; de Boor, "Römische Kaisergeschichte in byzantinischer Fassung I. Der Anonymus post Dionem."
44 de Boor, pp. 19–21.
45 Ibid., p. 17.
46 Ibid., pp. 17–19.
47 Ibid., p. 21, with Banchich and Lane, *The* History *of Zonaras*, n. 62, pp. 214–15.
48 Ibid., pp. 22–23. Cf. especially, Peter F 173 (*ELRG* 1, p. 3.4–10), Zonar. XII.23 (II, pp. 593.23–594.11), and the commentary of Banchich and Lane, *The* History *of Zonaras*, p. 109, n. 63.
49 *Zosimi Comitis et Exadvocati Fisci Historia Nova*, n. 1, pp. xxxiv–xxxv.
50 de Boor, pp. 31–33, *contra* Sotiriadis and Görres, "Zur Kritik einiger Quellenschriftsteller der spätern römischen Kaiserzeit," p. 219.
51 *ES*, p. 11, n. 1; Iamblichus *ES*, pp. 238–40.
52 *ES*, pp. xiv–xv.
53 Cf. *Vat. Gr.* 73, p. 323 = Mai, pp. 233–4, where | signifies line breaks and ||| page breaks in the manuscript, and Boissevain (*ES*, p. 264.5), who marks page breaks with | and does not signify line breaks, which the lines of his printed text are not meant to reflect.
54 Antonopoulos, Πέτρος πατρίκιος, pp. 240–41; Mazzarino "*L'Anonymus post Dionem* e la '*Topica*' delle Guerre Romano-Persiane 242/4 d.C.–283/(4?) d.C.," pp. 655–78; Potter, *Prophecy and History in the Crisis of the Roman Empire*, pp. 395–97. Antonopoulos, on the basis of a profile of what he thought one could expect in fragments from Peter's *History*, found that 38 percent of the fragments explicitly drawn from Peter in the *ELGR* and *ELRG* fit this profile in contrast to about 25 percent of the 191 *ES* fragments. From this he reasoned that "although the arguments in favor of Peter's authorship are strong, it is difficult to accept that from a single historical work a collection of so profoundly different fragments could be extracted." Mazzarino used what he, as had Mendelssohn, thought were mutually exclusive versions of the capture of Valerian in Zonaras and the *Anonymus* to suggest that the latter was Eustathius of Epiphania (*FHG* IV, pp. 138–42). For criticism, see Martolini, *L'*Anonymus post Dionem, *Pietro Patrizio e la* Leoquelle, pp. 95–100. Potter's acceptance of some of Müller's problematic

arguments against the identification of Peter with the *Anonymus*, his reliance on one of several ways to understand *ES* 166 (= F 183 below) on Odenathus' death, and his confusion of *ES* 191 (= F 212 below) – the chronological terminus of the *ES* Augustus-to–Constantine excerpts in consequence of the loss of part of the manuscript – and Peter *ELGR* 16 (= F 215 below) on Julian – the final selection of the compilers of the *ELGR* – with the discrepant termini of two distinct works drawn upon by the excerptors led him to conclude that the excerptor of the *ES* was using a manuscript of Dio already supplemented from Book XLV by an *Anonymus* whose account "derived from a number of sources, including Petrus."

55 Bekker's *Georgii Cedreni Historiarum Compendium* and Sathas' Ἀνωνύμου Σύνοψις Χρονική remain the standard editions. Tocci's *Theodori Scutariotae Chronica*, forthcoming in 2016, will soon supplant the latter. For Psellus, see Aerts' *Michaelis Pselli Historia Syntomos*. John Burke, Roger Scott, and Paul Tuffin are preparing the first modern translation of Cedrenus, on which Treadgold, *MBH*, p. 341, n. 136, comments, "Roger Scott ... has informed me that his team's findings indicate Cedrenus adapted, abridged, and supplemented his sources more than has usually been assumed."

56 Roberto, *Ioannis Antiocheni Fragmenta ex Historia Chronica*; Mariev, *Ioannis Antiocheni Fragmenta Quae Supersunt Omnia*; Walhgren, *Symeonis Magistri et Logothetae Chronicon*; Bekker, *Leonis Grammatici Chronographia*; Banchich and Lane, *The* History *of Zonaras*.

57 Paschoud, *Zosime Histoire Nouvelle*; Blockley *FCH*, Vol. II, pp. 2–150.

58 Brecht, *Die römische Reichskrise*; Bleckmann, especially *Die Reichskrise des III. Jahrhunders* and "Zu den Quellen der Vita Gallieni duo."

59 Németh, *Imperial Systematization of the Past*; Treadgold, *EBH* and *MBH*.

60 *The Last Pagans of Rome*, pp. 627–90. The force of Cameron's arguments against the importance of Nicomachus Flavianus, which seem to me decisive, in no way depend on his acceptance or rejection of the identification of Peter with the *Anonymus*.

61 Cf. Lenclavius' *Dionis Cassii Cocceiani Historiae Romanae Libri XLVI*. For an admirably clear treatment of this and other related points, see Murison, *Rebellion and Reconstruction*, pp. 1–5.

62 *Dionis Cassii Cocceiani Historia Romana*, Vol. V.

PETER'S *HISTORY*

TESTIMONY

T 1

John Lydus *De Magistratibus* II.25–26 (Wünsch, pp. 80.19–82.10 = T 1 Müller *FHG* IV, p. 183): And to those longing not to be ignorant of the succession of *magistri* up to our day, Peter, the consummately great intellect and trusty teacher of general history suffices for instruction through the things which he composed about what is referred to as the *magisterium*.

The power of the office advanced, then, to a higher degree. For not only is the *magister* entrusted to be in charge of the embassies of the nations arriving under him, both the public post and weighty multitude of those formerly *frumentarii* but now *magistriani*, but also the production of and authority over weapons and, furthermore, over matters of state. Standing out is Peter, the grand, second to none in virtues in any respect. For he preserves and guards the court and does not spurn Roman majesty, which, nearly having been destroyed by his predecessors' stupidity, in as much as he is wise and ever devoting himself to the books, he restores. And knowing the laws, if anybody does, in which he was reared from childhood, defending those in need, he showed himself both a magistrate most great and exuding due pride of his authority and a juryman keen and knowing absolutely how to judge the just, fortune in no way prostrating him. For he is mild and gentle, but not manipulable nor inclining toward requests outside the laws, and at once trusty and discerning in advance the desires of those approaching him, conceding not a moment to amusements, devoting the night to the books, the day to matters of business, and not thoughtlessly whistling away the day in chats between the court and his home, wrapping himself in intellectual inquiries and in narrations of more ancient matters with those who occupy themselves about these things. And not a moment for him is free of lessons, so the expounders of intellectual things fear their conversation with him. For he surrounds them with data and convolutions, in due measure rebuking them gently that "they are only said to be, but are not the sort of men rumor reports them to be." And for me in particular, the time together with him stirs up vertigos not insignificant. For I delight in him, because he is simultaneously noble and liberal and free from conceit and snootiness, both urbane and with a common touch. But he launches at me, as has indeed been said, anxieties not insignificant, offering for inquiry none of what I seem to know about, but introducing things totally unknown, with the result that in my head I recite the strongest prayers of all that he not, precisely as is his custom, launch at me any inaccessible speculation.

T 2

Procopius *Gothic War* I.3.30 (Huary and Wirth II, p. 19.16–21 = T 2 Müller *FHG* IV, p. 183): Now the sovereign, having become ecstatic about these things, immediately sent to Italy Peter, by kinship Illyrian, originating from Thessalonica, being, on the one hand, one of the orators in Byzantium, both intelligent and mild besides and sufficiently fitted by nature for persuasion.

T 3

Procopius *Gothic War* II.22.23–24 (Haury and Wirth III, pp. 250.21–251.6): And these ambassadors Belisarius did not release to the enemy first until they, too, gave up Athanasius and Peter and their personnel, whom, indeed, having reached Byzantium, the sovereign deemed worthy of the greatest rewards, having, on the one hand, appointed Athanasius praetorian prefect in Italy, to Peter, on the other hand, having granted the office of the so-called *magister*.

T 4

Procopius *Anecdota* 24.22–23 (Haury and Wirth III, p. 150.13–20 = T 3 Müller *FHG* IV, p. 183): And Peter, too, the whole time he was holding the office of the so-called *magister*, always every day kept wearing them [the *Scutarii*] down with unheard-of thefts. For while he was mild and, to the least degree, cognizant of how to give offense, he was of all men a consummate thief and absolutely full of shameful sordidness. Of this Peter I have also made mention in my prior accounts as having caused the murder of Amalasuntha, the daughter of Theodoric.

T 5

Procopius *Anecdota* 16.5 (Haury and Wirth III, pp. 100.25–101.2): And for this [arranging the murder of Amalasuntha] he came to the rank of *magister* and to the greatest degree of power and, most of all, of everyone's hatred.

T 6

Suda s.v. Πέτρος = Π 1406 (Adler IV, p. 117.20–23 = T 4 Müller *FHG* IV, p. 183): Peter, the orator, the *magister* and historian, an ambassador, when sent to Chosroes, was very weighty and invincible in the practice of oratory, in the mollification of barbaric spirits both obstinate and inflated. He wrote a *History* and *About State Protocol.*

Cf. *Suda s.v.* Εμβριθές = E 958 (Adler II, p. 255.7–9): Also: "Peter, the orator, the *magister* and historian, an ambassador, when sent to Chosroes, was very weighty and invincible in the practice of oratory for the mollification of barbaric spirits."

Chosroes = Chosroes 1 Anoushirvan, *PLRE* IIIA, pp. 303–6. For its estimation of Peter's oratorical virtuosity, the *Suda* copies Menander 6.2.25–26 (Blockley, *Men.*, p. 88) = *ES* 11, p. 20.9–11. Eudocia Augusta *Violarium* (Flach, p. 353), reproduce *Suda* Π1406. On the *Violarium*, see Krumbacher, I, pp. 578–79.

T 7

Men. 6.1.17–19 (Blockley, *Men.*, p. 54 = T 5 Müller *FHG* IV, p. 183 = F 11 Müller *FHG* IV, p. 206 = *ELRG* 3, p. 171.29–31): And Peter, the ambassador of the Romans, being in sufficient possession of the rest of culture and of the culture of the laws, spoke as follows ...

T 8

Men. 6.1.489–92 (Blockley, *Men.*, p. 80 = T 6 Müller *FHG* IV, p. 183 = F 11 Müller *FHG* IV, p. 215 = *ELRG* 3, p. 185.2–5): [Chosroes to Peter] Then, therefore, I, ambassador of Romans, should not be faulted by anybody, just as would make sense if I had been nurtured in that wisdom by which you have learned to excel in declamations, I myself not having learned to be persuasive.

T 9

Men. 9.1.59–62 (Blockley, *Men.*, p. 100 = T 7 Müller *FHG* IV, p. 183 = F 15 Müller *FHG* IV, p. 221 = *ELRG* 5, p. 190.11–15): For Peter, the ambassador before us, who, having lately been at hand, secured the terms of the peace, was able, by experience in words and by awesomeness of persuasiveness, to fend off both the things concerning the Saracens who are currently making accusations and other matters which were disputed.

The speaker is John (Ioannes 81, *PLRE* IIIA, pp. 672–74), Justin's (Iustinus 5, *PLRE* IIIA, pp. 754–56) ambassador, to Chosroes.

T 10

Men. 6.2.1–6 (Blockley, *Men.*, pp. 86–8 = T 8 Müller *FHG* IV, p. 183 = F 12 Müller *FHG* IV, p. 217 = *ES* 11, p. 19.15–20): Menander the historian says about Peter the ambassador and Chosroes: "Well then, these words issued from both, and no other thoughts were spoken about Suania. Truly, I have not employed some expressions in place of others rather than, where there is too low a level of the words, as far as was possible for me, rephrase them in better Attic."

T 11

Cassiodorus *Variae* X.19.4 (Mommsen p. 310.11–12) = T 9 Müller *FHG* IV, p. 183, a letter probably of 535 from the Gothic king Theodahad (Theodahadus, *PLRE* II, pp. 1067–68) to Justinian (Fl. Petrus Sabbatius Iustinianus 7, *PLRE* II, 645–48): ... so that the most eloquent man Peter, legate of Your Serenity, both foremost in learning and distinguished by a reputation of uprightness, may, without some accusation, receive proposals and not, against your will, sustain unsuitable delays.

T 12

Ibid. X.20.3 (Mommsen p. 310.29–30), a letter of 535 from Theodahad (Theodahadus, *PLRE* II, pp. 1067–68) to Theodora (1, *PLRE* IIIB, pp. 1240–41): It also has been added to my joy that Your Serenity has selected such a man as it is proper that such great glory send and fit that Your Obedience retain.

T 13

Ibid. X.22.1 (Mommsen p. 311.29–30) = T 10 Müller *FHG* IV, p. 183, a letter probably of 535 from the Gothic king Theodahad (Theodahadus, *PLRE* II, pp. 1067–68) to Justinian (Fl. Petrus Sabbatius Iustinianus 7, *PLRE* II, 645–48): You remember, wisest of princes, both through our legates and through the most eloquent man Peter, whom your piety recently assigned to us ... .

T 14

Ibid. X.23.1 (Mommsen p. 312.21–22) a letter probably of 535 from King Theodahad (Theodahadus, *PLRE* II, pp. 1067–68) to Theodora (1, *PLRE* IIIB, pp. 1240–41): Receiving of your legates Peter, a man most eloquent and, what is more estimable than dignities themselves, closely adhering to your indulgences, ... We learn through him that what it is established to have happened in this state is agreeable to you.

T 15

Ibid. X.24.1 (Mommsen p. 313.5) = T 11 Müller *FHG* IV, p. 183: a letter probably of 535 from Queen Gudeliva (*PLRE* II, p. 520) to Theodora (1, *PLRE* IIIB, pp. 1240–41): "When Peter, a man most wise, arrived ... "

T 16

Stephanus of Byzantium *Ethnica* A163/61.5–8 (Billerbeck, Gaertner *et al.*, Vol. I, p. 116.2–5 = T 12 Müller *FHG* IV, p. 183): Aconae: ... For thus [is named] a certain island belonging to the wholly praiseworthy patrician and consummately wise *magister* Peter and situated exactly opposite the blessed city and Chalcedon.

Meineke, *Stephani Byzantini Ethnicorum Quae Supersunt*, Vol. I, p. 61.6–9 with apparatus, thought Stephanus' epitomator had added the sentence.

T 17

Corippus *In Laudem Iustini Augusti Minoris* I.25–6 (Cameron, p. 37 = T 13 Müller *FHG* IV, p. 184): Successor and renewed glory of the good Peter, here present is, a *magister* with his father's gravity.

Theodorus is Theodorus 34, *PLRE* III, pp. 1255–56.

T 18

ELGR p. 390.5: From the *History* of Peter, *Patricius* and *Magister*.

T 19

ELRG p. 2.20: Peter, *Patricius* and *Magister*.

T 20

ELRG p. 3.3: From the *History* of Peter, *Patricius* and *Magister*.

T 21

Scorialensis (= *Haenelianus*) R II 13: The Peter who was one of the *magistri*, in the ninth book of his *Treatise on the Ceremony of the Palace*, says ...

The gloss was copied in 1574 from a manuscript no longer extant. See Laniado, "Un fragment peu connu de Pierre le Patrice," pp. 405–12, esp. pp. 405–8, on the passage and its importance for the study of the *scholia* to the *Basilica*.

T 22

Leidenensis Vossianus Gr. F 19 = *Scholium* 6, *Scholia Basilicorum* VIII.2.1, (Scheltema, *Basilicorum Libri* LX, Series B 1, p. 96): The same *magister* Peter, in the ninth book of his *Treatise on the Ceremony of the Palace*, says ...

FRAGMENTS AND COMMENTARY

F 1 (40 B.C.)

Dio XLVIII.24.5–6 (II, p. 265.12–19): He happened to have joined forces with Cassius and Brutus, and, having been sent to Orodes before the battle in order to receive some assistance, was delayed a long time by him while he [Orodes] was carefully observing what was going on and, on the one hand, hesitating to make a pact with him but, on the other hand, fearing to refuse. And subsequently, when the news of the defeat arrived and the victors were appearing to spare none of those who had warred against them, he remained among the barbarians, having preferred life with barbarians to destruction at home.

Peter *ES* 1, p. 241.1–5: ... having been sent on an embassy to Persia in order to request an alliance in respect of Brutus and Cassius. And as time began to pass, the sovereign of Persia being uncertain and awaiting the outcome of events, Labienus chose to remain among them, having preferred life with barbarians to destruction at home.

Before the Battle of Philippi (42 B.C.), Brutus and Cassius had dispatched Q. Labienus to Orodes, King of Parthia, in an effort to win his support. Labienus ultimately perished in Cilicia after a defeat in 39 at the hands of Antony's commander P. Ventidius Bassus. For more historical context, see Pelling, "The Triumviral Period," *CAH*² X, pp. 9–13 and 21. The passage reflects Peter's interest in Rome's dealings with her neighbors in the East.

F 2 (36 B.C.)

Dio XLIX.31.3 (II, p. 313.11–17): And ultimately, since the troops were not able to endure a further march and these things were happening in winter and, at the same time, too, since they were likely to suffer to no purpose – for he was intending to turn back to Armenia in not too long – , he flattered him very much and also made very many promises to him so that he might allow them to winter in the place, saying that come spring he would again campaign against the Parthians.

On Syntax = Περὶ Συντάξεως, *Lexica Segueriana*, ed. Bekker, *Anecdota Graeca*, Vol. I, p. 149.3–4, *s.v.* Θωπεύω = F1 Müller *FHG* IV p. 184: I flatter: with the accusative. In Peter's treatment of Antony: "At any rate, having flattered him very much ... "

The object of Antony's flattery was Artavasdes II of Armenia (*PIR*² A 1162, reigned 54–33) and its context the Roman campaign in 36 against the Parthians and their king, Phraates IV (*PIR*² P 296), and Artavasdes, king of Media Atropatene. Antony deposed Artavasdes II in 34 and took him to Egypt, where he remained a prisoner until 30, when, in the aftermath of Actium, Cleopatra ordered his execution. In 33, Phraates set one of Artavasdes II's sons, Artaxias (= Artaxes *PIR*² A1167, reigned 33 [33–30 *in absentia*]–20), on the vacated Armenian throne. On Antony's Parthian campaign and its aftermath, see Pelling, "The Triumviral Period," *CAH*² X, pp. 30–4, 38–40, and 59–61, and Reinhold, *From Republic to Principate*, pp. 55–60, 74–6, and 81–2.

F 3 (30 B.C.)

Dio LI.16.5 (II, p. 367.7–11): And next he looked at the body of Alexander and even touched it, with the result, so they say, that a bit of the nose was broken. But, in truth, the remains of the Ptolemies, though the Alexandrians had been zealously wishing to display them, he did not view, having said, "It was a king, but not corpses, I wanted to see."

Peter *ES* 2[a], p. 241.6–8: When Caesar was looking at the tomb and the body of Alexander, and the Alexandrians were urging him to see the body of Ptolemy, too, he said, "I wish to view kings, not corpses."

The occasion was Augustus' arrival in Alexandria after the victory at Actium and Antony's suicide. For Augustus' motivation, see F 4 below and, on this episode and Augustus in Memphis, Reinhold, *From Republic to Principate*, pp. 139–40.

F 4 (30 B.C.)

Dio LI.16.5 (II, p. 367.11–13): And for this same reason he did not want to meet with Apis, declaring that he was accustomed to worship gods, not cattle.

Peter *ES* 2[b], p. 241.9–10: When they are urging him, in turn, to meet with Apis, he says, "I am worshiping gods, not cattle."

Memphis was the home of Apis, the sacred bull. Augustus' snub of Apis and, by extension, of the priests of Memphis, served to distance his rule of Egypt from that of the Ptolemies. On this point, see, for example, Takács, "Cleopatra, Isis, and the Formation of Augustan Egypt," pp. 78–95, esp. pp. 80–2.

F 5 (29 B.C.)

Dio LII.42.6 (II, p. 411.18–20): He, then, both did these things and, furthermore, forbade all senators to travel outside Italy.

On Syntax = Περι Συνταξεως, *Lexica Segueriana*, Bekker, *Anecdota Graeca*, Vol. I, p. 130.10–12, *s.v.* Ἀνεῖπε = F1 Müller *FHG* p. 184: he forbade: with the dative. In Peter's treatment of the monarchy of Caesar: "He forbade senators to travel outside Italy."

If the reference in *On Syntax* to the source of its citation reflects the actual wording of the *History*, Peter may have taken his cue from Dio LII.1.1 (II, p. 379.6–8), where Dio begins his treatment of the events of 29 B.C. with the observation that after a period of seven hundred and twenty-five years the Romans began again to be ruled by a monarchy. On Augustus' directive, see Reinhold, *From Republic to Principate*, pp. 169–70 and 212–13, and Drogula, "Controlling Travel," pp. 230–66.

F 6 (26 B.C.)

Dio LIII.23.5 (II, p. 432.18–22):
But, in truth, Cornelius Gallus, too, engaged in all kinds of insolent behavior in consequence of his office. For, on the one hand, he was engaging in much idle chatter and did many blameworthy things besides. For, in fact, he both erected images of himself through the whole of Egypt, so to speak, and also inscribed his accomplishments on the pyramids …

Dio LIII.24.2 (II, p. 433.6–13):
Proculeius, however, was so disposed to him [Largus] that once, when he had encountered him, he covered his own nose and mouth with his hand, indicating to those with him that it was not safe for anyone to breath when he was around.

Peter *ES* 3, p. 241.11–18:
Cornelius became insolent and unjust, having been honored by Caesar. For in the exercise of his office he kept slandering and mistreating everyone, with the result, too, that a certain Proculus, having encountered him once, covered his own nose and mouth, implying that around him it was impossible to speak or breath. And someone else, having brought along witnesses, approached him in public and was asking him if he knew him. And when he said that he did not know him, having turned toward the witnesses, he said, "You see that he does not know me. Therefore, when speaking about me, in no way is he to be trusted."

F 6 as we have it mistakenly makes C. Cornelius Gallus (*PIR*^{2} C 1369), rather than Valerius Largus (*PIR* V 66), Gallus' "companion and intimate" (Dio LIII.23.6 [II, p. 432.23–4)]), the object of C. Proculeius' (*PIR*^{2} P 985) disgust. This confusion and F 6's "Proculus" for Dio's correct "Proculeius" are, if not Peter's or his exemplar's error, the fault of the Constantinian excerptor or of some earlier or later copyist.

The Caesar of F 6 is Augustus, who, in 30 B.C., had made Gallus the first prefect of Egypt. Proculeius, an *eques* and friend of Augustus, was trusted enough by the latter to have been dispatched to arrest Cleopatra. Apart from Dio LIII.23.6–24.3 (II, pp. 432.22–433.13) and Xiphil. 87.20–88.2 (III, p.

526), nothing else is known of Largus, who, according to Dio, had been the first accuser of Gallus. After Gallus' ruin and suicide, Largus had become an object of a general adulation to which Proculeius took exception.

Daly and Reiter, "The Gallus Affair and Augustus' *lex Iulia maiestas*," pp. 289–311, treat Gallus' fall. For commentary on Dio's handling of these events, see Rich, *Cassius Dio: The Augustan Settlement*, pp. 157–58, and, on Gallus in general, Boucher, *Caius Cornélius Gallus*, and Thompson and Koenen, "Gallus as Triptolemos on the Tazza Farnese," pp. 111–56.

F 7 (15 A.D.)

Dio LVII.14.1–2 (II, pp. 570.23–571.4): In the consulships of Drusus, his [Tiberius'] son, and of Gaius Norbanus, he paid to the populace what had been bequeathed by Augustus after someone, having approached a corpse being borne through the agora and having leaned down toward its ear, whispered something, and, when those who saw this asked what he had said, said that he had admonished Augustus that they had not yet been paid anything. In consequence, he [Tiberius] immediately had that man killed, in order that he might become a bearer of his own message to him, as he – mocking him, too, I suppose – said, and not much later reconciled with the others, having distributed sixty-five drachmas apiece.

Peter *ES* 4, p. 241.19–25: For a long time, Tiberius did not pay the legacies bequeathed by Caesar. And, when a corpse was being borne through the agora, someone, having approached, seemed to whisper in its ear, and, when he had been asked by those present why he had done this, said that they had disclosed to Augustus that to date the legacies had not been granted, on the one hand, he immediately had that man killed, in order that he might become a bearer of his own message to him, just as, mocking him, <he said>.

C. Norbanus Flaccus (*PIR*[2] N 168) and Drusus Julius Caesar (*PIR*[2] I 219) were *consules ordinarii* in A.D. 15. The anonymous man employs the corpse as a medium through which he can communicate the news of Tiberius' delinquency to Augustus (died August 19, 14 A.D.). Suet. *Tib*. 57.2 recounts the same incident. With Dio and Peter, cf. Xiphil. 131.30–132.9 (III, p. 551) and Zonar. XI.2 (II, p. 437.4–10). On Augustus' bequests, see Suet. *Aug*. 101.2, which specifies Augustus' order for immediate payment, and Tac.

Ann. I.8. Furneaux, *The Annals of Tacitus*², Vol. I, pp. 191–92, notes some implications of Dio's figure of sixty-five drachmas.

F 8 (17 or 18 A.D.)

Peter *ES* 5, p. 242.1–3: The senate also resolved that the month November, in which Tiberius was born, be called "Tiberius." But he did not acquiesce, having said to them, "And if you have thirteen Caesars, what will you do?"

Xiphil. 135.1–4 (III, p. 553) = Dio LVII.18.2 (II, p. 576.1–3): When the senate was pressing Tiberius, and, case in point, was requesting that the month November, on the sixteenth day of which he had been born, be called "Tiberius", he said, "What will you do if there come to be thirteen Caesars?"

Suet. *Tib.* 26.2 makes September the month in question. Tiberius' day of birth was November 16, 42 B.C.

F 9 (20 A.D.)

Peter *ES* 6, p. 242.4–9 = Dio LVII.19.1^{b} (II, p. 580.5–10): Tiberius used to berate bitterly those charged with something, uttering the following, "Nobody is ruled willingly, but he is forced to this against his will." For those who are ruled not only do not submit happily, but they also conspire against those who rule them. And he used to receive with favor those who were bringing charges, not distinguishing whether a slave speaks against a master or a son <against a father>.

The gloss that follows the quotation attributed to Tiberius could be Dio's or, perhaps, Peter's. Dio LIX.16.7 (II, p. 635.13–15), reproduced by Xiphil. 162.1–3 (III, p. 568), puts in Caligula's mouth a variation of the sentiment F 9 assigns to Tiberius.

F 10 (26–29 A.D.)

Peter *ES* 7, p. 242.10–13: Once when Livia was leading the way, some naked men came fully into her view, and, in consequence, were being led off to death. But she commanded that they be released, having said: "To the chaste, these seem to be statues."

Xiphil. 143.26–30 (III, p. 558) = Dio LVIII.2.4 (II, pp. 589.19–590.2): And other deft sayings of hers are in circulation, even that she once saved some naked men who had encountered her and, in consequence, were going to be put to death, having said, "For the chaste, such men differ not at all from statues."

This particular anecdote appears only in Peter, Xiphilinus, and at Zonar. XI.2 (II, pp. 441.21–442.2). Barrett, *Livia*, pp. 120–25, situates it, together with other celebrations of Livia's chastity, within the context of Augustus' social legislation and the maintenance of his public image. On Greek and Roman views of public nudity, see Hurschmann, "Nudity, § C, Everyday Life and Sport," col. 874.

F 11 (29 A.D.)

Peter *ES* 8, p. 242.14–18: The same woman [Livia], when she had been asked what sorts of methods she employed to exert so much control over Caesar, said, "Doing all the things he approves of with pleasure and not busying myself in any of his other affairs and pretending not to notice his sexual playthings."

Xiphil. 143.30–144.4 (III, p. 558) = Dio LVIII.2.5 (II, p. 590.2–5): When someone had asked her how and by what means she dominated Augustus to such a degree, she replied, "Keeping myself scrupulously chaste, gladly doings everything which seems right to him, not meddling in any of that man's other affairs, and pretending <neither to hear> nor to notice his sexual playthings."

Only Peter, Xiphilinus, and Zonar. XI.2 (II, p. 442.2–7) preserve this story.

F 12 (30 A.D.)

Peter *ES* 9, p. 242.19–22: Tiberius, when he was violently torturing someone on false charges and had discovered that he was tortured without cause, commanded that he be summarily executed, for he said that deliverance from life was beneficial to one who had been abused thus.

Xiphil. 145.16–19 (III, p. 559) = Dio LVIII.3.7 (II, p. 592.3–5): Moreover, when he had very severely tortured some other man, then discovered that he had been unjustly accused, he very curtly condemned him to death, having said, "He is too grievously abused to be able to live happily."

The episode is otherwise unattested. The context in Dio is Tiberius' elimination of C. Asinius Gallus (*PIR*[2] A 1229) and Vallius Syriacus (*PIR* V 171).

F 13 (30 A.D.)

Peter *ES* 10, p. 242.23–27 = Dio LVIII.4.9 (II, p. 594.8–11): Tiberius, having feigned a disease, sent Sejanus ahead to Rome, asserting that he too would follow, saying that a portion of his own body and soul was being torn from him, and he embraced him and, with tears, kissed him, with the result that Sejanus was more confident.

Tiberius's alleged ruse and remark to Sejanus are otherwise unknown.

F 14 (31 A.D.)

Dio LVIII.10.8–11.2 (II, p. 599.11–25): In truth, Regulus did not put the vote about his [Sejanus'] death either to all or to any one of them, frightened lest somebody oppose it and from this there also be some dustup, for, of course, he had many kinsmen and friends. But after he had inquired of someone and received the same verdict that he should be bound, he, together with the other magistrates and with Laco, led him from the senate and down to the prison. Then, indeed, one could to the fullest extent view human frailty, so as never to be swollen with conceit. For he whom everyone had escorted at dawn to the senate chamber inasmuch as he was even mightier than them, this man they then were dragging off to the pen as no one's better, and he whom they were formerly deeming worthy of many crowns, on this man they then placed bonds; and he whom they used to attend as a bodyguard like a master, this one they were guarding like a runaway slave and were uncovering his head whenever he was covering it, and

Peter *ES* 11, p. 242.28–33: Regulus and Laco, having seized Sejanus, bound him and led him to the prison. And from this one should have more compassion for human frailty and learn not to be elated about the good and not to feel revulsion about those who seem to be the opposite. For those who formerly honored him like a master were then guarding him like a runaway slave.

he whom they had decked out in the purple-edged toga, this one they were striking on the side of the head, <and> he to whom they used to do obeisance and to whom, as to a god, they used to make offerings, this one they were leading on with the intention of putting him to death.

Boissevain (II, p. 599, apparatus to 15–22) thinks that from "and will be taught" to "revulsion about those who seem to be the opposite" are Peter's own words. The arrest, prosecution before the senate in the Temple of Apollo, condemnation, and execution of Sejanus – L. Aelius Seianus (*PIR*^{2} A 255) – , occurred in October of 31, during which year he was *consul ordinarius* with Tiberius. P. Memmius Regulus (*PIR*^{2} M 468) was a *consul suffectus*, P. Graecinius Laco (*PIR*^{2} G 202) *praefectus vigilum*. Dio's detailed account comprises LVIII.9–13.3 (II, pp. 597.16–602.14). Seager, *Tiberius*, pp. 214–23, provides a modern overview. See, too, Syme, *Tacitus*, Vol. II, pp. 752–54.

F 15 (32 A.D.)

Dio LVIII.14.1–2 (II, p. 602.17–19): And then his kin and companions and all the rest who had flattered him in any way and those who had proposed honors for him began to be prosecuted.

Peter *ES* 12, p. 243.1–3: After the death of Sejanus, Tiberius had many of his friends executed, and many he punished. So too, in consequence, are all these things attributable to fortune.

Since Fortune appears in *ES* 12 but not Dio, "So too, in consequence, all these things are attributable to fortune" may be Peter's addendum. For Dio's references to Fortune, see *s.v.* Τύχη in W. Nawijn's *Index Verborum* to Boissevain's edition (V, pp. 807–8).

F 16 (32 A.D.)

Dio LVIII.19.3–4 (II, p. 606.14–23): ... now, of Terentius, because, being examined with reference to Sejanus' friendship, not only did he not deny it, but even said he had regarded him with the utmost respect and did him service, since he was honored thus, too, by

Peter *ES* 13, p. 243.4–10: Terentius, being examined with reference to Sejanus' friendship before Tiberius, said, "I did nothing unjust if I used to have this man as a friend, seeing him being honored by you. For if you, the ruler who knows all things

Tiberius himself, "with the result" he said, "that if, on the one hand, he [Tiberius] was behaving properly in having such a friend, I have not done anything unjust; on the other hand, if the ruler who knows all things accurately erred, what wonder is it if I, too, was deceived along with him? For, in point of fact, it certainly behooves us to feel affection for those honored by him, not being much concerned about what sort certain individuals are, but making the single standard of their friendship that they please the ruler."

accurately, erred, what wonder is it if I, too, was deceived along with you? For, in point of fact, it behooves us to feel affection for all those honored by you, not ever being much concerned about what sort they are, but making a single standard of their friendship that they please the ruler."

Tac. *Ann.* VI.8–9.1 has the *eques* Marcus Terentius deliver a speech in his own defense before the senate in which he makes the same point in much the same fashion, particularly at VI.8.4. According to Tacitus, Terentius' forthrightness resulted in the banishment of his accusers. On the relationship between the presentations of Terentius in Dio/Peter and in Tacitus, see Koestermann, *Cornelius Tacitus* Annalen, Vol. 2, p. 256.

F 17 (33 A.D.)

Dio LVIII.23.3 (II, p. 610.4–6): For he was ignorant of nothing that had to do with Gaius, but even said to him once, as he was quarreling with Tiberius, "You will kill him and others you."

Peter *ES* 14, p. 243.11–13: Once when Gaius and Tiberius, his [Tiberius'] descendant, were sparring, Tiberius the grandfather said to Gaius, "Why hurry? You will slay him and others you."

Excerpta Anonymi Byzantini ex Codice Parisino Suppl. Gr. 607 A, ed. Treu, p. 31.15–17 = Cumont, *Testimonia de Astrologis Romanis ex Codice Parisino Suppl. Gr. 607 A*, p. 100.6–8: "Once when Gaius, the son of Germanicus, and Tiberius, the son of Tiberius, were sparring, Tiberius said to Gaius, "Why hurry? You will kill him and another you."

Xiphil. 154.7–8 (III, p. 564): "For it is said that he once said to Gaius, as he was quarreling with Tiberius, "You will kill him and others you."

Zonar. XI.3 (II, p. 443.4–6): "For he was ignorant of nothing that had to do with Gaius, but even said to him once, as he was quarreling with Tiberius, "You will kill him and others you."

Tac. *Ann.* VI.46.4 places the same comment – "*occides hunc tu*," *inquit*, "*et te alius*." – in the context of verbal sparring between Caligula and Tiberius Gemellus, the son of Nero Claudius Drusus Germanicus (*PIR*[2] C 857) and Claudia Livia Julia (*PIR*[2] L 303). For the emperor Tiberius' ill feelings toward his grandson Gemellus and Caligula, see Suet. *Tib.* 62.3. After adopting Gemellus in 37, Caligula had him killed either in that year or in 38. On Gemellus' death, see Barrett, *Caligula*, pp. 108–11.

Since neither Dio, the Anonymous Treu, Xiphilinus, nor Zonaras styles the emperor Tiberius "grandfather" (πάππος), the word's presence in *ES* 14 is probably the excerptor's clarification or, less likely, Peter's. Likewise, either the excerptor or Peter must be responsible for the replacement of "you will kill" (ἀποκτενεῖς) with "you will slay" (φονεύσεις). The presence of "Why hurry?" in both Peter and the Anonymous suggests that they depended directly or indirectly on a different manuscript from that employed by Xiphilinus and Zonaras.

F 18 (33 A.D.)

Dio LVIII.23.4 (II, p. 610.10–12): At any rate, he is said <on the one hand> often to have recited this well-known old bit: "When I have died, let earth be mixed with fire."

Peter *ES* 15, p. 243.14–15: Tiberius was continuously repeating this iambidic: "When I have died, let earth be mixed with fire."

Suet. *Ner.* 38.1 attributes the same quotation to Tiberius. Cf. John of Antioch F 159.1.34–35 (Roberto, p. 280/Mariev, p. 185). Nauck *TGF, Adespota* 513, p. 940, provides references to other instances. "Iambidic" (τὸ ἰαμβίδιον), a *hapax legomenon*, may be Peter's term. In contrast to τὸ ἰαμβίδιον, τὸ ἰάμβιον, which stands in *ES* 51 = F 56 and *ES* 118 = F 130, below, also appears in a *scholium* to Plato *Republic* VIII.568b1 (Greene, *Scholia Platonica*, p. 266).

F 19 (33 A.D.)

Dio LVIII.23.4 (II, p. 610.13–14): Often, too, [he is said] to have counted Priam blessed, because he perished together with his country and his sovereignty.

Peter *ES* 16, p. 243.16–17: The same man, too, used to count Priam blessed because he perished along with his country and his sovereignty.

Tiberius' sentiment also appears at Suet. *Tib.* 62.3, to which cf. John of Antioch F 159.1.35–6 (Roberto, p. 280/Mariev, p. 185).

F 20 (34 A.D.)

Dio LVIII.24.3–4 (II, pp. 611.15–612.4): And Mamercus Aemilius Scaurus, in truth, who had never been in charge of anything or accepted bribes, was condemned because of a tragedy and met with misfortune more terrible than that which he composed. The poetic work was *Atreus*, and, in the manner of Euripides, it advised one of those ruled by him to bear the folly of he who was in control. Then, when he had learned this, Tiberius said that the verse had referred to him, having alleged himself to be Atreus because of his bloodthirstiness, and, explaining, "And I, then, shall make him Ajax," he brought pressure upon him to perish by his own hand.

Peter *ES* 17, p. 243.18–24: Aemilius Mamertius made a drama he titled *Atreus* in which he introduced someone saying, in the manner of Euripides, "One must bear the stupidities of those who rule." And, when he had learned this, Tiberius understood that verse was about him, having considered himself to be called Atreus because of the abominations of the slayings which he wrought, and he kept saying, "This man made me Atreus, and I shall make him Ajax." Therefore, he brought pressure upon him, with the result that he killed himself.

Tiberius quotes Eur. *Phoen.* 396. Tac. *Ann.* VI.29.3–4 has Q. Naevius Cordus Sutorius Macro (*PIR*[2] N 12) denounce Mamercus Aemilius Scaurus' (*PIR*[2] A 404) play and a Cornelius (*PIR*[2] C 1307 or 1342) and a Servilius (*PIR* 408, perhaps Tuscus) charge Scaurus with magic and adultery with Livilla, i.e., Livia Julia (*PIR*[2] L 303). Suet. *Tib.* 61.3 alludes to this incident.

F 21

Peter *ES* 18, p. 243.25–26: What someone wishes and desires, this, too, he very quickly believes.

Boissevain (III, p. 736) attributes these words to Peter.

F 22 (35 A.D.)

Dio LVIII.26.1–4 (II, p. 613.4–19): At the very same time, Artabanus the Parthian, when Artaxes had died, gave Armenia to Arsaces, his own son, and, when there was no punishment for this from Tiberius, began to try for Cappadocia and also to treat the Parthians very haughtily. Therefore, having rebelled from him, some sent an embassy to Tiberius, requesting a sovereign for themselves from those being held hostage. And to them, then, on the one hand, he sent Phraates, the son of Phraates, and when he had died en route, Tiridates, he too being from the royal line. And precisely so that he might assume control of the realm with the greatest ease, he wrote to Mithridates (the one in Iberia) to attack Armenia, in order that Artabanus, coming to the aid of his son from his own realm, would march forth. And so it was, though Tiridates, too, did not reign for long, for Artabanus, having enlisted Scythians, drove him out without difficulty. On the one hand, then, thus were the affairs of Parthia, on the other hand, Mithridates, a child of Mithridates of Iberia, so it seems, and a brother of Pharasmanes, the one who had become sovereign of the Iberians after him, took Armenia.

Peter *ELGR* 1, p. 390.6–15 = F2 Müller *FHG* IV, p. 180: The Parthians were requesting through an embassy to Trajan that he give them a sovereign from those being held hostage. And he sent them Phraates, the son of Phraates. And when he had died en route, he sent Tiridates, from the royal line, and, <so> that he might assume control of the realm with ease, wrote to Mithridates, sovereign of Iberia, to attack Armenia in order that Artabanus, coming to the aid of his son from his own realm, would be at hand. And, when he had arrived, Tiridates took control of the realm. However, he too did not reign for long, for Artabanus, having enlisted Scythians, drove him out without difficulty. And these, on the one hand, were the affairs pertaining to Parthia.

With Dio and Peter, cf. Tac. *Ann.* VI.31–32.3. Anderson, "The Eastern Frontier from Tiberius to Nero," *CAH* X, pp. 747–50, provides context.

F 23 (37 A.D.)

Dio LVIII.27.4 (II, p. 614.16–20): ... and Lucius Arruntius, distinguished both in age and in learning, perished voluntarily, although Tiberius was already sick and thought not to recover. For when he had perceived the evilness of Gaius, he was eager, before he experienced him, to die beforehand, having said, "I am not able in old age to serve a master who is new and of this sort."

Peter *ES* 19, p. 243.27–31: A certain Lucius Arruntius, distinguished for his age and his culture, having seen Tiberius sick to the point of death and being at risk and the sovereignty moving to Gaius, killed himself, having said, "I am not able in old age to serve a master, especially a younger one of this sort."

Tacitus' L. Arruntius (*PIR*[2] A 1130) voices similar sentiments at *Ann.* VI.47–48.3, where he maintains that the charges against Arruntius included complicity in Sejanus' planned coup and adultery with Albucilla (*PIR*[2] A 487), whom Dio LVIII.27.4 (II, p. 614.14–16) mentions, though not by name.

F 24 (37 A.D.)

Dio LVIII.28.4 (II, p. 615.4–8): For, in as much as Tiberius already was badly ill, he [Macro] was playing to the youth [Caligula], and, most of all, he had led him to a desire of his own [Macro's] wife, Ennia Thrasylla. And Tiberius, having suspected this, once said, "Well, indeed, it is that, having abandoned the one in descent, you hurry toward the one on the ascendant."

Peter *ES* 20, pp. 243.32–244.2: Once Tiberius, when he had observed the friendship of Macro and Gaius, said, "You do well indeed, leaving the one in descent behind and running toward the one on the ascendant."

Tac. *Ann.* VI.46.4 mentions the same censure by Tiberius. It was the praetorian prefect Q. Naevius Cordus Sutorius Macro (*PIR*[2] N 12) who, according to Tac. *Ann.* VI.50.5, ordered Tiberius' murder. In contrast, Suet. *Calig.* 12.2 makes Caligula the killer, while Dio LVIII.28.3 (II, pp. 614.31–615.4) names both. Dio and Suetonius agree about an illicit affair between Caligula and

Ennia (*PIR*^{2} E 65). Suetonius, unlike Dio, makes Macro the initiator. Tiberius' alleged comment is perhaps meant to echo Pompey's supposed quip about Sulla that more people worship the rising than the setting sun (Plut. *Regnum et Imperatorum Apophthegmata* 203 E).

F 25 (37/40 A.D.)

Dio LIX.8.8 (II, p. 626.18–21): And, indeed, after he had granted that ten slaves be furnished to Piso, then, when he asked for more, he granted that he have as many as he wanted, having said, "The same number of soldiers also will join you."

Peter *ES* 21, p. 244.3–6: Gaius, having banished Piso, gave him ten slaves alone. And when that one began to beg that he give more to him, he ordered him to have as many as he decides he needs, having said, "However, the same number of soldiers will also join you."

Dio says that Caligula seized Cornelia Orestilla (*PIR*^{2} C 1942) during the celebration of her marriage to C. Calpurnius Piso (*PIR*^{2} C 284), then, within two months (more probably two years) and on the grounds that Cornelia and Piso were having an affair, banished both. In 65, Piso committed suicide after the failed conspiracy against Nero in which he had played an important, if ineffective, part. On Piso's death, see Tac. *Ann.* XV.59.1–5, on the so-called Pisonian Conspiracy, Griffin, *Nero*, pp. 166–70.

F 26 (39 A.D.)

Dio LIX.16.1–4 (II, pp. 634.14–635.2): Up to this time, then, he [Caligula] was constantly and before all speaking ill of Tiberius, and he did not just give a pass to the others who were maligning him in private or in public but even took delight in them. But then, having entered the council chamber, he roundly commended him and roundly chastised the senate and the populace on the grounds that they were wrongly censuring him. "For," he said, "while it is permissible for me, being ruler, to do this, too, you, to be sure, not only act unjustly <but

Peter *ES* 22, p. 244.7–13: After many second-thoughts, Gaius at last began to turn upon the senate and brought charges against them that they had slandered Tiberius. "For," he said, "while it is permissible for me, being ruler, to do this, too, you not only act unjustly but also impiously, being so disposed toward the one who ruled you, and if he did some wrong, he acted at your urging. And Sejanus, having been inflated by you, was destroyed."

also impiously>, being so ill-disposed towards the man who once ruled you." And after this, going individually through those who had perished, he began proclaiming that it seemed, in fact, that the senators had been the causes of the destruction of most of them, because they prosecuted some of them, because they testified against others, and because they pronounced sentence on all. And these things, too, supposedly from those same letters which he once said he had burned, he read through his freedmen, and he added, "And if Tiberius had done anything unjust, you ought not to have honored him while he lived, by Zeus, nor to have reversed your position about what you often discussed and voted on. But you both dealt with that man capriciously and, having inflated and corrupted Sejanus, you condemned him, with the result that it is necessary that I, too, accept no kindness from you."

An immediate result of Caligula's invective was to cow the senate (Dio LIX.8–11 [II, p. 635.15–32]). Barrett, *Caligula*, pp. 130–2, offers a critical overview. Suet. *Calig.* 30.2 also connects Caligula's aspersions to senatorial support of Sejanus.

F 27 (39 A.D.)

Dio LIX.18.5 (II, p. 638.3–7): And, on the one hand, a certain Junius Priscus, a commander, was accused of some other things but killed because he was wealthy. And, in this case, Gaius, when he

Peter *ES* 23, p. 244.14–16: Gaius, when he had killed Priscus on account of his possessions and discovered that these were few, uttered an amazing statement: "He deceived me and needlessly had learned that he had acquired nothing worthy of the death, uttered an amazing statement: "He deceived me and needlessly perished, for he could have survived."

perished. For he could not survive under these circumstances."

If wittiness is the measure, Peter's version of what Caligula said is preferable to Dio's, the point of the former being that Priscus might have avoided execution had Caligula known that his true circumstances alone would have done him in. In any case, some modern scholars doubt that Caligula's primary motive in this or parallel instances was the acquisition of wealth. Junius Priscus (*PIR*² I 801), a praetor in 39, is unknown apart from Dio, Peter, Xiphil. 164.2–6 (III, p. 570), and Zonar. XI.5 (II, p. 452.18–21).

F 28 (39 A.D.)

Dio LIX.19.1–2 (II, p. 638.8–14): Among these men who had then been judged, Domitius Afer also experienced incredible danger and a more wondrous salvation. For Gaius hated him for other reasons too, because under Tiberius he had accused a certain woman who was related to Agrippina, his mother. No doubt as a result of this, she, having once encountered him and having noticed he stood aside from the road through shame, summoned him and said: "Courage, Domitius, for to me it is not you who are culpable, but Agamemnon."

Peter *ES* 24, p. 244.17–21: Dometius, an orator most excellent and awesome, a base man, under Tiberius informed against a woman of the notables, with the result that she came close to death. And, having encountered her once, being ashamed, he got out of the way. And she, having come near him, said, "Courage, Dometius, because to me you are not to blame, but Agamemnon."

Cn. Domitius Afer (*PIR*² D 126) was one of the consummate orators of his age. Tac. *Ann.* IV.52.1–4 names Claudia Pulchra (*PIR*² C 1116) as Afer's target and recounts Vipsania Agrippina's (*PIR* V 463) visceral reaction. Tiberius condemned both Claudia Pulchra and Furnius (*PIR*² F 589), her alleged lover, on the charge of adultery. Afer's accusation would have been in 26. Tac. *Ann.* IV.66.1–2 describes Afer's subsequent prosecution of Claudia Pulchra's son, Quinctilius Varus (*PIR*² Q 30) in 27. Agrippina, whose "Agamemnon" is Tiberius, perhaps alludes to Hom. *Il.* XIII.112.

F 29 (39 A.D.)

Dio LIX.19.2–7 (II, pp. 638.14–639.7): And then, when he [Domitius] had erected an image of him, he inscribed an epigram on it, making manifest that in his twenty-seventh <year> he was consul for the second time, he [Caligula] was irritated on the grounds that he [Domitius] was reproaching his youth and lawlessness, and immediately concerning this act, about which he actually expected to the honored, he [Caligula] brought him to the council and read a long speech against him. For generally he thought that he surpassed all the orators and, knowing that that man was an awesome speaker, he was eager to surpass him. And he surely would have had him killed, if he had been moved however much to jealousy. And he now made no reply nor offered any defense, but actually, having affected to wonder at and to be astounded by the awesomeness of Gaius, and repeating the charge point by point, just as if being some listener but not under examination, he was commending him, and, when the right to speak was given to him, he resorted to entreaty and lamentation, and, in the end, fell to the ground and, lying prostrate, supplicated him on the grounds that he was more frightened of him as an orator than as the Caesar. And so, he, seeing and hearing this, was softened, having actually believed he had overpowered him

Peter *ES* 25, p. 244.21–35: This Domitius, having made an inscription for a statue of Gaius, said, "In his twenty-seventh year he was consul for the second time." When he had received this, Gaius brought charges against him on the grounds that he was disparaging his youth and lawlessness, and he brought him to the senate for the purpose of having him killed and delivered an ornately composed speech, and if he had defended himself, he would have been put to death. And he was in awe of him as he spoke and kept applauding like someone listening but not someone being charged; and when he had finished, in an exaggerated fashion he seemed to be amazed at the awesomeness of the speech. And when an opportunity for a defense had been given, he began to turn to lamentation and, in the end, fell to the ground, supplicating him and saying he feared him as a speaker more than as a Caesar. And he, seeing and hearing this, was softened, having believed that he had prevailed by the disposition of his words, and released him, saying, "No longer consider yourself an awesome speaker." He also appointed him a consul.

by the disposition of his words. And, because of this and because of Callistus, the freedman, whom he was holding in esteem and to whom Domitius had paid court, he ceased being angry. And, in fact, he replied to Callistus, having blamed him later because he even accused him in the first place, "It was unfitting that I keep such a speech to myself." Domitius, on the one hand, convicted, in truth, of no longer being an awesome speaker, was saved.

Apart from Dio, Peter, Xiphilinus, and Zonaras, this incident goes unmentioned. For Domitius Afer, see on F 28. C. Julius Callistus (*PIR*² I 229), Caligula's most influential freedman, later aided in his assassination and afterwards became *a libellis* of Claudius (*PIR*² C 942). Xiphil. 164.15–165.10 (III, p. 570) treats both Domitius and Callistus, while Zonar. XI.5 (II, pp. 452.21–453.7) omits mention of the latter. Caligula did, in fact, appoint Domitius a *consul suffectus* for 39 (cf. Dio LIX.20.1 [II, p. 639.13]).

F 30 (39 A.D.)

Dio LIX.19.7–8 (II, p. 639.7–12):
On the other hand, Lucius Annaeus Seneca, having excelled in wisdom all the Romans who were his contemporaries and many others, too, was, in truth, nearly destroyed, neither having done nor having seemed to do any wrong, because he delivered a certain case beautifully in the council when he [Caligula] was present. Then, on the one hand, after he had ordered him to be put to death, he pardoned him, having believed one of the women with whom he was intimate, that he was sorely afflicted by empyema and would soon meet his end.

Peter *ES* 26, p. 245.1–6:
Seneca Anneus, excelling all his contemporaries in wisdom, when he delivered before him [Caligula] a finely composed speech, on account of this alone was almost destroyed. But he pardoned him, persuaded by a woman with whom he was sleeping who was present, who said, "He is afflicted with empyema and will soon die." And having considered this true, he conceded to him only that he was not going to die yet.

These are the only versions of this alleged incident. L. Annaeus Seneca (*PIR*^{2} A 617) is, of course, the famous orator, tragedian, proponent of Stoicism, and tutor of Nero. Suet. *Calig.* 53.2 maintains that Caligula regularly disparaged Seneca's eloquence. On the grounds for Caligula's criticism, see Barrett, *Caligula*, p. 69, and, on the possibility of Julia Agrippina – Agrippina the Younger (*PIR*^{2} I 641) – as the anonymous woman, pp. 149 and 155, n. 101, and Barrett's *Agrippina*, pp. 68–9. Seneca's eventual suicide occurred in 65. Griffin, *Seneca*, p. 42, treats Seneca's health and, pp. 52–6, offers an insightful analysis of Dio's testimony.

F 31 (39 A.D.)

Dio LIX.22.1–3 (II, p. 642.1–9): For he gathered two-hundred thousand, but as some say, two-hundred and fifty thousand [soldiers], and seven times by them was acclaimed emperor, as, I suppose, also seemed right to him, having neither won any battle nor having slain any enemy. For, while once, when he had captured a few of them by some trickery, these he bound, and actually did away with a large part of his own, cutting down some one by one, others, too, in groups simultaneously, having murdered all of them. For once, when he had noticed a crowd either of prisoners or some others, he gave this very order, that, from the bald one to the bald one, they all be slaughtered.

Peter *ES* 27, p. 245.7–11: Gaius was so indiscriminate about the slayings that once, when many accused had been brought before him, on the condition that he examine them, on the one hand, he stood them in a row, and delivered the howler repeated to this day, "From the bald one to that longhaired one, slay all."

Suet. *Calig.* 27.1 records the same comment as Dio and Xiphil. 166.15–17 (III, p. 571). It is impossible to tell whether or not the variant in the *ES* is due to Peter, his exemplar, or the excerptor.

F 32 (39 A.D.)

Dio LIX.22.3–4 (II, p. 642.9–14): And once, when he was playing dice and had learned that there was no money, he demanded the registries of the Gauls and, when he had ordered the wealthiest from these put to death, he returned to the dice players and said: "You compete about a few drachmas, but I gathered about 150,000,000."

Peter *ES* 28, p. 245.12–16: The same man, playing dice once in Gaul and having learned there was no money, having gotten up, sought a register of the wealthy and ordered that many from these be murdered and their wealth brought in. And, having approached his fellow dice players, he said, "While you strive over a pittance, I amassed a fortune."

Note that the point of the comment, rather than the precise amount involved, was important to Peter or the excerptor. Xiphil. 166.21–23 (III, p. 571) and Zonar. XI.6 (II, p. 453.14–15) retain the figure. Only Peter or the excerptor actually sets the incident in Gaul, though Caligula was, indeed, in Gaul by October of 39. Suet. *Calig.* 41.2 records a slightly similar story involving Caligula and two Roman *equites*.

F 33 (40 A.D.)

Peter *ES* 29, p. 245.17–31: The same Gaius, after he had arrested Cerialius and his son, Papinius, tortured senators, with the result that they declared the plots that were being fomented against him. And Cerialius, on the one hand, said absolutely nothing, and before his eyes they were immediately killed – among whom was Bassus, too. And he [Caligula] produced his [Bassus'] father [Capito], who had

Xiphil. 167.23–7 (III, p. 572) = Dio LIX.25.6 (II, pp. 647.24–648.10): When he [Caligula] had ordered Beltinus Cassus to be slain, he forced his father, Capito, who had not done anything unjust and had not been indicted, to be with him while he was being murdered. And when he inquired if it was permissible for him at least to shut his eyes, he commanded that that man also be slain.

Zonar. XI.6 (II, pp. 454.13–455.7) = Dio LIX.25.5b–7 (II, pp. 647.13–648.23): Having lived in this fashion, he was altogether likely to be plotted against. And he detected that attack, and, after he had arrested Anicius Cerialis and his son, Sextus Papinius, he tortured him. And when he had divulged nothing, promising salvation and a pardon to him, he persuaded Papinius to denounce certain people, either neither been falsely accused nor issued a summons, in order that he might observe his son's execution. And when the old man had inquired if it was possible for him to shut "the lecherous," he [Caligula] commanded that, after their murder, he also be murdered. And, having disguised his true feelings, he kept repeating that the judgment of the sovereign was just, for, in truth, both they and he himself were among the murderers and many others were our accomplices. And, when he had been ordered to speak, he said that all those near him were also collaborators in these evils. And he would have accomplished the greatest things, if, after he had been brought forward, he had not also named those really close to him [Caligula]. For he thus was distrusted about the rest. And that man [Bassus' father] was killed.

truly or falsely, and immediately he gave a command to kill that man and the rest before his eyes. And being in danger, he affected to be one of the men who had plotted against him, promised to expose all the rest, and named both Gaius' companions and the accomplices in his licentiousness and cruelty. And he would have brought many to ruin, except that, when he had slandered the prefects and Callistus and Caesonia, he was distrusted. And he, on the one hand, was executed, but prepared this very same destruction for Gaius.

For the principals and problems of interpretation, see Barrett, *Caligula*, pp. 249–50 and 265, nn. 17–20. The excerptor's "us" may be a trace of direct statement. "Lecherous," whether Dio's, Peter's, or the excerptor's word, is a circumlocution for the tamer "eyes" of Xiphilinus and Zonaras. Suet. *Calig.* 27.4 mentions Caligula compelling parents to watch the executions of their sons.

F 34 (40 A.D.)

Peter *ES* 30, pp. 245.32–246.5: Gaius himself, having called the prefects and two others, entered in a tunic and says to them, "Behold! You three are armed, but I am alone and unarmed. If you hate me, murder me." And as those men fell at his feet and kept proclaiming that they had no such thing in mind about him, he withdrew, feigning he had been persuaded. And yet he himself remained suspicious about their friendship, and they were full of fear. And he was keeping them at odds with one another.

Zonar. XI.6 (II, pp. 455.7–15) = Dio LIX.25.8 (II, pp. 648.23–649.12): For, having summoned the prefects and Callistus in private, he said, "I am one, and you are three; while I am unarmed, you have weapons. Therefore, if you hate me and want to kill me, slay me." As a result of this, having considered himself to be hated and that they were angered by what he was doing, he began to suspect them and to wear a sword in his belt even in the city, and he was engaging them with one another, in order that they not be of one mind, talking to each one individually about the rest, on the grounds that he was most trustworthy, until, understanding what he was up to, they delivered him to the conspirators.

These are the only accounts of this alleged incident. Callistus is C. Julius Callistus (*PIR*^{2} I 229).

F 35 (40 A.D.)

Peter *ES* 31, p. 246.6–9 = Dio LIX.25.9 (II, p. 649.13–16): He [Caligula] himself ordered that senate be convened, and he pretended he had given amnesty to them, having said that there were few, in fact, with whom he was still angry. And in the judgment of all, he was giving these men twice the anxiety, for each was thinking of himself.

Barrett, *Caligula*, pp. 307–12, offers an overview of Caligula's relationship with the senate.

F 36 (40 A.D.)

Peter *ES* 32, p. 246.10–18: Protogenes, one of the harshest *delatores*, always carried two scrolls in which he wrote the accusations, and the larger he named *Sword*, the smaller *Dagger*. The man [Protogenes] entered the council chamber, and, when the senators saw him, through fear all ran forward and began to greet him and to welcome him with a kiss. And when Scribonius, too, was advised to do this, having glared fearsomely, he [Protogenes] said, "Do you too greet me thus, despising Caesar?", with the result that all the senators surrounded Scribonius and tore him to pieces. And having learned this, Gaius was conciliated.

Xiphil. 167.27–168.4 (III, p. 572) = Dio LIX.26.1–3.1 (II, pp. 649.19–650.3): Now there was a certain Protogenes who was assisting him with all the harshest matters, with the result that he always carried about two books and named one of these *The Sword*, the other *The Dagger*. This man once entered the council chamber as if about something else, and, when all, as was natural, greeted him and were welcoming him, he observed something bitter in Scribonius Proculus and said, "Do you too greet me, hating the emperor thus?" And having heard this, those who were present surrounded their senatorial colleague and tore him to pieces. And when Gaius was gladdened by this and said he was reconciled with them, they both voted for some festivals and that he use the high speaker's platform even in the senate chamber itself, so that no one get to him, and a military guard, even there.

Suet. *Calig.* 28 probably alludes to the murder of Scribonius Proculus (*PIR* S 215). At *Calig.* 49.3, he says that *The Sword* and *The Dagger* were discovered after Caligula's death, after which Claudius had Protogenes (*PIR*[2] P 1017), the former emperor's freedman, executed.

F 37 (40 A.D.)

Peter *ES* 33, p. 246.19–23: Some Gaul, after he had beheld Gaius, was laughing loudly at him. And, having considered him to be laughing through pleasure, he ordered him to be led forward and says, "Who do you think I am?" And he – I will quote him verbatim – said, "You are an immense absurdity," and suffered nothing terrible, for he was a shoemaker and poor.

Xiphil. 168.26–169.1 (III, p. 572) = Dio LIX.26.8–9 (II, pp. 651.14–652.4): And once some man, a Gaul, after he had seen him holding court upon a lofty platform in Zeus's form, laughed. And Gaius summoned him and asked, "What do I seem to you to be?" And he replied – for I shall quote him verbatim – , "An immense absurdity." And, nevertheless, he suffered nothing terrible, for he was a shoemaker. So, I suppose, it is easier that such men more easily bear the outspokenness of the undistinguished than of those being in any repute.

Only Peter, Xiphilinus, and Zonar. XI.7 (II, pp. 457.16–457.1) preserve the story, Xiphilinus alone with the appended musing.

F 38 (39 A.D.)

Dio LIX.23.7 (II, p. 644.10–14): And then, having divorced Paulina on the pretext that she was not bearing children, but really because he had had his fill of her, he married Milonia Caesonia, with whom, on the one hand, he formerly was having an affair, on the other hand, then he wished also that she be made a wife, since she was pregnant, in order that she bear a child for him over a period of thirty days.

Peter *ES* 34, p. 246.24–26: Milonia, after thirty days of marriage, bore a son, whom she had from her former husband. And she kept saying that it had been born to god himself, because in thirty days he became both a husband and a father.

Caligula had married the older and reputedly once-beautiful Lollia Paulina (*PIR*² L 328) after he had compelled her divorce from her husband P. Memmius Regulus (*PIR*² M 468). The child here in question was Julia Drusilla (*PIR*² I 665). Milonia Caesonia (*PIR*² M 590) had previously borne three other daughters. For all this, see Suet. *Calig.* 25.1–4.

F 39 (41 A.D.)

Peter *ES* 35, p. 246.27–29: After the death of Gaius, the populace, on account of his statement that he wished everyone had one throat, mocking him, kept saying, "While we do not have one neck, we do have many hands."

Xiphil. 172.23–6 (III, p. 575) = Dio LIX.30.1[c] (Boissevain II, p. 660.1–12): Those present were recalling the statement once made by him [Caligula] to the populace: "Would that you had one neck," showing him that, while he had one neck, they, in truth, had many hands.

Only Peter, Xiphilinus, and Zonar. XI.7 (II, p. 459.1–7) preserve the famous riposte.

F 40 (41 A.D.)

Peter *ES* 36, pp. 246.30–247.5: Many of those who were his companions in debauchery and had shared in his wrongdoings were angry and disturbed, and, having made many attempts, were not able to settle the soldiers down, and Valerianus Asiaticus, a man who had been a consul, stopped it in a remarkable fashion. For while they were running about and asking who had slain Gaius so that they might exact justice from him, he went up to a conspicuous place and shouted to them, "Would that I had killed him." And dumbstruck as a result of this and in awe of the man, they quieted down.

Xiphil. 172.26–31 (III, p. 575) = Dio LIX.30.2 (II, p. 660.18–31): And when the guardsmen began to become agitated and, having run about, were asking: "Who slew Gaius?", Valerius Asiaticus, a man who had held a consulship, calmed them in a fashion wondrous indeed, having gone up to some conspicuous place and having shouted out, "Would that I had killed him!" For, dumbstruck, they ceased the disturbance.

With Peter and Xiphilinus, cf. Zonar. XI.7 (II, p. 459.8–11). Because Tac. *Ann.* XI.1.1–2 has Sosibus (*PIR* S 552) allude before Claudius to D. Valerius Asiaticus' (*PIR* V 25) claim to have been a principal figure in Caligula's murder, it seems likely that Tacitus treated the alleged incident described in F 40 in a lost section of the *Annales*. See further Barrett, *Caligula*, pp. 254–5, and Levick, *Claudius*, pp. 61–4.

F 41 (42 A.D.)

Dio LX.16.4–7 (II, p. 678.5–18): It was then that a certain Galaesus, a freedman of Camillus, after he had been led into the senate, spoke freely about many different things, but, this one thing, too, certainly worthy of remembrance. For, when Narcissus had taken center stage and said to him "What would you have done, Galaesus, if Camillus had become monarch?", he replied, "I would have stood behind him and been silent." Consequently, he became famous for this and Arria, in turn, for another. For she, the wife of Caecina Paetus, being unwilling to live after he had been put to death, even though able to be in some repute, for she was very close to Messalina, furthermore, too, even encouraged her husband, who was very frightened. For, after she had taken the sword, she stabbed herself and handed it to him, having said, "Behold, Paetus, I am not in pain." And some began applauding them, for by this time the succession of evil affairs had come to this, that virtue was considered nothing else than the act of dying nobly.

Peter *ES* 37, p. 247.6–16: A freedman of Sabinus was produced for questioning and talked freely. And Narcissus asked him, "What would you have done, if Sabinus had become monarch?" He replied, "Stood behind him and been silent." Condemned as a result of this, he was killed. And a certain Ariame, when she saw her husband in extreme danger, not only did not flinch but killed herself and called upon her husband to do the same. For, after she had taken the sword, she applied it to her own stomach and pushed, saying, "See, I do not suffer. This is nothing. You do it too!" Then, having seen her dying, he, too, slew himself. For matters had come to such a state that suicide had come to be considered a virtue.

Arria's character is the subject of Mart. I.14 and Plin. *Ep*. III.16. On this episode, see Levick, *Claudius*, pp. 59–60.

F 42 (42 A.D.)

Dio LX.16.7 (II, p. 678.18–21): And Claudius was, I suppose, so disposed both to their punishment and that of the others that he

Peter *ES* 38, p. 247.17–19: When these things had happened, Claudius was repeatedly reciting the Homeric line: "a man defends also repeatedly gave this verse as a watchword to the soldiers, that it is incumbent "that a man defend himself when one offers some prior provocation."

himself when one offers some prior provocation."

The content of F 42 continues that of F 41. Suet. *Claud.* 42 records Claudius' fondness for the same Homeric watchword. Cf. *Il.* XXIV.369 and *Od.* XVI.72 and XXI.133.

F 43 (44–45 A.D.)

Peter *ELGR* 2, p. 390.16–22 = F 3 Müller *FHG* IV, pp. 184–85 = Dio LX.28.7 (II, p. 690.1–8): Mithridates, the sovereign of the Iberians, launched an insurrection and began to prepare for the war against the Romans. When his mother had voiced opposition and, when she was unable to dissuade him, had resolved to flee, wishing to conceal what was afoot, he himself, on the one hand, was continuing the preparations, but sent Cotys, his brother, in an embassy ostensibly to convey kind words to Claudius. And he, after he had dishonestly discharged the diplomatic mission, told him everything and became sovereign of Iberia in place of Mithridates.

The Mithridates in question was Mithridates of Bosphorus (*PIR*^{2} 635), not Mithridates of Iberia (*PIR*^{2} 643). The excerptor is probably responsible for the confusion. The embassy of Cotys (*PIR*^{2} 1156) dates to 44 or 45. The anonymous mother – Gepaepyris (*PIR*^{2} G 168, known through coins alone) – was the wife of Aspurgus (*PIR*^{2} A 1265). Levick, *Claudius*, pp. 157–58, provides context.

F 44 (47 A.D.)

Peter *ES* 39, p. 247.20–2: A certain Gallus, eligible to be a senator and spending time abroad, he [Claudius] quickly summoned and said, "I shall bind you in golden shackles," and he bestowed the rank on him.

Xiphil. 142.3–6 (III, p. 579) = Dio LX.29.2 (III, p. 1.5–8): And when a certain Surdinius Gallus, eligible to be a senator, went abroad to Carthage, he [Claudius] quickly summoned him and said "I shall bind you in golden shackles." And thus, shackled by his rank, he remained in his country.

Apart from Peter, Xiphilinus, and Zonar. XI.9 (II, p. 466.11–14), Claudius' comment to Surdinius Gallus (*PIR* S 747) is otherwise unknown. Levick,

Claudius, pp. 100–3, sets this instance within Claudius' broader policy of election to the senate.

F 45 (47 A.D.)

Peter *ES* 40, p. 247.23–28: In the theater, a certain actor quipped, "Intolerable is a successful rogue," with the result that the entire populace looked toward Polybius, his [Claudius'] freedman, who then was perpetrating many acts of violence. And Polybius, after he had stood up, shouted, "The same poet says, 'Those formerly goatherds kings became.'"

Xiphil. 142.7–13 (III, p. 579) = Dio LX.29.2–3 (III, pp. 1.10–2.2): ... When a certain actor in the theater had once quipped, "Intolerable is a successful rogue," and when the entire populace had looked toward Polybius, his [Claudius'] freedman, and when he had shouted out, "The same poet says, 'Those formerly goatherds kings became,'" he did him no harm.

Suet. *Claud.* 28 mentions Claudius' special regard for Polybius (*PIR*^{2} P 558), his *ab studiis*. On *ab studiis*, see Levick, *Claudius*, p. 212, n. 5. Zonar. XI.10 (II, 467.15–18) notes that Polybius was killed at the command of Valeria Messalina (*PIR* V 161), Claudius' wife. Polybius' quotation is very close to Men. *Epit.* 333. The quotations are *Adespota* 487–88, respectively, in Koch, *CAF*, p. 498.

F 46 (49 A.D.)

Peter *ES* 41, p. 247.29–35 = Dio LX.32.4[a] (III, pp. 9.15–10.1): Mithridates, the sovereign of the Iberians, when he had engaged a Roman army and been defeated and despaired for himself, begged that a plea be granted him, in order that he neither be executed perforce nor be led in victory processions. And, in truth, when it had thus come to pass, Claudius, in Rome, upon a tribunal, received him and began to speak threateningly to him. But he, with frankness, both said some other things in reply and added this, "I was not brought to you, but I came. And if you do not believe me, release me and try to find me."

Tac. *Ann.* XII.15–21 supplies context and, at XII.21, recounts Mithridates' riposte to Claudius.

F 47 (52 A.D.)

Peter *ES* 42, p. 248.1–6 = Dio LX.33.3[c] (III, p. 12.7–17): The ruler of the Britons, Cartaces, when he had been captured, was sent up to Rome. Upon a tribunal, Claudius, wearing a cloak, tried him. And he obtained pardon, staying with his wife and children in Italy. And once, when he had gone round the city and seen its magnitude and the splendor of the houses, said, "Why, when you possess things of such quality and quantity, do you want our tents?"

Boissevain prints the more truncated Zonar. XI.10 (II, pp. 470.16–471.2) beside Peter. Cf. Tac. *Ann.* XII.36–7 and Levick, *Claudius*, pp. 144–46. Cartaces = Caratacus (*PIR*² C 418).

48 (52/53 A.D.)

Peter *ES* 43, p. 248.7–10: <After> Gallicanus the rhetor had been thrown into a river by Claudius, Afer, a rhetor esteemed in acting as an advocate, called upon by someone to advocate before Claudius on his behalf, said, "Who told you that I swim better than Gallicanus?"

Xiphil. 145.11–17 (III, p. 582) = Dio LX.33.8 (III, p. 14.1–7): Once, Claudius, when he had become angry with a certain Julius Galicus, a rhetor, who was pleading a case, ordered him to be thrown into the Tiber, for it was near where he happened to be holding court. In truth, in reference to it, Domitius Afer, foremost of his contemporaries in advocating for anyone, after he had prevailed, got off an exquisite jest. For when a certain man was in need of help from him when he was abandoned by Galicus, he said to him, "Who told you that I swim better than that man?"

Apart from Peter, Xiphilinus, and Zonar. XI.10 (II, p. 471.2–7), the incident and Gallicanus/Galicus = Iulius Gallicus (*PIR*² I 335) are otherwise unattested.

F 49 (54 A.D.)

Peter *ES* 44, p. 248.11–14: Nero spoke wittily about Claudius. For, when mushrooms had been brought into a certain dinner, when someone had said, "Mushrooms are the food of gods," he said, "True, for, to be sure, my father, when he had eaten a mushroom, became a god."

Xiphil. 146.30–32 (III, p. 583) = Dio LX.35.4 (III, pp. 18.20–19.2): Nero, too, left behind a comment not unworthy of recollection. For he used to say that mushrooms were the food of gods because that man [Claudius], too, through the mushroom, had become a god.

Suet. *Ner.* 13.1, too, notes Nero's alleged quip.

F 50 (54 A.D.)

Peter *ES* 45, p. 248.15–18: When Nero was born, someone is said to have predicted from the movement of the stars, "He will both reign and will murder his mother," having heard which, Agrippina is said to have shouted in reference to these things, "Only let him reign and kill me." And later she certainly changed her mind.

Xiphil. 147.20–7 (III. p. 583) = Dio LXI.2.1–2 (III, pp. 19.24–20.6): There occurred the following signs of rulership for him. For, as he was being born, toward dawn, rays from the not-yet-visible approach of the sun encompassed him, and a certain astrologer, as a result of these things and of the motion of the stars at that time and their relation to one another, divined two things at once about him: that he would reign and that he would murder his mother. And when she heard this, Agrippina, immediately went so out of her senses that, on the one hand, she actually cried this out "Let him kill me, only let him reign!" But later, too, she was certainly going to repent her prayer.

On predictions occasioned by Nero's birth, see Suet. *Ner.* 6.1–2 and Griffin, *Nero*, p. 23.

51 (55 A.D.)

Peter *ES* 46, p. 248.19–26: Acte had been purchased from Asia, and she was exceedingly beloved by Nero, above Octavia, his wife. And when, doing many things, she [Octavia] was incapable of changing him, at every opportunity she vehemently inveighed against him, shouting that she herself had rendered him ruler, just as though she were able, through this, to take the monarchy from him, not

Xiphil. 150.11–22 (III, p. 585) = Dio LXI.7.1–3 (III, p. 26.6–17): And indeed Acte, on the one hand, had been bought from Asia, and having been beloved by Nero, she was adopted into the family of Attalus and was much beloved, even above Octavia, his wife. Therefore, Agrippina, indignant both for other reasons and for these, first attempted to admonish him, and began to knowing that monarchy, once bestowed by a private individual, immediately establishes the one who has received it master of the one who has given it, and that, because of him, most of the time, too, those who have given it are destroyed.

mistreat some of his associates with beatings and to put others out of the way. And when she accomplished nothing, she was deeply pained and said to him, "I rendered you ruler," just as though she were able to take the monarchy from him. For she did not recognize that every absolute power, once bestowed by a private individual on anyone, departs immediately from the one who has given it and attaches itself to the one who has received it against him.

On Claudia Acte (*PIR*[2] C 1067) and Iulia Agrippina (*PIR*[2] I 641), see, too, Tac. *Ann.* XIV.2.1–2, Griffin, *Nero*, pp. 72–5, and Barrett, *Agrippina*, pp. 167–69. Attalus is Attalus I Soter. For Octavia, see *PIR*[2] C 1110.

F 52 (58 A.D.)

Peter *ES* 47, p. 248.27–31: Nero and Otho both used to have sex with one woman, for they seemed to be exceedingly fond of themselves because of the similarity of their way of life, with the result that Otho once said to him, "Would that you see me thus a Caesar," and suffered no punishment as a result, and heard only so much in response, "Not even a consul shall I see you."

Xiphil. 152.16–21 (III, p. 587) = Dio LXI.11.2 (III, p. 33.1–7): There was a certain Marcus Salvius Otho, who, because of the similarity of their ways and the commonality of their crimes, was so intimately connected to Nero that once, even having said to him "Would that you see me thus a Caesar," suffered no punishment as a result, but heard only so much in response: "Not even a consul shall I see you." To this man he gave Sabina, being from patricians, after he had separated her from her husband, and both used to have sex with her at the same time.

Cf. Tac. *Ann.* XIII.45–46, Suet. *Otho* 3, Plut. *Galb.* 19.2–5, and Griffin, *Nero*, p. 45, p. 247, n. 51. Sabina = Poppaea Sabina (*PIR*[2] P 850).

F 53 (59 A.D.)

Peter *ES* 48, pp. 248.32–249.4: After the plot, Agrippina, when she had survived and saw Anicetus, who had been dispatched by Nero upon her, immediately leaped from her bed and rent her clothing and, having bared her belly, said, "Strike this, Anicetus, strike, for it has borne Nero!" And seeing her dead, Nero uttered an impious statement, "I did not know that I had such a becoming mother."

Xiphil. 154.3–11 (III, p. 588) = Dio LXI.13.4–5 (III, p. 35.14–21): When he had heard this, Nero did not restrain himself, but punished the one who had been sent as if he punished one who had come for the purpose of his own murder, and against his mother he immediately dispatched Anicetus with the sailors, for he did not trust her death to the guardsmen. And she, when she had seen them, both knew what they came about and, when she had leaped from her bed, rent her clothing and, when she had bared her belly, said, "Strike this, Anicetus, strike, for it bore Nero!"

Cf. Tac. *Ann.* XIV.7, Suet. *Ner.* 34.2, Sen. *Octavia* 371–72, Griffin, *Nero*, pp. 75–7, and Ginsburg, *Representing Agrippina*, pp. 50–3. Anicetus (*PIR*^{2} A 589) was Nero's freedman, pedagogue, and prefect of the fleet.

F 54 (59 A.D.)

Peter *ES* 49, p. 249.5–10: Thrasea, a senator, while being killed by Nero, said, "If Nero were going to murder me alone, I would suffer it, but if he does <not> spare those who lavishly praise him, in consequence, nothing worse will come to pass for me; but while those men are totally obliterated, at least there will be some memory of me in the time hereafter. For while Nero is able to kill me, he is not able to obliterate me."

Xiphil. 155.5–13 (III, p. 589) = Dio LXI.15.3–4 (III, p. 37.10–18): For he used to say: "If Nero were going to murder me alone, I would make allowance for the others who are flattering him. But if, indeed, with respect to many of those who lavishly praise him, he has destroyed some and will slay others, why should someone, humiliating himself in vain, perish like a slave while he has the power to render what is owed to nature like a free man? For, on the one hand, in my case, afterwards, too, there will be some talk of me, but of them – except this very thing, that they were slaughtered – none." Such was Thrasea, and he used to always say this to himself, "Nero is able to kill me, but not to harm me."

P. Clodius Thrasea Paetus (*PIR*[2] 1187) was devoted to the philosophy of the Stoa and, it seems, particularly taken with its stance against tyranny and tyrants. According to Tac. *Ann.* XIV.12.1, he found it difficult to dissimulate after the murder of Agrippina. Cf. Griffin, *Nero*, pp. 171–77, and Griffin, *Seneca*, pp. 100–3 and 424–25.

F 55 (59 A.D.)

Peter *ES* 50, p. 249.11–15 = Dio LXI.16.2[a] (III, p. 38.5–7): As Nero was entering Rome, they took down the statues of Agrippina. And when they had not had enough time to decapitate one, they threw a ragged garment over it so that it seemed to be veiled, and immediately someone, when he had composed an epigraph, fastened to the statue: "I am modest and you have no shame."

The quotation is otherwise unknown. Ginsburg, *Representing Agrippina*, pp. 79–91, discusses sculptural representations of Agrippina.

F 56 (59 A.D.)

Peter *ES* 51, p. 249.16–7: An iambic, too, began to circulate: "Nero, Orestes, Alcmaeon: matricides."

Xiphil. 155.19–21 (III, p. 589) = Dio LXI.16.2[a] (III, p. 38.9–10): And, on the one hand, one was able, too, to read in many places, similarly inscribed: "Nero, Orestes, Alcmeon: matricides."

Suet. *Ner.* 39.2 quotes the same verse. For "iambic," see F 18, above.

57 (59 A.D.)

Peter *ES* 52, p. 249.18–20: Nero, murdering many during his tyranny, is deterred by Seneca, having said this to him: "As many as you may murder, you are unable to murder the one who is going to reign after you."

Xiphil. 157.3–5 (III, p. 590) = Dio LXI.18.3 (III, p. 40.24–6): And many he would have eliminated straightway, if Seneca had not said to him, "As many as you may slay, you are unable to kill your successor."

The maxim does not appear in Seneca's writings or elsewhere.

F 58 (62 A.D.)

Peter *ES* 53, p. 249.21–24: Once when Nero was saying, "I totally release Octavia and I do not cohabit with her," Burrus forthrightly said to him, "Well then, return to her her dowry, too, that is, the monarchy. For the monarchy is from her father himself."

Xiphil. 165.21–25 (III, p. 596) = Dio LXII.13.1–3 (III, pp. 51.8–52.3): ... and in Rome, Nero first divorced Octavia Augusta, on account of his concubine Sabina, and later had her killed, although Burrus was opposing him and impeding the divorce, at one point even having said, "Well then, return to her her dowry, too," that is, the hegemony.

Octavia (*PIR*[2] C 1110) was the daughter of the emperor Claudius and Valeria Messalina (*PIR* V 161). For the sordid details of the fall of Octavia and the rise of Poppaea Sabina (*PIR*[2] P 850), cf. Suet. *Nero* 35.1–3, Tac. *Ann.* XIV.59.3–64.2, and Griffin, *Nero*, pp. 98–100. For a parallel to the riposte of Sextus Afranius Burrus (*PIR*[2] A 441), Nero's praetorian prefect, see *SHA Marc.* 19.8–9, where it is attributed to Marcus Aurelius with reference to Annia Galeria Faustina (*PIR*[2] A 716), his wife and the daughter of Antoninus Pius.

F 59 (62 A.D.)

Peter *ES* 54, p. 249.25–26: Once Burrus, when he had been asked twice about the same matter, said, "Do not ask me twice about things which I spoke of once."

Xiphil. 165.26–28 (III, p. 596) = Dio LXII.13.2 (III, p. 52.3–5): For so vigorously did he employ it that once, when he had been asked by him [Nero] an opinion about things concerning which he had declared his view, he bluntly said, "About whatever I spoke once, never inquire of me again."

Only Peter and Xiphilinus preserve Burrus' alleged command.

F 60 (62 A.D.)

Peter *ES* 55, pp. 249.27–250.2: Pythias, who was one of those in the bedchamber of Octavia, was refusing to lie against her, but, even after he had submitted to many tortures, kept swearing that she had never done a wrong to Nero's bed. And once, when Tigillinus was pressuring her vigorously and telling her to confess the evils which her mistress did, having spat in his face, she even said, "Tigillinus, my mistress's privates are purer than your mouth."

Xiphil. 165.31–166.7 (III, p. 597) = Dio LXII.13.3–4 (III, pp. 52.15–53.3): For when all the rest of those around Octavia except Pythias were siding with Sabina against her, on the one hand, having disdained the one because she was suffering from misfortune, on the other hand, flattering the other because she was powerful, Pythias alone did not tell any lie against her, though tortured most cruelly, and finally, when Tigellinus kept pressing her, she both spat at him and said, "My mistress has privates purer than your mouth."

For context, see F 58, above. Except for Tac. *Ann.* XIV.60.3 (without naming Pythias [*PIR*² P 1108]), the insult is otherwise unknown. See Griffin, *Nero*, pp. 103–4, on the notorious praetorian prefect Ofonius Tigillinus (*PIR*² O 91).

F 61 (62 A.D.)

Peter *ES* 56, p. 250.3–4: Nero used to regard the evils of his own kinsmen as subjects for jokes and witticisms.

Xiphil. 166.7–8 (III, p. 597) = Dio LXII.14.1 (III, p. 53.4–5): Nero used to make the evils of his women a subject for jokes and jests.

What follows in Xiphilinus makes no mention of jests about "kinsmen" or "women." Cf. Xiphil. 166.8–18 (III, p. 597) = Dio LXII.14.1–3 (III, p. 53.4–18).

F 62 (62 A.D.)

Peter *ES* 57, p. 250.5–7: When the head of Paul the apostle had been brought to Nero, he said, "I did not know that he had such a big nose," just as if he would have spared him, if he had known this beforehand.

Xiphil. 166.8–11 (III, p. 597) = Dio LXII.14.1 (III, p. 53.5–8): At any rate, after he had killed Plautus, then, after he had seen his head, which had been brought to him, he said, "I did not know he had <so> big a nose," just as if he would have spared him if he had known this earlier.

Tac. *Ann.* XIV.59.3 is lacunose at this point. However, given that the context in Tacitus is Rubellius Plautus' (*PIR*[2] R 115) execution, Xiphilinus' version is obviously correct. The addition of the gloss "the apostle" may be Peter's or the excerptor's work or, far more likely, the addition of a copyist of the *ES*. In any case, the version of *ES* 57 is unique.

F 63 (64 A.D.)

Peter *ES* 58, p. 250.8–9: = Dio LXII.15.1[a] (III, p. 54): A certain Thrasea expressed an opinion that, for a man of senatorial rank, exile was the ultimate punishment.

The alleged view of Thrasea – probably P. Clodius Thrasea Paetus (for whom, see on F 54, above) – is otherwise unknown. On his eventual forced suicide in 66, see Tac. *Ann.* XVI.21–35 and Griffin, *Nero*, pp. 170–77.

F 64 (64 A.D.)

Peter *ES* 59, p. 250.10–12: In the time of the great and famous conflagration of Rome, an oracle something like this was spoken, "Last of the sons of Aeneas, a matricide shall reign."

Xiphil. 169.2–5 (III, p. 599) = Dio LXII.18.4 (Boissevain III, p. 57.1–4): And when Nero, encouraging them, kept saying that these verses could not be found anywhere, they, when they had made a substitution on the grounds that it was truly Sibylline, began chanting another oracle. And this is it: "Last of the sons of Aeneas, a matricide shall govern."

The oracle appears, too, at *Anthologia Graeca, Appendix* 218, ed. Cougny, *Epigrammatum anthologia Palatina cum Planudeis et appendice nova*, Vol. III, p. 512, at Ced. I, p. 360.9, and as a copyist's addition to Symeon Magister's notice of Nero at *Chronicon* 54.1. On the last, see *Symeonis Magistri et Logothetae Chronicon*, ed. Wahlgren, p. 85, *apparatus criticus*.

F 65 (64 A.D.)

Peter *ES* 60, p. 250.13–15: Under him, the clan of Julius, which was descended from Aeneas, came to an end. For after Nero no longer did the clan of Julius reign, but other Romans.

Xiphil. 169.7–8 (III, p. 599) = Dio LXII.18.4 (III, p. 57.1–8): For, last of the Julians descended from Aeneas, he reigned.

Suet. *Galb.* 1 notes other portents that Nero would be the last of his line to rule.

F 66 (65 A.D.)

Peter *ES* 61, p. 250.16–19: Many plotted against Nero. And when, as this became known to Nero, Sulpicius Asper, the centurion, when asked the cause of the attempt, said, "I was not able to help you in any other way nor to keep you from disgracing yourself except through your death."

Xiphil. 170.4–14 (III, p. 600) = Dio LXII.24.1–2 (III, p. 63.4–12): And indeed, Seneca and Rufus, the prefect, and some other distinguished men plotted against Nero; for they were not able to bear his disgraceful behavior, his licentiousness, and his cruelty any longer. And, at the same time, they wished to be delivered from these evils and that he be freed, just as Sulpicius Asper, a centurion, and Subrius Flavius, a military tribune, both being of the bodyguards, confessed to Nero himself. For the latter, asked by him the reason for his attempt, said: "I was not able to help you in any other way ... "

Tac. *Ann.* XV.68.1 also mentions the reply. Cf. Xiphil. 170.4–172.1 (III, pp. 600–2) = Dio LXII.24.1–27.4 (III, pp. 63.4–66.5), Tac. *Ann.* XV.48–73, and Griffin, *Nero*, pp. 171–77, where (p. 173), Griffin calls Asper's retort "the only trace" of a philosophical justification for the Pisonian Conspiracy consistent with Stoicism. The principals are L. Faenius Rufus (*PIR*² F 102), Subrius Falvus (*PIR* S 684), and Sulpicius Asper (*PIR* S 710).

F 67 (65 A.D.)

Peter *ES* 62, p. 250.20–23: Flavius Subrius, too, when he had been asked, said, "We loved you, having hoped you would be a good ruler. And I hated you because you did this-and-that. For I cannot be a slave either to a charioteer or citharist."

Xiphil. 170.14–17 (III, p. 600) = Dio LXII.24.2 (III, p. 63.12–15): ... and Flavius [said], "I both loved you more than anyone and hated you. While I loved you, having hopes you would be a good ruler, I hated you because you did this and that. I cannot be a slave to a charioteer or citharist."

Nero had posed a question of motive. With Peter and Xiphilinus, cf. Tac. *Ann.* XV.67.2, which purports to quote Subrius Flavus verbatim: "I loathed you. No soldier was more faithful to you, so long as you deserved to be loved. I began to loathe you after the parricide of a mother and wife and you showed yourself to be a charioteer, actor, and arsonist."

F 68 (65 A.D.)

Peter *ES* 63, p. 250.24–30 = Dio LXII.28.3[a] (III, p. 67.5–10): When Nero was holding Sporus the eunuch as a wife, one of those with him in Rome and who had prepared himself for philosophy, having been asked if he was satisfied with these nuptials and the cohabitation, said, "You do well, indeed, Caesar, cohabiting with such sorts. Would that your father, too, held the same zeal and cohabited with such a spouse," signifying that, if this had happened, he would not have been born and the state would be free of great evils.

For the eunuch Sporus (*PIR* S 582) and the jest, see Suet. *Ner.* 28.1.

F 69 (65 A.D.)

Peter *ES* 64, pp. 250.31–251.3: When Nero had commanded that he write four hundred books, Anneas Cornutus said that these were many and then nobody would be able to read them. And when Nero had said, "Yet Chrysippus, whom you praise and emulate, wrote more by far," he replied, "But those are a mode of life of people of the best sort." And through this he was banished.

Xiphil. 172.22–173.1 (III, p. 602) = Dio LXII.29.2–4 (III, pp. 67.19–68.9): And he [Nero] began preparing to write all the deeds of the Romans in epic verse, too, and, before composing, when he had summoned Annaeus Cornutus, then most famous for learning, among others, he even meditated about the precise number of books. And he nearly killed him, but then banished him to an island, because, when some men were urging him [Nero] to write four hundred books and he [Cornutus] said that these were many and that nobody would read them, and someone said, "And yet Chrysippus, whom you praise and emulate, composed many more," he replied, "But those are useful for the conduct of people's life." While Cornutus, then, incurred exile for this, Lucan, on the other hand, was, in fact, prevented from writing, since he was being strongly commended for his work.

We know nothing of the Stoic L. Annaeus Cornutus' (*PIR*^{2} A 609) career after his exile. On the poet Lucan = M. Annaeus Lucanus (*PIR*^{2} A 611) – a pupil of Cornutus – and on Lucan's attitude toward Nero and vice versa, see Griffin, *Nero*, pp. 156–59. Diog. Laert. *Vitae Philosophorum* VII.189–202 gives an impressive list of Chrysippus' works.

F 70 (66 A.D.)

Peter *ES* 65, p. 251.4–5: Tiridates gave the sword to Nero, after he had said that he would recover it when he departed.

Vologases I of Parthia (*PIR* V 629) had placed his brother Tiridates (*PIR*^{2} T 238) on the throne of Armenia. Anderson, "The Eastern War from Tiberius to Nero," *CAH* X, pp. 758–73, provides historical context. The incident described in *ES* 65 does not appear in Xiphilinus' long account of Tiridates' stay in Italy. Cf. Xiphil. 173.5–175.26 (III, pp. 602–4) = Dio LXIII.2–7.1 (III, pp. 68.14–72.12). Boissevain (III, p. 72, apparatus) raises but rejects the possibility that this is because the excerptor took this extract from another spot in Dio and inserted it here. But if the order of the excerpts accurately reflects Peter's *History*, Peter himself may be behind the anomaly, either having mentioned here what he had read later in Dio or having included material he knew from some other author. With Xiphilinus, cf. Suet. *Ner.* 13.

F 71 (66 A.D.)

Peter *ES* 66, p. 251.6–15: Tiridates said to Nero, "Master, I am a descendant of Arsaces and a brother of the sovereigns Vologesus and Pacorus and your slave. And I came to you, doing obeisance to you, my god, as I do obeisance to Mithras, too, and will be whatever you enjoin. For you are my fate and fortune." And Nero said, "You did well indeed, having come here, in order that, being present, you gladden me and have enjoyment from me being present. For neither what your father left you nor your brothers, having given, preserved, these do I bestow, and I make you sovereign of Armenia, so that both you and they may know that I am able both to take realms away and to grant them."

Xiphil. 174.20–29 (III, p. 603) = Dio LXIII.5.2–3 (III, p. 70.10–19): For thus did he speak: "Master, I am a descendant of Arsaces and a brother of the sovereigns Vologesus and Pacorus and your slave. And I came to you, my god, doing you obeisance as I do obeisance to Mithras, too, and will be whatever you enjoin. For you are my fate and fortune." Nero answered him thus: "But you certainly did well, having come here yourself in order that you, being present, benefit from me being present. For neither that which your father left you nor your brothers, having given, preserved, these things do I bestow, and I make you sovereign of Armenia, so that both you and they may know that I am able to take realms away and to grant them."

After the death *c.* 34 of the Roman-appointed Armenian favorite Artaxias (*PIR*^{2} A 1168) as King of Armenia, Artabanus of Parthia (*PIR*^{2} A 1155) made Arsaces (*PIR*^{2} A 1153), his own son and the brother of Pacorus (*PIR*^{2} P 31), ruler. This had precipitated a series of intrigues, diplomatic missions, and military operations which led, in 60, to the abandonment of Armenia by Tigranes (*PIR*^{2} T 207), who had Rome's backing, in the face of Armenian and Parthian actions. Inconclusive campaigns by all involved followed. After a truce, negotiations mainly between Rome and Vologases resulted in 63 in the installation of Tiridates as Armenia's king and his kingdom becoming a protectorate of Rome. The latter's journey to Italy would permit Nero to receive homage from an Arsacid while, at the same time, allowing Vologases, the Arsacid ruler of Parthia, to avoid any appearance of subservience to Rome. See further Anderson, *supra*, on F 70.

F 72 (66 A.D.)

Peter *ES* 67, p. 251.16–20: Because of his [Nero's] cithara playing and the rest of his shameful actions, Tiridates turned from Nero and gave Curbulo much praise, blaming him for one thing alone: that he was putting up with such a master. This, in fact, he did not conceal from Nero himself. For he once said to him, "Master, it is a good slave you have in Curbulo."

Xiphil. 175.8–14 (III, pp. 603–4) = Dio LXIII.6.3–4 (III, p. 71.7–13): Afterwards Nero performed on the cithara in public, and, dressed in the raiment of the Greens and wearing a charioteer's helmet, drove a chariot. Tiritdates, loathing him because of this but praising Corbulo, was faulting him for this one thing alone: that he was putting up with having such a master. And he did not conceal this from Nero himself, but once said to him, Master, it is a good slave you have."

Cn. Domitius Corbulo (*PIR*[2] C 141) had been the principal Roman commander against Parthia and was largely responsible for the resurgence of Rome's power and prestige on and beyond this border of her empire. See further Anderson, *supra*, on F 70.

F 73 (66 A.D.)

Peter *ES* 68, p. 251.21–23 = Dio LXIII.7.1[a] (III, p. 72.3–5): Tiridates, watching a boxing match once, when he saw one of the boxers had fallen and was being struck by his opponent, said, "The fight is unjust, for it is not just to strike the one who has fallen."

Peter alone records this alleged incident. Is this Peter's own contribution? For the possibility, see above, on F 70.

F 74 (66 A.D.)

Peter *ES* 69, p. 251.24–28: Nero wrote Vologases about him [Vologases] coming to him. But he did not accept. And yet, being often bothered by him, he responded to him, "It is far easier for you than for me to sail across so great a sea. Therefore, if ever you come to Asia, then we shall arrange

Xiphil. 175.27–31 (III, p. 604) = Dio LXIII.7.1[a] (III, p. 72.3–5): But, in truth, Vologesus was not willing to come to Nero, though summoned often, and finally, when it became burdensome to him, he responded to him: "It is far easier for you than for me to sail across so great a sea. Therefore, if ever you where we are able to meet each other."

come to Asia, then we shall arrange where we are able to meet each other."

Only Peter and Xiphilinus note this purported exchange.

F 75 (66 A.D.)

Peter *ES* 70, p. 251.29–30: Nero used to say he was "Champion of the Circuit," for he was not satisfied with the rest of the theaters, but kept going abroad, too.

Xiphil. 176.6–8 (III, p. 604) = Dio LXIII. 8.2–3 (III, p. 73.4–10): For Rome did not suffice for him, nor did the Theater of Pompey or the Great Hippodrome, but he required a campaign abroad, too, in order that he become, as he used to say, "Champion of the Circuit."

Cf. Suet. *Ner.* 22–4, Xiphilinus' "Great Hippodrome" is the Circus Maximus. The Pythian, Isthmian, Nemean, and Olympic games comprised the so-called "Circuit."

76 (67 A.D.)

Peter *ES* 71, pp. 251.31–252.3 = Dio LXIII.10.1[a] (III, p. 76.1–5): When he had become upset with someone because, while he [Nero] was speaking, he looked sullen and did not zealously praise him excessively, he drove him away after he had commanded that he not come into his sight. And since he kept turning him away, when he said, "And where am I to go?", Phoebus, the freedman of Nero, replied to him, "To the crows."

Peter *ES* 103 = F 109, below, shows that Phoebus' (*PIR*[2] P 391) unnamed target was the future emperor Vespasian. Suet. *Vesp.*14 recounts the alleged exchange, though the prescribed destination there is Morbovia, a pun on the Latin *morbus*.

F 77 (67 A.D.)

Peter *ES* 72, p. 252.4–5: When someone was asked, "What is the emperor doing?" He replied, "He is in labor." For he was playing the part of Canace.

Xiphil. 177.10–14 (III, p. 605) = Dio LXIII.10.2 (III, p. 76.7–11): None of them dared to pity or to hate the wretch. But one certain soldier, seeing him in chains, was angered and, having run up, released him and, when somebody asked, "What is the emperor doing?" replied, "He is in labor." For Nero was, in fact, playing the part of Canace.

Suet. *Ner.* 21.3 recounts Nero's practice of singing the roles of tragic heroines while wearing masks in the likenesses of certain of his lovers. Among these heroines, Suetonius includes "Canace in labor." Canace had fallen in love with her brother Macareus and together they had produced a child. When Aeolus discovered this, he compelled Canace to take her own life and had the baby exposed. In consequence, Macareus, too, committed suicide. For references, see Stoll, "Kanake (1)," Roscher, *Lex.*, Vol. II.1, col. 946. The Canace of Euripides' *Aeolus* was Nero's likely model. For testimony and fragments, see Nauck, *TGF*, pp. 291–97. For the sequence of *ES* 72, 73, and 74, see below on F 79.

F 78 (67 A.D.)

Peter *ES* 73, p. 252.6–7: From Delphi he quickly departed, saying that Apollo was envious of his voice.

Cf. Xiphil. 178.22–29 (III, p. 606) = Dio LXIII.14.1–2 (III, p. 79.9–14):

> This same man [Nero], because she declared some oracles that pleased him, gave to the Pythia 400,000 (which Galba recovered). And, indeed, from Apollo, on the other hand, either, then, having been annoyed because she predicted some distressing things to him or having been otherwise enraged, too, he both confiscated the territory of Cirrha and gave it soldiers and also brought an end to the seat of the oracle, having let the blood of slaughtered men run into the cavern from which the sacred vapor used to rise.

On these and other aspects of Nero's real or purported dealings with Delphi, see Parke and Wormell, *The Delphic Oracle*, Vol. I, pp. 283–84. Cirrha was the port of Delphi. For the sequence of *ES* 72, 73, and 74, see below in F 79 and Boissevain III, p. 79, apparatus.

F 79 (67 A.D.)

Peter *ES* 74, p. 252.8–9: Nero once said that neither he himself lived apart from Tigillinus nor Tigillinus apart from Nero.

Xiphil. 177.32–178.1 (III, p. 605) = Dio LXIII.12.3 (III, p. 78.6–7): For I reckon Tigillinus, in turn, an appendage of Nero, because he was with him.

Unlike Xiphilinus' version of Dio, either Peter or the excerptor makes Nero the source of the sentiment about Tigillinus (*PIR*[2] O 91). Boissevain (III, p. 78, apparatus) notes that, based on the order events in Xiphilinus, *ES* 74 seems out of sequence, i.e., *ES* 72 parallels Dio LXIII.10.2 and *ES* 73 parallels Dio LXIII.14.1–2, while *ES* 74 parallels Dio LXIII.12.3.

F 80 (68 A.D.)

Dio *EV* 257 (I, p. 354.16–26) = Dio LXIII.26.1 (III, p. 89.3–8): Nero, watching the gymnastic contest after lunch, when he had learned of the matters concerning Vindex in Naples, was not troubled, but, having leaped down from his seat, vied with some athlete. Nor did he hasten to Rome, but, having merely sent a letter to the senate, he asked forgiveness that he had not come, saying that he had a sore throat, as if, even then, he was going to be required to sing something to them.

Peter *ES* 75, p. 252.10–13: Nero wrote the senate in Rome with respect to Galba's plot and the proclamation. But he himself was not present. And he was adding falsely, in his defense, that he had a sore throat, as if in reference to singing, too, upon his arrival in Rome.

Suet. *Ner.* 40.4–41.1 exhibits some points of contact, though Nero does not compete with an unnamed athlete and, unlike *ES* 75, has Nero write the senate about Vindex rather than about Galba. For context, see Griffin, *Nero*, pp. 180–81.

F 81 (68 A.D.)

Peter *ES* 76, p. 252.14–20: The senate, when it had learned of this – the matter about Vindex and Galba – , decreed against Vindex everything customary in reference to those engaged in revolution. And Nero promised

Xiphil. 183.9–13 (III, p. 609) = Dio LXIII.23.2 (III, pp. 89.19–90.13): It is said that when Nero had proclaimed two and a half million for Vindex, Vindex, when he had heard this, said, "He who has killed Nero and brought his

Zonar. XI.13 (II, p. 480.6–12): For he [Vindex] possessed such a great desire for this that, when Nero had proclaimed two and a half million for the one who would bring him Vindex's head, he said, "He who has killed Nero that he would give to the man who killed Vindex and brought his head to him two and a half million drachmas. When he had learned this, Vindex replied to those who had told him, "And to the one who brings the head of Domitius I give my own in return."

head to me will receive mine in return."

and brought his head to me will receive mine in return."

For context, see Griffin, *Nero*, p. 181. Peter's Domitius is Nero and probably reproduces what he found in Dio.

F 82 (68 A.D.)

Peter *ES* 77, p. 252.21–24: Affairs being in much turmoil, Nero blamed the senators. And those who were expecting to give him some counsel about what was going on, convened with haste. And he said to them, "I have discovered a way by which the water-organ will make a louder and more harmonious sound."

Xiphil. 184.10–14 (III, p. 610) = Dio LXIII.26.4 (III, p. 91.5–9): One night, when he had suddenly summoned in haste the foremost senators and knights as if he were going to share with them something about what was going on, he said – for I shall quote him verbatim – , "I have discovered a way by which the water-organ will produce louder and more musical tones."

The turbulent situation of *ES* 77 is Vindex's rebellion. Suet. *Ner.* 41.2 also tells the story of the special meeting at which Nero discussed a new type of water-organ.

F 83 (68 A.D.)

Peter *ES* 78, p. 252.25–28: Nero often used to say to his confidants, "Even if we fall from rule, another skill will sustain us." To such a

Xiphil. 184.24–29 (III, p. 610) = Dio LXIII. 27.2 (III, p. 92.7–20): And when he had been abandoned by all alike, he planned both to

degree of madness had he come that, after his autocratic rule, he was planning to leave it, to live as a private citizen, and to play the cithara.	kill the senators and to sail to Alexandria, having suggested, "Even if we fall from rule, yet this very skill will sustain us there." For he had come to such a degree of insanity that he actually believed he would be able to live differently as a private citizen and to play the cithara besides.

On Nero's death, see Griffin, *Nero*, p. 182. The version of Nero's words at Zonar. XI.13 (II, p. 480.15–16) agrees with Xiphilinus.

F 84 (68 A.D.)

Peter *ES* 79, p. 252.29–30 = Dio LXIII.27.4 (III, p. 99.15–16): Control of the realm, having come to be in such great confusion, was beyond no one's hope.

ES 79 contains the sole instance of ἐγχείρησις, here rendered "seizure," in Dio or Xiphilinus. This and the absence of a parallel in Xiphilinus or Zonaras suggest that the words of *ES* 79 are Peter's.

F 85 (68 A.D.)

Peter *ES* 80, pp. 252.31–253.2: To the guardsmen who were demanding of Galba what Nymphidius was promising, he said, "We are accustomed to levy soldiers, but not to purchase them."	Xiphil. 187.23–25 (III, p. 612) Dio LXIV.3.3 (III, pp. 101.18–102.2): And, at any rate, he did not give money to the guardsmen who were demanding it, and he even said, "We are accustomed to levy soldiers, but not to purchase them."

Tac. *Hist.* I.5 and Suet. *Galb.* 16.1 both report the same comment. For the circumstances, see Murison, *Rebellion and Reconstruction*, pp. 37–8. Nymphidius = C. Nymphidius Sabinus (*PIR*^{2} N 250).

F 86 (68 A.D.)

Peter *ES* 81, p. 253.3–4 = Dio LXIV.3.4^b (III, p. 102.15–16): Some disdained their own slaves, wishing to rid themselves of bad slaves.

Zonar. XI.14 (II, p. 482.10–13), lines 12–14 of which = Dio LXIV.3.4^a (III, p. 102.11–14), certainly comes from the portion of Dio directly before *ES* 81 and, consequently, clarifies its meaning. See further Murison, *Rebellion and Reconstruction*, p. 39.

F 87 (69 A.D.)

Peter *ES* 82, p. 253.5–6: When he had learned from a soldier of Galba that Otho had been beheaded, he said, "And who ordered you to do this?"

Xiphil. 188.29–189.3 (III, p. 613) = Dio LXIV.6.2 (III, p. 104.9–14): And Galba, when he had learned what was being done, sent some men to the camp, thinking he would be able to persuade them to change their minds. Meanwhile, a certain soldier, lifting his bare and bloodstained sword, approached him and said, "Take heart, emperor! For I have killed Otho, and there is no further danger for you." Having believed this, Galba then said to him, "And who ordered you to do this?"

Tac. *Hist.* I.35.2 and Plut. *Galb.* 26.1–2 identify the soldier as Julius Atticus (*PIR*^{2} I 184). Suet. *Galb.* 19.2 recounts the incident but does not name the soldier. See further Murison, *Rebellion and Reconstruction*, pp. 47–8.

F 88 (69 A.D.)

Peter *ES* 83, p. 253.7–8: The same man, being put to death by those who had plotted against him, said only this, "For what evil did I do?"

Xiphil. 189.8–10 (III, p. 613) = Dio LXIV.6.4 (III, pp. 104.20–105.1): And thus, having been struck in the neck in the very litter in which he was being carried and having leaned out of it, he was wounded, having said only this, "And what evil did I do?"

Tac. *Hist.* I.41.2 records the same comment. On Galba's death and variant accounts of his last words, see Murison, *Rebellion and Reconstruction*, p. 48.

F 89 (69 A.D.)

Peter *ES* 84, p. 253.9–12: As justice was about to dispose of Otho, then, just as though he had been consigned to punishment, he kept repeating this popular proverb, "Why was it necessary that I play long pipes?" This is said about those trying to do something outside what is fitting for them.

Xiphil. 190.9–17 (III, p. 614) = Dio LXIV.7.1 (III, p. 106.11–16): Accordingly, for Galba this was the end. But justice, then, was about to come looking for Otho, too, as he quickly learned. For the omens were unfavorable to him as he was offering the first sacrifice, with the result that, being repentant about what had been done, he said, "Why was it necessary that I play long pipes?" And this is a popular saying referring to a proverb about those doing something outside of what is suitable for them.

Suet. *Otho* 7.2 gives in Greek a slightly different and metrical version of the same proverb. That the explanation of the proverb stands both in the excerpt from Peter and in Xiphilinus tells against the possibility that the comment is a post-Dio gloss. Cf. Murison, *Rebellion and Reconstruction*, pp. 54–5.

F 90 (69 A.D.)

Peter *ES* 85, p. 253.13–14: And he kept being disturbed in his dreams, but there was not a refuge from the future.

Xiphil. 190.17–25 (III, p. 614) = Dio LXIV.7.2–3 (III, pp. 106.17–107.5): And after this, he was, in fact, so troubled in his dreams that he even fell out of bed and terrified those who were guarding him. In truth, when they had rushed in, they discovered him lying on the ground. For, once he had gained control, he was able to retire, and he remained in charge and rendered justice ...

Cf. Suet. *Otho* 7.2 and Murison's commentary, *Rebellion and Reconstruction*, p. 55.

F 91 (69 A.D.)

Peter *ES* 86, p. 253.15–17: The soldiers, when they had obtained freedom to speak their mind, voted to kill the senators and kept declaring that as long as this council existed Otho could not be monarch.

Xiphil. 191.6–12 (III, pp. 614–15) = Dio LXIV.9.2–3 (III, pp. 107.18–108.8): Moreover, he brought the soldiers to such a degree of daring and lawlessness as a result of the things which he gave them and with which he extravagantly flattered them that once they even forced their way into the palace while a group of the senators was dining there with Otho and finally, after they had killed those who had barred the way, even burst into the banquet itself and would have murdered all those who were within, if they had not jumped up and hidden in advance.

Xiphilinus' "he" is Otho. Cf. Plut. *Otho* 3.4–5, Tac. *Hist.* I.81, and Suet. *Otho* 8.2. See Murison, *Rebellion and Reconstruction*, pp. 58–9, for the difficulties posed by the accounts of this incident.

F 92 (69 A.D.)

Dio *EV* 262 (I, p. 365.9–12) = LXIV.10.2 (III, p. 109.10–13): Otho withdrew from the battle, saying that he could not bear the sight of a battle between men of the same stock, as if he had become emperor as a result of some just action but not after he had murdered the consuls, the Caesar, and the emperor in Rome herself.

Peter *ES* 87, p. 253.18–20: Otho, after he had arrayed himself against Vitellius and said he could not bear the sight of a battle between men of the same stock and retired, was defeated.

Suet. *Otho* 10.1 attributes like sentiments to Otho and names his own father, Suetonius Laetus (*PIR* S 691), as the source of this information. The engagement in question was the so-called First Battle of Bedriacum between the forces of Otho and Vitellius. On the confusing course of the campaign, see Murison, pp. 63–4.

F 93 (69 A.D.)

Peter *ES* 88, p. 253.21–22: Otho, after he had lived a brief time, in consequence of this shrouded the lewdness of his life.

Xiphil. 193.1–5 (III, p. 616) = Dio LXIV.15.1a–2[2] (III, p. 113.8–15): This was the end that befell Otho, when he had lived thirty-seven years minus eleven days and had reigned ninety days. For, in truth, after he, of humankind, had lived most basely, he died most nobly.

Plut. *Otho* 18.2 closely parallels Xiphilinus. Zonar. XI.15 (II, p. 486.12–13), probably following Dio, says that by the manner of his death Vitellius "overshadowed the impiousness and wickedness of his life." *ES* 88, on the other hand, suggests that Peter saw nothing redeeming in Vitellius' death and, departing from Dio's version, chose to make that point. Murison, pp. 65–71, discusses the often contradictory testimony about Vitellius' end.

F 94 (69 A.D.)

Peter *ES* 89, p. 253.24–7: Vitellius expelled the sorcerers and the astrologers through an edict, having told to them to depart all of Italy on the specified day. And they, during the night, set up a counter edict stating that he was going to depart from life on the day in which he died.

Xiphil. 193.24–30 (III, p. 616) = Dio LXV.1.4 (III, p. 116.1–11): When Vitellius was in Rome, he was, I suppose, managing other matters as seemed right to him, and he issued an edict through which he expelled the astrologers, having told them to leave from all Italy within this day, having posted the specified one. And they, when they had issued a counter notice at night, in turn ordered him to depart from life on the day in which he died. And thus, on the one hand, they accurately prognosticated what was going to occur ...

Cf. Tac. *Hist.* II.62.2 and Suet. *Vit.* 14.4, to be read with Murison, *Rebellion and Reconstruction*, pp. 75–7.

F 95 (69 A.D.)

Peter *ES* 90, p. 253.28–30: Those who dined with Vitellius repeatedly came to very bad ends. So, for example, Crispus, after he had become ill and absented himself for some days, then, after he had appeared, said, "If I had not been ill, I would have absolutely perished."

Xiphil. 194.7–11 (III, pp. 616–17) = Dio LXV.2–3 (III, p. 117.9–15): Yet it was from precisely this [regurgitation of his meals] that he was able to persist, since those very men who were dining with him all met a bad end. For this reason, one of them, Vivius Crispus, uttered a most humorous remark, and, after he had been forced for some days by sickness to absent himself from the dining, said, "If I had not been ill, I would have absolutely perished."

Suet. *Dom.* 3.1 records another of Q. Vivius Crispus' (*PIR* V 379) witticisms, for which see F 105, below. On Crispus' interesting career and character, see Murison, *Rebellion and Reconstruction*, pp. 78–9.

F 96 (69 A.D.)

Peter *ES* 91, pp. 253.31–254.2: Vitellius used to say that he praised and admired Nero but faulted him because he had furnished his residences modestly and used little wealth for the sake of luxury.

Xiphil. 194.25–29 (III, p. 617) = Dio LXV.4.1 (III, pp. 118.15–119.2): And since I have mentioned these things a single time, I shall also add that he was not even satisfied by the Golden House of Nero. But though he very much admired and lauded Nero's name and all his life and all his pursuits, he nevertheless faulted him, saying that he lived basely and employed minimal and cheap furnishings.

On Vitellius, Nero, and the Golden House, see Murison, *Rebellion and Reconstruction*, pp. 80–1, and Griffin, *Nero*, pp. 137–42.

F 97 (69 A.D.)

Peter *ES* 92, p. 254.3–4: His wife Galleria kept criticizing the decoration found in the palace for being minimal.

Xiphil. 194.29–31 (III, p. 617) = Dio LXV.4.2 (III, p. 119.3–4): And his wife Galeria, because she had found the decoration in the palace minimal, ridiculed them.

Murison, *Rebellion and Reconstruction*, p. 81, notes: "This is the only item in all our sources which is remotely hostile to Galeria Fundana" (*PIR*^{2} G 33).

F 98 (69 A.D.)

Peter *ES* 93, p. 254.5–8 = Dio LXV.4.4 (III, p. 120.18–21): Vitellius ascended the Capitoline and greeted his mother. She was a proper sort, and, when she first heard her son referred to as Germanicus, said, "I bore a Vitellius, but not a Germanicus."

Tac. *Hist.* II.89 mentions Vitellius' meeting with his mother Sextilia (*PIR* S 460) on the Capitoline, though there is no notice of her reaction to the title "Germanicus."

F 99 (69 A.D.)

Peter *ES* 94, p. 254.9–12: Too much did Vitellius retain and consort with his old friends, behaving a little unusually. For many, after they have unexpectedly ascended to great importance, despise those who had been acquainted with them in their former humble state.

Xiphil. 195.21–25 (III, pp. 617–18) = LXV.7.1 (III, p. 121.13–19): And he was habitually mindful of his old companions and honored them greatly, not disdaining to seem to recognize any of them, just as other men would. For many, after they have unexpectedly ascended to great importance, despise those who had been acquainted with them in their former humble state.

Cf. Tac. *Hist.* II.87.2 and Suet. *Vit.* 12.1 on alleged friends from Vitellius' disreputable past. Murison, *Rebellion and Reconstruction*, p. 88, raises the possibility that Dio's observation about how the successful often treat their longtime friends may reflect the historian's personal experience. Whether this is so or not, Peter felt it worthy of inclusion in his *History*. Was he out to make a point with his own contemporaries? Of course, whatever Dio's and Peter's motives, they are not necessarily dependent on one another.

F 100 (69 A.D.)

Peter *ES* 95, p. 254.9–12: Alienus, when he had deserted Vitellius, allied himself with Vespasian. And later, when he had repented, again acclaimed Vitellius emperor. For such things are accustomed to happen in civil wars.

Xiphil. 197.3–12 (III, p. 619) = Dio LXV.10.3–4 (III, pp. 124.18–125.2): After this, when friendly proposals came to him from Primus, he summoned the soldiers and, when he had described the weakness of Vitellius and the strength of Vespasian and the character of each, he convinced them to change sides. And then, on the one hand, they took down the images of Vitellius from their standards and swore they would be ruled by Vespasian, but, after they had been dismissed and returned to their tents, after they had suddenly reassembled in much haste and confusion, they again haled Vitellius emperor and took Alienus into custody on the grounds that he had betrayed them, having taken no heed of his rank as consul. For such are the works of civil wars.

Cf. Tac. *Hist.* III.13–14. M. Antonius Primus (*PIR*^{2} A 866), a prominent commander in Pannonia, had supported Vespasian against Vitellius and, in 69 near Hostilia in Italy, began negotiations with Caecina Aelianus (*PIR*^{2} C 99) and Fabius Valens (*PIR*^{2} F 68), both of whom backed Vitellius and may have been consuls. After Aelianus had transferred his and his troops' allegiance to Vitellius, the soldiers decided against the shift and arrested Caecina. On the complex course of events and the issue of the characters of the principals, see Murison, *Rebellion and Reconstruction*, pp. 96–100.

F 101 (69 A.D.)

Peter *ES* 96, p. 254.16–18: Terrified, Vitellius put on a ragged tunic, wishing to escape detection. But it was impossible that a man who had been emperor escape detection for long.

Xiphil. 201.21–26 = Dio LXV.20.1–2 (III, p. 132.14–19): ... Vitellius, terrified, put on a ragged and filthy tunic, and hid himself in a dark room in which dogs were being kept, having an intention to escape during the night to Tarracina and to his brother. And the soldiers, when they had investigated and discovered him, for, having been an emperor, he was not able to escape detection very long, seized him ...

The room was in the palace and the context Vespasian's consolidation of his hold on the city of Rome. Cf. Tac. *Hist.* III.84.4 and Suet. *Vit.* 16, to be read with Murison, *Rebellion and Reconstruction*, pp. 118–19.

F 102 (70 A.D.)

Peter *ES* 97, p. 254.19–20: Each day Mucianus used to say, "Resources are the sinews of sovereignty."

Xiphil. 204.10–13 (III, pp. 623–24) = Dio LXVI.2.5 (III, p. 136.12–15): And Mucianus was also very zealously collecting in the treasury indescribable resources from everywhere, in every way possible, bringing censure about it upon himself instead of upon Vespasian. For he used to say that it was always the case that resources were the sinews of sovereignty.

Tac. *Hist.* II.84.1 has C. Licinius Mucianus (*PIR*[2] L 216) say "sinews of civil war." The characterization of resources or wealth as the "sinews of war" or "sinews of affairs of state" is a commonplace in Greek, Latin, and Byzantine literature. On the other hand, the "sinews of sovereignty" version of F 102 is unique to Peter and Xiphilinus. See further Murison, *Rebellion and Reconstruction*, pp. 129–30.

F 103 (70 A.D.)

Peter *ES* 98[a], p. 254.21–4: The Alexandrians were not happy under Vespasian, but kept reviling him and jeering at his avarice and shouting to him, "You seek six obols on top of this," with the result that he, though very mild-mannered, became enraged.

Xiphil. 205.19–206.2 (III, pp. 624–25) = LXVI.8.2–5 (III, pp. 140.15–141.12): Moreover, the Alexandrians, too, were not happy with him, but were even very angered, with the result that not only in private, but also in public, they jeered and reviled him. For, when they had expected they would receive something great from him because they had made him emperor first, they not only gained nothing but also had monies exacted besides. For, on the one hand, he collected much from them in other ways, having neglected no source of revenue, not even if someone was a beggar, but raising funds both from the other sources and from the temples alike. And often, too, he renewed some taxes which had been discontinued and increased others which were customary. And afterwards he did this same thing in the other subject territory and in Rome. The Alexandrians, at any rate, began hurling other things at him, along with "You seek six obols on top of this," with the result that he, though very mild-mannered, became enraged, and commanded, on the one hand, that the six obols per man be exacted and also ordered that they be punished.

Suet. *Vesp.* 19.2 tells a story similar in some respects. On the purpose of the six-obol payment of F 103 and its possible implications for the history of Roman fiscal policy with respect to Alexandria and Egypt, see Murison, *Rebellion and Reconstruction*, pp. 143–46.

F 104 (70 A.D.)

Peter *ES* 98[b], p. 254.25–27: When Titus had sought their pardon, they kept reviling him no less and yelling, "We feel for him, for he does not know how to be Caesar."

Xiphil. 206.2–5 (III, p. 625) = Dio LXVI.8.6 (III, p. 142.1–4): At any rate, after Titus had sought their pardon, Vespasian spared none of them. And they did not leave him alone, but, gathered in a sort of meeting, they shouted very loudly in unison to Titus, having said exactly this, "We feel for him, for he does not know how to be Caesar."

Titus had requested pardon for the Alexandrians from Vespasian. Titus' presence in Alexandria fixes chronological parameters of the winter of 69–70 for the incident. See Murison, *Rebellion and Reconstruction*, p. 146.

F 105 (70 A.D.)

Peter *ES* 99, p. 254.28–30: Someone gracefully opined to the man who had asked Vespasian, during his reign, "With what does Caesar busy himself?" He said, "He is retired, and not even a fly lands by him."

Xiphil. 206.16–18 (III, p. 625) = Dio LXVI.9.4–5 (III, p. 143.12–14): Consequently, someone not unseemingly said to one who had asked, "With what does Domitian busy himself?", "He is both retired and not even a fly lands by him."

Suet. *Dom.* 3.1 attributes the comment to Vibius Crispus, for whom see F 95, above.

F 106 (70 A.D.)

Peter *ES* 100, p. 254.31–32 = Dio LXVI.3[a] (III, p. 144.17–18): Vespasian was laughed at whenever, paying an expense, he used to say, "I shall buy these with my own money."

Though Suet. *Vesp.* 16 and 19.2 and Zonar. XI.17 (II, pp. 494.20–495.4) address Vespasian's attitude toward money, the quotation assigned him by Peter is unparalleled.

F 107 (70 A.D.)

Peter *ES* 101, p. 255.1–2: Vespasian used to tell jokes like a commoner and regale in being the butt of jokes.

Xiphil. 207.14 (III, p. 626) = Dio LXVI.11.1 (III, p. 145.7–8): For he used to tell jokes like a commoner and regale in being the butt of jokes.

With F 107 cf. Suet. *Vesp.* 12–13 and 22–3.

F 108 (70 A.D.)

Peter *ES* 102, p. 255.3–5: The same man did not become angry with the person who brought him the reproachful letters, which they call *anonyma* and in the language of Latins *famosa*, but was responding to them and appending additions.

Xiphil. 207.14–16 (III, p. 626) = Dio LXVI.11.1 (III, p. 145.8–11): And if – as *anonyma* are accustomed to – any letters to the emperors which reproached him were ever posted publicly, he publicly posted in response what he was in agreement with, being not at all agitated.

On this type of lampoon, see Murison, *Rebellion and Reconstruction*, p. 156. The odd "they call" and the transliteration of the Latin *famosa* into Greek characters – unique in all of Greek literature – may be the wording of Peter or the excerptor.

F 109 (70 A.D.)

Peter *ES* 103, p. 255.6–9: A certain Phoebus, when he had become frightened, came to him [Vespasian] requesting that he not be angry about what he told him once under Nero – to go off to the crows. And he laughed and replied, "But would that you go to the crows." Yet up to this time, too, he did not punish him.

Xiphil. 207.17–23 (III, p. 626) = Dio LXVI.11.2 (III, p. 145.11–17): And Phoebus, when he had approached him and apologized because under Nero he had once looked angrily at him in the theater in Greece about things which he was seeing the emperor doing disgracefully, he [Phoebus] angrily commanded him to depart, and, when he was asked where to, he said, "To the crows," then, when Phoebus began apologizing about this, he [Vespasian] neither did him any harm nor said anything else to him in reply except precisely this, "Be off to the crows."

See F 76, above, and Murison, *Rebellion and Reconstruction*, pp. 156–57.

F 110 (70 A.D.)

Peter *ES* 104, p. 255.10–14: When Vologesus, sovereign of the Persians, had written thus to

Xiphil. 207.23–26 (III, p. 626) = Dio LXVI.11.3 (III, p. 145.17–20): And when Vologesus had him, "Sovereign of Sovereigns Vologesus sends greetings to his friend Vespasian," having titled him neither Autocrator nor Augustus, he did not abuse him in return, but wrote back to him thus, "To Sovereign of Sovereigns Vologesus, Vespasian Caesar."

written to him thus, "King of Kings Arsaces to Flavius Vespasian, greetings," he did not censure him at all, and he wrote back in the same fashion, having prefaced none of the titles of the realm.

Murison, *Rebellion and Reconstruction*, p. 157, raises the possibility that Vologases (*PIR* V 629) wrote before he knew of Vitellius' death and Vespasian's acclamation. The account of the exchange should, then, be taken as a comment on Vespasian's character rather than on any haughtiness on Vologases' part. Dio, as reflected in Xiphilinus, has Vologases I use the regnal name of the Arsacid dynasty of Parthia. Peter or the excerptor retained "Vologesus" in the citation.

F 111 (70 A.D.)

Peter *ES* 105, p. 255.15–18: When some men had come under suspicion about tyranny and were discussing matters very boldly, he was not angered but, having broken into tears, departed the senate house, having said only this besides, "My son succeeds me or no one."

Xiphil. 207.30–208.1 (III, p. 626) = Dio LXVI.12.1 (III, p. 146.5–8): And once, because of this, the tribunes, after they had seized him, delivered him to their attendants, and Vespasian was confounded and, having broken into tears, left the senate house, having added only this, "Either my son will succeed me or nobody else"

Xiphil. 207.26–27 (III, p. 626) = Dio LXVI.12.1 (III, p. 146.1) specifies C. Helvidius Priscus (*PIR*[2] H 59) as the individual seized. On him, see Dio *EV* 273 (I, pp. 360.17–361.4) = Dio LXVI.12.2 (III, p. 148.10–24). Suet. *Vesp.* 25 has "sons" rather than "son" and connects the statement to the emperor's confidence in the predictions of horoscopes. For more on the principals and context, see Murison, *Rebellion and Reconstruction*, pp. 157–59.

F 112 (71 A.D.)

Peter *ES* 106, p. 255.19–28 = Dio LXVI.13.1[a] (III, p. 147.8–15): Mucianus said a great number of amazing things to Nero against the Stoics, that "They are full of empty boasting;" "If any of them lets his beard grow, raises his eyebrows, throws his mantelet over his shoulder, and walks barefoot, he immediately says he is wise, brave, just, and gives himself great airs even if, as this well-known saying goes, he knows neither letters nor how to swim;" and "They look down on everyone and call the well-born, on the one hand, spoiled, the commoner slim-witted, and the handsome, on the one hand, licentious, the base simple, and the wealthy greedy, and the poor servile." ...

For Mucianus, see F 102 and Murison, *Rebellion and Reconstruction*, pp. 162–63, on Mucianus, Stoics, and Cynics. Due to the absence of leaves discarded from *Vat. Graec.* 73, Peter's treatment of the rest of Vespasian's reign through a portion of the initial year of Hadrian's is missing. See Boissevain, *ES*, p. 255.28–29, and his diagram of foliation at p. xii.

F 113 (87–88 A.D.)

Peter *ELGR* 3, pp. 390.23–391.2 = Dio LXVII.6.5 (III, p. 172.1–7) = F 4 Müller *FHG* IV, p. 185: Decebalus, sovereign of Dacia, promising peace, dispatched a herald to Domitian. Against him, Domitian sent Fuscus with a large force. Having learned this, Decebalus sent a delegation to him again, saying in mockery that, if each of the Romans should take two obols to Decebalus to pay as tribute each year, peace would be established with him. But if he should not take this, he would make war and cause great evils to be inflicted on them.

Decebalus' (*PIR*^{2} D 19) rule began *c.* 87, and F 113 probably refers to Cornelius Fuscus' (*PIR*^{2} C 1365) operations of that year. Consequently, Decebalus' alleged arrogance precedes his destruction of Fuscus' forces in 88. The suggestion of a Roman tribute would serve as a presage to Domitian's agreement in 89 to an annual payment to Decebalus. See Bennett, *Trajan*, p. 86, for narrative and sources.

F 114 (102 A.D.)

Dio *ELGR* 46 (pp. 426.16–427.7) = Dio LXVIII.9.1–2 (III, p. 194.1–14): Even before his defeat, Decebalus, on the one hand, had sent envoys, not the best of the longhairs, as before, but of the cap-wearers. And these, when they had thrown both their weapons and themselves to the ground, begged of Trajan especially to submit to go to Decebalus himself for an

Peter *ELGR* 4, p. 391.3–8 = F 5 Müller *FHG* IV, p. 185 = Boissevain III, p. 195, apparatus: Decebalus sent as envoys to Trajan cap-wearers. For these, among them, are held in higher honor. For he formerly sent longhairs, apparently less worthy among them. But those men, after they had come before Trajan, threw their weapons down and, when audience and talks, even on the grounds that he would do everything he would be ordered to do, and if not, at any rate, to send someone to him to make a settlement.

they had bound their hands behind them in a manner of prisoners of war, began to entreat Trajan to come to Decebalus for talks.

Müller prints *ELGR* 4 and 5 as a single fragment. F 114 and F 115 afford a rare opportunity to compare an excerpt of Dio himself with an excerpt of Peter. The historical context is Trajan's First Dacian War of 101–102, for which see Bennett, *Trajan*, pp. 86–97, in general, and specifically for F 114, p. 92 and p. 247, n. 37. The "longhairs" (κομήτες) seem to have comprised a broad reservoir of the Dacian populace from which warriors were drawn, while "cap-wearers" (πιλοφόροι) were individuals prominent at a local level and distinguished by the *pilleus*, a conical cap of felt. Bennett, *Trajan*, Plates 10B and 10A, provides images of the former and latter, respectively.

F 115 (102 A.D.)

Dio LXVIII.9.2–6 (III, pp. 194.14–196.2): And Sura and Claudius Livianus, the prefect, were sent. And nothing was accomplished, for Decebalus did not dare meet them but then sent envoys, too. Trajan seized mountains that had been fortified and on them found the weapons, the engines that had been captured, and the standard that had been taken in the time of Fuscus. Then, because of this and also since Maximus, at the same time, had captured his sister and a strong position, Decebalus was ready to agree to anything whatsoever of the things which had been prescribed – not that he was going to abide by these, but in order to catch his breath from the present state of affairs. For to surrender his weapons and engines and engine makers and to return deserters,

Peter *ELGR* 5, p. 391.9–20 = F 5 Müller *FHG* IV, p. 185 = Boissevain III, p. 195, apparatus: Decebalus again sent an embassy to Trajan, gaining a cessation of the present state of affairs. And he was promising to surrender to Trajan all his arms and engines of war and the Roman makers of those engines who were with him and the deserters, and to destroy all the defenses he built, and also to concede the ground which Trajan controlled, and to consider personal enemies both his enemies and those of the Romans, and not to receive a deserter, nor to have a Roman soldier near himself. Trajan then accepted the delegation upon these articles of agreement. And Decebalus threw his weapons before him and, having fallen to the ground, prostrated himself and sent envoys to Rome, and they and to dismantle his fortifications and to withdraw from captured territory, and furthermore to consider the same people as the Romans enemies and friends, and neither to receive any deserter nor to employ any soldier from the realm of the Romans – for, persuading the most and the best from there, he was attaching them to himself – he, after he had come to Trajan, fallen to the ground and done him obeisance, and thrown down his weapons, pledged, though unwillingly.

similarly bound their hands as in a manner of prisoners of war.

For context, see on F 114. For Cornelius Fuscus, see on F 113.

F 116 (117 A.D.)

Peter *ES* 107, pp. 255.29–256.2 = Dio LXIX.8.11 with apparatus + 9.3 (III, apparatus, pp. 228 and 229): ... On the roads. For, for the most part, he used to walk or ride and very seldom used a chariot. And he used to breakfast without wine and eat much. And often, trying cases, he would partake of food during a break and he used to breakfast and dine with everyone and for him the common meal was full of all sorts of discussions.

Xiphil. 245.29–33 (III, p. 652) = Dio LXIX.7.3 (III, p. 228.7–13): Both in Rome and abroad he used to always have the noblest men about him, and he was with them even in the banquets, and, for this reason, a fourth often was riding with him. And he used to go hunting as often as possible, and he used to breakfast without wine and eat much. And often, even trying cases, he would partake of food during a break and he used to dine with all the first and foremost, and to him the common meal was full of all sorts of discussions.

ES 107 marks the end of the lacuna in *Vat. Graec.* 73, for which see Boissevain, *ES*, p. 255.28–29, and his diagram of foliation at p. xii. The subject of F 116 is the behavior of Hadrian. Either Peter or the excerptor has mistaken Dio's "foremost" (ἀρίστων) for "breakfast" (ἤριστα).

F 117 (117 A.D.)

Peter *ES* 108, p. 256.3–5 = Dio LXIX.8.1[a] (III, p. 229.1–3): When the Alexandrians had rioted, they did not cease at all until they received a letter of Hadrian rebuking them. Thus, perhaps, word of an emperor can be more influential than arms.

Hadrian probably was in Gaul when word reached him of unrest in Alexandria, prompted, it seems, by some disagreement about the identification of a new Apis bull. On the precise circumstance, see Birley, *Hadrian*, p. 142.

F 118 (121 A.D.)

Peter *ES* 109, p. 256.6–9 = Dio LXIX.10.3[a] (III, p. 231.9–12): After Plotina died, Hadrian was praising her, saying, "Though she requested many things from me, there was nothing she failed to gain." And this meant nothing other than that; "She used to request such things as neither burdened me nor allowed me to object."

Pompeia Plotina (*PIR*[2] P 679), wife of Hadrian's adoptive father Trajan, had been instrumental in Hadrian's rise. He probably was in Spain when he learned of her death. See Birley, *Hadrian*, pp. 144–45.

F 119 (134 A.D.)

Peter *ES* 110, p. 256.10–13: When the populace had shouted to Hadrian in the hippodrome that a certain charioteer who was a slave should be freed, he said, "It is not fitting that you implore us to free a slave who is not our own nor for me to coerce his master."

Xiphil. 252.11–15 (III, p. 656) = Dio LXIX.16.3 (III, p. 236.9–13): And after he had come to Rome, when, during some spectacle, the populace, crying out, was insisting that a certain charioteer be freed, he responded through a written public notice, having said, "It is not fitting that you implore us to free another's slaves or to coerce his master to do this."

For context, see Birley, pp. 280–81.

F 120 (136 A.D.)

Peter *ES* 111, p. 256.14–18: A certain Similis, commander of the guards, being in high repute for prudence and fairness, Hadrian

Xiphil. 253.14–19 (III, p. 656) = Dio LXIX.19.1 (III, p. 238.13–18): And while Similis certainly was surpassing him [Turbo] in age used to honor exceedingly. And, when he had summoned him while still a centurion, he was conversing with him while the prefects were standing outside. And he said, "It is shameful, Caesar, that you converse with a centurion while the prefects are standing outside."

and rank, he was, to be sure (as I, at any rate, think), in character second to none of them. And it is possible to infer this even from the smallest things. For to Trajan, when he had once summoned him inside while still a centurion ahead of the prefects, he said, "It is shameful, Caesar, that you converse with a centurion while the prefects are standing outside."

Note that Peter or the excerptor has mistakenly shifted the context of C. Sulpicius Similis' (*PIR* S 735) remark from the reign of Trajan to that of Hadrian. If due to Peter, this undoubtedly is a result of the passing mention of Trajan within the portion of Dio from which Peter drew. If due to the excerptor, it is a consequence of the allusion to Trajan in a series of excerpts dealing with affairs under Hadrian. Dio's point (Xiphil. 252.31–253.14 [III, p. 656] = Dio LXIX.18.1–4 [III, pp. 237.11–238.13]) had been to contrast the career and character of the out-going prefect Sulpicius Similis with those of Q. Marcius Turbo Fronto Publicius Severus (*PIR*^{2} M 249). For these two and for broader context, see Birley, pp. 90–2 and 95–6. On the basis of Dio's expositon as reflected in Xiphilinus, *ES* 111 and 112 should have followed *ES* 113.

F 121 (136 A.D.)

Peter *ES* 112, p. 256.19–22: The same Similis, after he had taken command of the guard under constraint, gave up the command and spent seven years in the country. And when he had died, he wrote on his monument, "Here lies Similis, fifty years old, on the one hand, but having lived seven years."

Xiphil. 253.19–23 (III, pp. 656–57) = Dio LXIX.19.2 (III, pp. 238.18–239.4): Moreover, he took command of the guardsmen unwillingly and, after had had taken it, resigned and, barely having been discharged, spent the seven remaining years of his life quietly in the country, and upon his tomb inscribed this: "Here lies Similis, who had a life of many years, but who lived seven years."

See above, F 120.

F 122 (136 A.D.)

Peter *ES* 113, pp. 256.23–257.2: Silvanus and Fuscus were killed by Hadrian. Sirvillius, when he had learned this, requested incense and fire and, after he had burned the incense, said, "Know, gods, on the one hand, that I do you no injustice, but die like one who has done the greatest injustices." For, not bearing the diseases and pains, Hadrian wanted to kill himself, with the result that, having cried out, he once said, "Zeus, how bad it is that one who desires to die be unable to."

Xiphil. 252.18–23 (III, p. 656) = Dio LXIX.17.1–2 (III, pp. 236.17–237.1): And Severianus and Fuscus, his grandson, he murdered, on the grounds that they had been displeased with this, the former being ninety, the latter eighteen. And before the execution, Severianus requested fire, and, burning incense, said at the same time, "Know, gods, that I, on the one hand, do you no injustice. But concerning Hadrian, I pray for this alone, that, having desired to die, he be unable to."

On the basis of the exposition in Xiphilinus, the content of *ES* 113 should have preceded *ES* 111 and 112. In 136, an ailing Hadrian had announced the adoption of L. Ceionius Commodus (*PIR*^{2} C 606), who, as L. Aelius Aurelius Commodus, became Hadrian's heir apparent. This seems to have precipitated an attempt to displace Aelius by Pedanius Fuscus (*PIR*^{2} P 198) and L. Iulius Ursus Servianus (*PIR*^{2} I 631), Fuscus' grandfather and the husband of Hadrian's sister, Domitia Paulina (*PIR*^{2} D 108). On all this, see Birley, pp. 289–92. Sirvillius is a corruption of Severianus.

F 123 (138 A.D.)

Peter *ES* 114, p. 257.3–9: After the senate had threatened to abolish the memory of Hadrian and not to enroll him among the heroes, Antoninus, weeping and lamenting, as he was not persuading them, [said] in conclusion, "I do not rule you, if, indeed, he became a man base and bad to you and an enemy. For it is clear that you will dissolve all the things which have been done by him. And one of these is also my adoption."

Xiphil. 256.15–23 (III, p. 658) = Dio LXX.1.2–3 (III, p. 243.5–13): And because the senate decided not to grant heroic honors to Hadrian, who had died, in consequence of some murders of prominent men, Antoninus, weeping and wailing, spoke much else to them and, in the end, said, "I, then, shall not rule you, if, indeed, that man became base and hateful to you and a foe. For it is clear that the things which have been done by him, one of which, too, is my adoption, you will dissolve."

Antoninus is Hadrian's successor, Antoninus Pius. Peter's "abolish the memory of" refers to *damnatio memoriae*.

F 124 (138 A.D.)

Peter *ES* 115, p. 257.10–12: Antoninus preferred to chastise none of the sycophants, having said, "I am not able to begin your leadership from murders."

Xiphil. 256.24–9 (III, p. 658) = Dio LXX.2 (III, pp. 243.14–244.3): ... the senate give him the eponym Augustus and Pius for this reason, since, at the beginning of his reign, when many had been summoned and some even ordered by name to appear, he nevertheless punished no one, having said, "There is no need that I should begin my leadership over you from such acts."

Boissevain (III, p. 243) notes that from this point on the text of Dio used by Peter does not seem to have been fuller than the one Xiphilinus and Zonaras employed some six centuries later. Antoninus Pius became emperor on July 10, 138.

F 125 (166 or 167 A.D.)

Peter *ELGR* 6, p. 391.21–28 = F 6 Müller *FHG* IV, p. 186 = Dio LXXI.3.1[a] (III, pp. 250.6–251.7): After six thousand Langiobards and Obii had crossed the Ister, when Vindex's cavalry had taken the field and Candidus' infantry had reached them first, the barbarians betook themselves to full-scale flight. After these things had so transpired, reduced to fear from the first attack, the barbarians sent to Iallius Bassus, who was managing Paeonia, envoys – both Vallomarius, sovereign of the Marcomanni, and ten others who had been selected, one per nation. And the envoys, after they had by oaths pledged peace, set off for home.

On this incursion, see Birley, *Marcus Aurelius*, pp. 201–2 and 230. For Candidus, Iallius Bassus, and Vallomarius, see *PIR*[2] C 384, I 4, and B 42, respectively.

F 126 (168 A.D.)

Peter *ES* 116, p. 257.13–17: Once, when he had been asked for money by the soldiers, Marcus did not give it, having said, "By as much more the soldiers receive than the established amount, by so much does it come out of the blood of their offspring and kinsmen. The power of rulership rests not in the soldiers, but in god."

Xiphil. 259.20–25 (III, p. 660) = Dio LXXI.3.3–4 (III, pp. 251.14–252.7): And yet, after a struggle most mighty and a brilliant victory had come about, nevertheless, the emperor, when he had been asked by the soldiers, did not give them money, having said this, "By as much more than whatever they receive beyond the established amount, this will be exacted from the blood of their parents and kinsmen. For, mark you, god alone is able to make judgments about absolute rulership."

The soldiers' request for a donative came after the successful repulse of a German incursion into Italy, probably in 168. Birley, *Marcus Aurelius*, pp. 211–14 and 230–31, provides context.

F 127 (171 A.D.)

Dio *ELGR* 56, p. 431.10–18 = LXXI.11.2–3 (III, p. 253.2–15): And those seeking peace, just as the Quadi, also gained it, in fact, both in order that they be detached from the Marcomani and because they gave many horses and cattle and both all the deserters and the prisoners of war – first, on the one hand, about 13,000 and later the rest, too – they submitted to return.

Peter *ELGR* 7, pp. 391.29–32 = F 7 Müller *FHG* IV, p. 186 = Dio LXXI.11.2 (III, p. 253.2–8): Quadi, seeking peace, sent envoys to Marcus, and gained it. And many horses and many cattle they gave, and 13,000 prisoners of war they then, on the one hand, released, and later, too, others galore.

See below, on F 128.

F 128 (171 A.D.)

Peter *ELGR* 8, p. 392.1–2 = F 7 Müller *FHG* IV, p. 186 = Dio LXXI.11.6 (III, p. 253.25): Astingi and Lacringi came to the assistance of Marcus.

For this diplomacy and its consequences, see Birley, *Marcus Aurelius*, pp. 231–33. Müller combines *ELGR* 7 and 8 into a single fragment.

F 129 (172 A.D.)

Peter *ES* 117, p. 257.18–22 = Dio LXXI.5.2 (III, p. 256.3–8): Marcus was speaking to someone in the language of Latins. And not only he but no one else at all of those present understood what had been said, in consequence of which Rufus, the prefect, said, "It is likely that he does not understand what has been said by you, for he does not know Greek either." For he himself did not understand what had been said.

Xiphil. 250.8–10 (III, p. 661) = Dio LXXI.5.2–3 (III, p. 256.3–13): And Rufus Basaeus was a prefect for Marcus, a good man in other respects, but uncultured in consequence of rusticity, and during the first part of his life, at any rate, because he had been raised in poverty.

Peter is the only witness to M. Bassaeus Rufus' (*PIR*^{2} B 69) alleged comment to Marcus Aurelius. Xiphilinus evidently thought it unworthy of notice.

F 130 (175 A.D.)

Peter *ES* 118, p. 257.23–26: Marcus was exceedingly ill, with the result that he held few hopes of deliverance, and often in his illness he kept reciting the iambic of tragedy: "Such things does wretched war bring to pass."

Xiphil. 262.5–9 (III, p. 663) = Dio LXXI.22.1 (III, p. 262.1–9): When Pertinax had received a consulship for his acts of bravery, nevertheless those who were resentful about him being from the obscure with respect to lineage kept citing from tragedy: "Such does wretched war produce," ignorant that he would also be emperor.

Pertinax was *consul suffectus* in 175. The quotation is Eur. *Supp.* 119. Of course, the point of the quotation in *ES* 118 differs from that of the parallel in Xiphilinus. It seems likely that the excerptor, working on material from the reign of Marcus Aurelius and concerned primarily about preserving the verse as a *sententia*, simply kept Marcus the focus rather than introducing a mention of Pertinax as had Dio. For "iambic," see on F 18, above.

131 (175 A.D.)

Peter *ES* 119, p. 257.27–30 = Dio LXXI.27.1[a] (III, p. 267.11–14): When Marcus was preparing for the war against Cassius, he accepted no barbarian alliance although many were hastening to him, saying that it was not proper for barbarians to know the evils in motion between Romans.

Around the beginning of April 175, a false report of the death of the ailing Marcus, then operating from Sirmium, may have prompted Avidius Cassius (*PIR*[2] A 1402), governor of Syria, to rebel. By late July, Cassius had been murdered by one of his officers. For these events, see Birley, *Marcus Aurelius*, pp. 252–59.

132 (176 A.D.)

Peter *ES* 120, p. 258.1–5: When the senate was urging that those who had collaborated with Cassius and their kinsmen be put to death, he wrote much back, including this: "I beg and implore, preserve my reign pure from any senatorial blood. For may it not come to pass that under me any of you be destroyed either by my or your vote."

Xiphil. 265.17–21 (III, p. 666) = Dio LXXI.30.1–2 (III, pp. 270.1–271.2): Having violently lamented Faustina, who had died, he wrote to the senate that none of those who had joined with Cassius were to be killed, as if he would be able to find from this alone some consolation about Faustina. "For," he said, "may it not come to pass that any of you be killed either by my or your vote."

The empress Annia Galeria Faustina (*PIR*[2] A 716) died at Halala (subsequently Colonia Faustinopolis) in Cappadocia early in the summer of 176, at which time Marcus was moving from Alexandria, where he had spent the winter of 175/6, through Asia Minor on his way back to Rome. For Avidius Cassius, see above on F 131. Birley, *Marcus Aurelius*, pp. 262–66, deals with Marcus in the East, Faustina's death, and the fates of those associated with Cassius.

F 133 (176 A.D.)

Peter *ES* 121, p. 258.6–11: And when he had come forth, Marcus began to apologize to the populace because he had been away from Rome for many years. And they began to shout "Eight, eight" and to show it with their fingers. For he

Xiphil. 266.5–11 (III, p. 666) = Dio LXXI.32.1 (III, p. 272.14–20): And after he had come to Rome and was giving a speech to the populace, when, in the midst of him talking among other things about the fact that he happened to have been away for eight years. And they began to request that they should receive eight gold pieces apiece. Perceiving this, Marcus, after he had smiled, said, "Eight, too" and gave them eight gold pieces apiece.

had been abroad for many years, they shouted "Eight" and began indicating this, too, with their hands, in order that they, indeed, also receive as much gold for the banquet, he smiled and he himself also said "Eight" and, after this, distributed two-hundred drachmas apiece to them, an amount they had not yet received before.

Marcus entered Rome near the end of November. The absence from the *ES* of Marcus' two-hundred-drachma largesse is probably due to the excerptor – who would have judged he had done what was required of him once he had recorded Marcus' *sententia* – rather than to any decision by Peter to ignore it.

134 (184 or 185/186 A.D.)

Peter *ES* 122, p. 258.12–14 = Dio LXXII.9.2[a] (III, p. 290.13–15): The soldiers in Britain chose Priscus, a junior officer, as emperor. And he declined, having said, "I am as much an emperor as you are soldiers."

The date could be any time between 177 and 190. Birley, *The* Fasti *of Roman Britain*, pp. 145 and 260–61, has, on the basis of *SHA Comm.* 8.4, suggested a date of 184 or, on the basis of *SHA Pert.* 3.5–6, 185 or shortly thereafter and has very cautiously posited a possible identification of Priscus with T. Caunius Priscus (*PIR*[2] C 590), legate of Legio III Augusta.

F 135 (189–190? A.D.)

Peter *ES* 123, p. 258.15–19: Comodus enrolled obscure and poor men in the senate after he had taken their wealth, with the result that Julius, when he had forfeited all his wealth, became a senator, and something of this sort was wittily remarked about him, that "Julius, after he had been deprived of his wealth, was exiled to the court."

Xiphil. 274.15–18 (III, p. 672) = Dio LXXII.12.3 (III, p. 294.7–10): And some, having already dissolved all their resources, became senators, so that it was even said about Julius Solon, a man most obscure, that "Bereaved of his wealth, he was exiled to the senate."

Note that, in contrast to F 135, Xiphilinus attributes these actions to Cleander, Commodus' *cubicularius*, rather than to Commodus himself. The difference is probably due to the Constantinian excerptor's concern with a *sententia* from Commodus' reign rather than with an accurate reflection of the context of the *sententia* in Peter's *History*. On M. Aurelius Cleander (*PIR*^{2} A 1481), see Eck, "Aurelius Cleander, M.," col. 384, *s.v.* Aurelius II.10. Julius is Julius Solon (*PIR*^{2} I 584).

F 136 (192 A.D.)

Peter *ES* 124, p. 258.20–24: Comodus, after he had removed the head from the colossus in Rome and added a club and a lion, wrote "Lucius Comodus Heracles," after which was the epigram bearing: "I, Lucius, am not Zeus's son, triumphant Hercules, but they contend that I am."

Xiphil. 280.20–25 (III, p. 676) = Dio LXXII.22.3 (III, p. 303.7–14): And let no one be in doubt. For after he had cut off the head of the colossus and substituted another of himself and given it a club and set underneath it a sort of lion of bronze to make it look like Hercules, he inscribed, in addition to the honorific names for him that had been exhibited, this, too: "Member of the *Secutores*, Lone Lefthander Who has Twelve Times" (I think) "conquered One Thousand."

The statue, about which see Griffin, *Nero*, p. 131, had been erected by Nero and later gave its name to the Colosseum. Perhaps as an indirect result of an earlier confusion of ΡΩΜΗΙ with ΡΟΔΩΙ, some authors – e.g., *Chron. Pasch.* I, p. 492.1–2, and Ced. I, p. 441.12–13 – make the monument modified by Commodus the Colossus of Rhodes. *SHA Comm.* 15.8 gives *Palus Primus Secutorum* as one of Commodus' titles. A *secutor* was a type of gladiator characterized by distinctive weaponry and protective gear. With Peter and Xiphilinus, cf. Herodian I.15.9. Peter *ES* 124 is the sole record of the epigram of F 136.

F 137 (193 A.D.)

Dio *EV* 329 (I, p. 380.20–23) = Dio LXXIII.6.1 (III, p. 310.17–22): Laetus, the consul, censured

Peter *ES* 125, p. 258.25–28: Comodus was accustomed to give barbarians much money. And having

Xiphil. 285.20–25 (III, p. 680) = Dio LXXIII.6.1 (III, p. 310.17–22): Laetus was upholding as much evil as Commodus did. At any rate, after he had summoned some barbarians who had received much gold from him in return for peace (for they were still en route), having said to them, "Tell those at home that Pertinax reigns" ...

sent for some envoys who had received money and were en route, Pertinax detained them and, when he had taken the money, said, "Tell those back home that Pertinax is sovereign."

Pertinax through panegyric and insulting Commodus. At any rate, after he had summoned some barbarians who had received much gold from him in return for peace (for they were still en route), he asked for it back, having said to them, "Tell those at home that Pertinax reigns," for, in point of fact, they certainly feared his name from the things which they had suffered when he was on campaign with Marcus.

In Dio, Xiphilinus, and Zonar. XII.6 (II, p. 541.5–9) it is Q. Aemilius Laetus (*PIR*² A 358), Commodus' and Pertinax' praetorian prefect, who tells unnamed barbarians to inform their people that Pertinax is in control, while Peter or the Constantinian excerptor transfers the comment to Pertinax, who makes the point that he "is sovereign." The shift in subject may have occurred during the composition of the *ES*, where the focus would have been on the *sententia* rather than on who spoke it. The broader wording of the *ES* may be Peter's or the excerptor's. The mistaken "consul" (ὕπατος) of Dio as preserved in the *EV* may be an error of transcription for "prefect" (ἔπαρχος). In any case, Laetus never held a consulship.

F 138 (193 A.D.)

Dio *EV* 331 (I, p. 381.10–14) = Dio LXXIII.8.5 (III, pp. 312.21–313.3): With respect to the plot against Pertinax, when the senators were about to vote

Peter *ES* 126, pp. 258.29–259.3: When Flaccus was about to proclaim himself sovereign and had been discovered and sentenced to death by the senate, he

Xiphil. 287.1–4 (III, p. 681) = Dio LXXIII.8.5 (III, pp. 312.21–313.3): But when we were about to vote to condemn Falco, Pertinax, having risen and cried out, in condemnation of Falco and were, in fact, already naming him an enemy, Pertinax, having stood up and cried out, said, "May it not come to pass that any senator unjustly be put to death during my reign." And, on the one hand, thus was he saved.

[Pertinax] began to shout, "With Pertinax holding the office of emperor, may it not come to pass that a senator be killed or exiled." And Flaccus, having become cautious and respectful, passed the time that remained in the country.

said, "May it not come to pass that any senator unjustly be put to death during my reign."

The prefect Laetus and the praetorians reacted against Pertinax' imposition of stricter controls over their behavior by conspiring to replace him with Q. Sosius Falco (*PIR* S 557), *consul ordinarius* and the Flaccus of *ES* 126. Laetus – the subject of the missing δὲ clause which would have followed the conclusion of *EV* 331 above – , was soon executed on the order of Pertinax' successor, Didius Julianus (Xiphil. 287.4–6 [III, p. 681] = Dio LXXIII.9.1 [III, p. 313.4–5]).

F 139 (193 A.D.)

Peter *ES* 127, p. 259.4–8: Pertinax, after he had attempted to correct in a short time all the things that had happened badly, perished, not having understood, although being most experienced in affairs, that it is impossible to bring an immediate, comprehensive correction to affairs, but, if anything does, the establishment of a political foundation requires time and wisdom.

Xiphil. 287.31–35 (III, p. 682) = Dio LXXIII.10.3 (III, p. 314.10–14): Thus did Pertinax, after he had attempted to restore everything in a short time, meet his end, and he did not know, though being most experienced in affairs, that it is impossible to correct a mass of things securely – but if, indeed, anything does, the establishment of a political foundation, above all, requires time and wisdom.

Pertinax died on March 28, 193, murdered by soldiers of the Praetorian Guard who had been angered by the executions of some of their comrades on the orders of Laetus in the latter's attempt to shift to them the responsibility for the failed attempt to elevate Falco to the purple. For this, see F 138, above.

F 140 (193 A.D.)

Peter *ES* 128, p. 259.9–16 = Dio LXXIII.14.2[a] (III, p. 318.10–16): Julianus, after he had seized the realm after Pertinax, began castigating everyone. When the senate had voted for a gold statue of him, he did not accept it, having said, "Give me a bronze, in order that it too survive. For I see, in fact, that while the gold and silver of the emperors before me have been demolished, the bronze remain," having erred in saying this, for the bronze which had been given was demolished after he had been killed.

Xiphil. 290.33–291.4 (III, p. 684) = Dio LXXIII.14.1 (III, p. 318.1–4): And Julianus, after he had seized the realm in this way, began managing affairs in a servile fashion, flattering the senate and those possessing any power and promising some things and granting others as favors, and he joked and bantered with those he happened to encounter.

The *sententia* of *ES* 128 was evidently meant as an example of servility and flattery of the senate attributed to Julianus by Dio apud Xiphilinus. Xiphil. 227.8–9 (III, p. 639) = Dio LXVIII.2.1 (III, p. 188.5–6) records a similar sentiment, though articulated in negative terms, credited to Nerva.

F 141 (194 A.D.)

Peter *ES* 129, p. 259.17–25: Cassius Clemens, a senator, being tried before Severus on account of his friendliness toward Niger, said, "I did not even know Niger, but when Niger undertook the war against Julianus, I happened to be there. And I chose that which the Daemon allotted me. And if you punish me because I did not desert him and come to you, reckon this too about those who are close to you, that it behooved them to desert you and support Niger. And everything whatsoever for which you condemn us, this you bring upon yourself." And Severus was not angered about these things.

Xiphil. 299.10–25 (III, p. 690) = Dio LXXIV.9.1–3 (III, pp. 333.9–334.4): Cassius Clemens, a senator, being tried by Severus himself, did not conceal the truth, but spoke freely in the following fashion. "I," he said, "knew neither you nor Niger, but, indeed, when I had been caught in that man's group, I necessarily attended to the situation at hand, not so I could fight you, but so I could depose Julianus. In this, then, I did nothing unjust, having in the beginning pursued the same things as you, nor, because, having abandoned him to whom I was allotted once and for all by the

Daemon, I did not subsequently go over to you. For neither would you have wanted those seated with you and any of those sharing in your decisions, after they had betrayed you, to desert to him. Therefore, put neither our bodies nor our names to the test, but the matters themselves. For in everything for which you condemn us, of this, too, you will find yourself and your companions guilty. For even if you are convicted, the majority of the time neither in any suit or sentence, yet in your reputation among mankind, memory of which will endure to eternity, you will seem to indict others for the things for which you are liable." To be sure, Severus, amazed by this man's forthrightness, allowed him to keep half of his wealth.

Only Peter, Xiphilinus, and Zonar. XII.8 (II, pp. 547.19–548.8) – the last more abbreviated than Xiphilinus but not as much so as *ES* 129 – mention Cassius Clemens (*PIR*[2] C 489). As is so often the case with the fragments of Peter's *History*, it is impossible to gauge how much compression is due to the excerptor as opposed to Peter himself. The context is the aftermath of Severus' defeat in 194 of C. Pescennius Niger (*PIR*[2] P 254), erstwhile governor of Syria, whose troops had proclaimed him emperor after Pertinax' death. On the clash with Niger, see Birley, *Septimius Severus*, pp. 171–82, and pp. 179–80, where Birley convincingly attributes Serverus' magnanimity in the case of Cassius Clemens to a fear of driving potential backers or neutrals into the arms of another rival, namely D. Clodius Albinus (*PIR*[2] C 1186).

142 (197 A.D.)

Peter *ES* 130, p. 259.26–31 = Dio LXXIV.8.5 (III, p. 345.10–15): While all were pretending to side with Severus, they were being confuted by the sudden announcements, being unable to conceal what was hidden in the soul. For when a report had suddenly come to their ears, they began reacting unguardedly, and by these things and by their countenance and characters, thus was each discovered. And some, too, were recognized more from excessive pretense.

ES 130, as is the case with *ES* 131 = F 143, seems to treat the situation in Rome just prior to Severus' defeat on February 19, 197 of the rival Augustus Clodius Albinus at Lugdunum. In 193, Severus, in an effort to secure his support, had raised Albinus, then *legatus pro praetore* in Britain, to the rank of Caesar. After receiving word late in 195 or early in 196 that Severus had bestowed the rank of Caesar on his own young son Caracalla (born in 188), Albinus had assumed the title of Augustus. For the war with Albinus, see Birley, *Septimius Severus*, pp. 184–95.

143 (197 A.D.)

Dio *EV* 344 (I, pp. 384.24–385.8) = Dio LXXIV.9.5–6 (III, pp. 345.16–346.10): Severus attempted in the case of those being punished by him ... to use Clarus Erucius as an informer against them, in order to compromise the man and to be thought to make the case more substantial in consequence of his family and reputation. And he promised he would give him both safety, in fact, and amnesty. And when he chose to die rather than to give any such testimony, he began to turn to Julianus and convinced him. And through this he pardoned him, at any rate so far as neither to kill nor disenfranchise him, for, in fact, he vigorously investigated all his testimony under torture, having made of no account his current rank.

Peter *ES* 131, pp. 259.33–260.5 = Dio LXXIV.9.5–6 (III, pp. 345.16–346.5): Severus, wishing to refute the senators who had written to Albinus against him, wished, too, to destroy Vibianus, a former consul and a man who seemed to side with Albinus, in order that, employing his testimony against the senators, he might make the charge worthy of belief. But he preferred to be slain rather than to do anything foreign to freedom. Then, after he had discovered Julianus, he seduced him to this and used him as an accuser.

The context is the aftermath of Septimius' victory over Albinus at Lugdunum, for which see F 142, above. C. Iulius Erucius Clarus (*PIR*[2] E 97) had been *consul ordinarius* in 193. Julianus (*PIR*[2] I 93) is otherwise unknown. Birley, *Septimius Severus*, pp. 198–200, discusses the purge.

144 (200 A.D.)

Peter *ES* 132, p. 260.6–10 (III, pp. 353–54 apparatus): Plotinianus was managing affairs with such fearlessness that he seemed to be an emperor and the emperor a consul. The result was that Severus said the following to the senate: "Your sovereign prays to die before him," and someone dared to address him in writing: "To a Fourth Caesar."

Xiphil. 312.23–31 (III, p. 699) = Dio LXXV.15.1–2 (III, pp. 353.16–354.2): The foremost cause of these things was Severus himself, who so yielded to him in all matters that the latter was held in the esteem of an emperor, the former of a prefect. For with respect to other matters, too, while he knew absolutely everything Severus was saying and doing, no one, in truth, knew any of the secrets of Plautianus. And he courted his daughter for his son, having left aside many fine maidens, and he appointed him consul, and, so to speak, prayed to have him as successor to his rule, and once even wrote in a letter, "I love the man so much that I even pray to die before he does."

C. Fulvius Plautianus (*PIR*^{2} F 554) was Septimius' kinsman and, from at least the beginning of 197, his praetorian prefect. Pu(blia) Fulvia Plautilla Augusta (*PIR*^{2} F 564), Plautianus' daughter, married Caracalla in 202, in spite of what appears to have been growing tension between Septimius and his prefect. In 203, Plautianus was *consul ordinarius*. See further Birley, *Septimius Severus*, pp. 200–4 and 212–13, on Caracalla's hostility toward Pompeia Plotina (*PIR*^{2} P 679), and 220–21 and 230–35, on Plautianus' fall from grace and eventual execution in January 205 at the behest of Caracalla.

F 145 (200 A.D.)

Peter *ES* 133, p. 260.11–13 = Dio LXXV.15.2^b (III, p. 354.6–8): When many resolutions to honor him had been made by the senate, he accepted few, saying, "Be fond of me in your souls, not in your resolutions."

The speaker appears to be Plautianus, for whom, see on F 144, above. The quotation, with its feigned modesty, is unparalleled.

F 146 (200 A.D.)

Peter *ES* 134, p. 260.14–16: In Tyana, Severus visited Plautianus, who had become ill. And his soldiers did not allow those who were with the sovereign to enter, but kept them outside.

Xiphil. 313.6–8 (III, p. 700) = Dio LXXV.15.4 (III, p. 354.15–18): Once, at any rate, in Tyana, when Severus was visiting him when he was ill, the soldiers who were around Plautianus did not allow those accompanying him to enter with him.

F 146 and 147 provide examples of Plautianus' status in the eyes of Septimius' staff and attendants. Cf. Birley, *Septimius Severus*, p. 212.

F 147 (200 A.D.)

Peter *ES* 135, p. 260.17–18: No one appeared before Severus, who had consented to hear a case, because Plautianus was not present.

Xiphil. 313.8–11 (III, p. 700) = Dio LXXV.15.5 (III, p. 354.18–21): And the man who was arranging the docket of cases before him, after he had been ordered once by Severus, when he had some free time, to introduce some case, was unwilling to do so, having said, "I am unable to do this unless Plautianus orders me."

See above on F 146.

F 148 (211 A.D.)

Peter *ES* 136, p. 260.19–24: Antoninus, after Geta's murder, after he had said many inappropriate things to the senate, declared this, too, "I prefer to live with you, but, if this is not to be, to die instead of you." And the next morning, when he had arrived at the senate chamber, he begged their pardon, not because he had slaughtered his brother, but because he had a sore throat and did not wish to give a public speech.

Xiphil. 328.9–14 (III, pp. 710–11) = Dio LXXVII.3.1–2 (III, p. 375.11–14): And, in fact, he said this, too, "Mostly I pray to live with you, and if not, otherwise to die with precisely you."

As Boissevain notes (III, p. 375, apparatus), *ES* 136's placement of Caracalla's sentiment in the senate (συνέδριον) rather than, as in Xiphilinus 328.3–5 (III, p. 710) = Dio LXXVII.3.1 (III, p. 375.3–4), before some of the soldiery is probably due to Peter himself or the excerptor. The probable date of Geta's murder by Caracalla's orders is December 26, 211. Septimius had died in February of the preceding year.

F 149 (212 A.D.)

Peter *ES* 137, p. 260.25–30 = Boissevain III, pp. 375.26–376.12: And being about to exit, at the door itself he turned about and says, "Hear a matter of importance, in order that the entire world rejoice! All who have been exiled by whatever charge, except if they have been exiled by my, as well as by your, divine father, return!" And he was thinking he was doing something great, bringing the malefactors and criminals of humankind back to Rome.

Xiphil. 328.14–19 (III, p. 711) = Dio LXXVII.3.3 (III, pp. 375.25–376.16): And after he had risen from the bench and come to the door, he said, "Hear from me a matter of importance, in order that the whole habitable world rejoice, all the exiles who have been condemned on whatever charge and in whatever way, may return." Well, after he had thus emptied the islands of exiles and given pardon to the most evil of those who had been convicted, not much later, he then filled them [the islands] ...

The speaker is Caracalla and his audience the senate – σύγκλητος in Xiphilinus, the probable source of the συνέδριον of *ES* 136. From "return" to the end of *ES* 137 are Peter's or the excerptor's words. The dead Septimius had been formally consecrated a *divus*. It is more difficult to explain why Peter or the excerptor would have added Caracalla's proviso than it is to assume that Xiphilinus omitted it. On this point, Zonar. XII.12 (II, p. 561.1–3) is no help.

F 150 (212 A.D.)

Peter *ES* 138, pp. 260.31–261.4 = Dio LXXVII.4.1[a] (III, p. 376.22–25): When the guardsmen had accused them of something, Antoninus turned Papianus and Patronius over to them to execute, having said the following, too, "I rule for you and not for myself, and, in consequence, I also rely on you, both as accusers and as judges."

This is the sole notice of Caracalla's alleged declaration. After Plautianus' execution (see on F 144), Aemilianus Papinianus (*PIR*[2] 388) – one of Rome's greatest jurists – had become praetorian prefect. Caracalla's failure to intervene on Papinianus' behalf seems more the result of a decision to appease the praetorians than the consequence of any special animus against Papinianus. Patronius is Valerius Patruinus (*PIR* V 103). For what it is worth, cf. *SHA Antoninus Geta* 6.1–2 with the comment of the author of *SHA Caracalla* 8.1: "I know that many have reported about Papinianus' death in writing thus, so as not to have knowledge of the cause of his fall, some reporting one thing, others something else." On the broader issue of the bloodbath unleashed upon Caracalla's accession, see Potter, *The Roman Empire at Bay*[2], pp. 134–37.

F 151 (212 A.D.)

Peter *ES* 139, p. 261.5–7: And he severely rebuked the man who had slain Papianus, not because he had slain him, but because he granted him an axe and did not decapitate him with a sword instead.

Xiphil. 328.23–24 (III, p. 711) = Dio LXXVII.4.2 (III, p. 377.1–5): And he censured the very man who had slain Papianus because he killed him with an axe and not a sword.

See on F 150 and, for Caracalla's comment, cf. *SHA Caracalla* 4.1, "Then, in his [Caracalla's] presence, Papinianus was beheaded with an axe by the soldiers and killed. He said to the man who had beheaded him, 'It was proper for you to have executed my command with a sword,'" and *SHA Geta* 6.3, "Papinianus himself had been beheaded with an axe, with Bassianus [i.e. Caracalla] disapproving, because the matter had not been executed with a sword." Since Roman law mandated that soldiers use swords for executions, the axe being reserved for lictors, the point of the story was probably to illustrate Caracalla's attempt to mock the learned Papinianus even after death. See further Johnson, "A Witticism of Antoninus Caracalla?", pp. 101–4.

152 (212 A.D.)

Peter *ES* 140, p. 261.8–11: Antoninus was accustomed to take everything from the living and dead, with the result that the Romans shouted in unison among many other things "We call on the living in order to bury the dead."

Xiphil. 331.12–15 (III, p. 713) = Dio LXXVII.10.3 (III, p. 383.20–24): And during the entire duration of his reign the whole world that was subject to him was so ravaged that once, in a hippodrome, the Romans shouted in unison among many other things: "We strip the living in order to bury the dead."

This alleged response to Caracalla's methods of amassing revenue is otherwise unknown. On this aspect of Caracalla's reign, see Potter, *The Roman Empire at Bay*², pp. 137–39.

F 153 (212 A.D.)

Peter *ES* 141[a], p. 261.12–13: The same man used to say often, "It is mandatory that no man have silver except me so that I may gratify the soldiers."	Xiphil. 331.15–17 (III, p. 713) = Dio LXXVII.10.4 (III, pp. 383.23–384.2): In fact, he used to say to the soldiers, "It is mandatory that no man except me have silver so that that I may gratify the soldiers with it."

Peter and Xiphilinus are the only witnesses to this sentiment.

F 154 (212 A.D.)

Peter *ES* 141[b], p. 261.14–17: When Julia, his mother, censured him because he gave much to the soldiers and said, "For us neither just nor unjust revenue has been left," after he had displayed his sword, he said, "Take courage, mother, while we have this, money will not fail us."	Xiphil. 331.17–20 (III, p. 713) = Dio LXXVII.10.4–5 (III, p. 384.2–6): And once when Julia was censuring him because he had spent much on them and had said, "No longer does either just or unjust revenue remain for us," he, after he had displayed his sword, replied, "Take courage, mother, for while we have this, not at all will money fail us."

As is the case with F 152 and 153, the quotation is otherwise unattested.

155 (212 A.D.)

Peter *ES* 142, p. 261.18–24 = Dio LXXVII.11.1[a] (III, p. 384.9–15): Julius Paulus was a man of consular rank and a slanderer and a mocker and a man who spared not even the emperors themselves whom Severus also released under supervision. And because, being under guard, he continued to mock the sovereigns, after he had summoned him, Severus swore that he would cut off his head. And he replied that he was able to cut it off, "but as long as I have it, neither you nor I am about to control it," in consequence of which, Severus laughed and released him.

The Julius Paulus of *ES* 142 may be the Junius Paullinus of Xiphil. 331.22 (III, p. 713) = Dio LXXVII.11.12 (III, p. 384.17) = F 156, itself probably a mistake for Junius Paulinus. The latter may be L. Junius Annius Maximus Paulinus (*PIR*² I 729). To be of consular rank does not mean one was a consul, and, in fact, neither Julius Paulus nor Junius Paulinus is attested to have been a consul. The explanation of the title may be that Junius Paulinus was a son of Annius Maximus (*PIR*² A 671), consul in 207.

F 156 (212 A.D.)

Peter *ES* 143, pp. 261.25–262.3 = Dio LXXVII.11.1² (III, pp. 384.17–385.4, col. 2): Antoninus, after he had summoned the same man, permitted him to write verses against him. And he artfully mocked him. For he said that he always seemed angry. Yet, while he said this as a jest, he pleased that man greatly, for he was wishing to appear terrifying and fierce and severe. And through this, to him twenty myriads ...

Xiphil. 331.22–25 (III, p. 713) = Dio LXXVII.11.1² (III, pp. 384.17–385.4): At any rate, he bestowed twenty-five myriads on Junius Paulinus because he unintentionally, being a jester, was induced to mock him a bit. For he said he looked like someone who was enraged, since, I suspect, he comported himself in the direction of anger.

See on F 155, above.

F 157 (213 A.D.)

Dio *EV* 377 (I, p. 394.25–29) = Dio LXXVII.14.1–2 (III, pp. 390.13–391.3): The women of the Chatti and, indeed, as many of the Alambanni who fell into their hands did not, in truth, submit at all passively, but when Antoninus asked whether they wished to be sold at some time or be slain,

Peter *ES* 144, p. 262.4–8 = Dio LXXVII.14.2 (III, pp. 390.10–391.2): Antoninus, when he had campaigned against the Albanni, purchased his apparent victory with money. And he also took women prisoners, among whom the women were marveled at. For when he had asked

Xiphil. 333.12–18 (III, p. 714) = Dio LXXVII.14.2 (III, pp. 390.10–391.2): But, however, even these, when they had sold the name of defeat for much money, conceded to him safe passage to Germany. Their women, after they had been captured by the Romans, when Antoninus asked

they chose the latter. Then, on the one hand, when they had been sold, all of them killed themselves, and there were those who even killed their children.	whether they wished to be sold or to be slain, they replied, "To be slain." And since they were sold, the majority cut their own throats.	them whether they wished to be sold or slain, chose the latter. Then, when they had been sold, all, on the one hand, killed themselves, and there were those who even killed their children.

Caracalla's operations around the Rhine may have begun late in 212 but were confined mostly to 213 and seem to have ended late in September of that year. Much of what we know of them depends on epigraphic, numismatic, and papyrological evidence, for which see Christol, *L'Empire Romain du III*[e] *Siècle*, pp. 39–40. The "Chatti" of *EV* 377 is an error for Cenni, so identified at Xiphil. 333.9 (III, p. 714) = Dio LXXVII.14.1 (III, p. 390.6) but otherwise absent from Dio and Peter, Xiphilinus, or Zonaras, whose content here derives from him. The *EH* correctly name the Chatti only at Dio *ELGR* 42 (p. 425.32) = Dio LXVII.5.1 (III, p. 176.3). "Alamanni" appears in the *EH* only at John of Antioch *EI* 78 (de Boor, p. 116.23) = F 186 Müller *FHG* IV, p. 608 = F 279.2 Roberto, p. 466/F 221 Mariev, p. 376.12. Elsewhere in the *EH*, "Alamanni" has become "Albanni" and "Alambanni," as in *EV* 377 and *ES* 144 of F 157 above or "Albanni" at John of Antioch *EI* 73 (p. 114.12) = F 169 Müller *FHG* IV, p. 603 = F 253.16 Roberto, p. 436, with apparatus/F 195.18 Mariev, p. 354.19, with apparatus, and Dio *EV* 373 (I, p. 394.1, with apparatus) = LXXVII.13.4 (III. P. 388.15 with apparatus). For "Alambanni," cf. Dio *EV* 374 (I, p. 394.13) = LXXVII.13.6 (III. p. 389.10 with apparatus), and Dio *EV* 381 (I, p. 395.16–17) = LXXVII.15.2 (III, p. 392.2 with apparatus). It seems clear, then, that the "Albanni" of *ES* 144 is not Peter's word, but that in the process of excerption it replaced "Alamanni." On the basis of the slaughter of their children alleged by Dio, Peter's seemingly redundant "women" in "among whom the women were marveled at" must refer narrowly to the wives among the captive women.

F 158 (213 A.D.)

Peter *ES* 145, p. 262.9–13 = Dio LXXVII.16.6 (III, pp. 394.16–395.4): Antoninus kept censuring and rebuking everyone because they were asking nothing of him. And he repeatedly said to all, "It is clear you do not have confidence in me from the things which you do not ask of me. And if you do not have confidence in me, you mistrust me, and if you mistrust me, you fear me, and if you fear me, you hate me." And he was making this an excuse for treachery.

The *sententia* of *ES* 145 is unique.

F 159 (213 A.D.)

Peter *ES* 146, p. 262.14–22 = Dio LXXVII.16.6[a] (III, p. 395.5–13): Antoninus, when he was about to kill Cornificia, as if he were actually honoring her, ordered her to choose a death she wished to die. And she, after she had wept profusely and recalled her father, Marcus, and her grandfather, Antoninus, and her brother, Commodus, in the end came out with this, "O, unhappy little soul, confined in a vile body, depart, be freed, show them that Marcus' daughter exists, even if they do not wish her to." And when she had set aside all the adornment in which she had attired herself and composed herself, she severed her veins and died.

According to Herodian IV.6.3 and *SHA Caracalla* 3.3, Caracalla had decided to kill Cornificia (*PIR*[2] C 1505), sister of Commodus, when he saw her mourning Geta shortly after his murder (December 26, 211). The quotation attributed to Cornificia is otherwise unattested.

F 160 (214 A.D.)

Peter *ES* 147, p. 262.23–31= Dio LXXVII.18.8 (III, pp. 395.21–396.5): Antoninus, after he had come to Pergamum and some people began arguing with him, seemed to bring to mind a verse of this sort from some oracular response, "Into Telephian land will enter an Ausonian beast." And because, on the one hand, he was called a beast, he was taking delight in and feeling it a pleasure that he, too, was killing very many all at once. And the person who had composed the verse kept laughing and saying that he made the verse himself as a means of demonstrating that no one can die contrary to destiny, but the popular adage is true that liars and deceivers, even if they never speak truly, are trusted.

The details of what transpired at Pergamum are beyond recovery. Late in the fall of 214, Caracalla crossed from Europe to Asia Minor. Though Xiphil. 337.14–18 (III, p. 717) = LXXVII.23.4 (III, p. 401.22–7) alludes to the "Ausonian beast" oracle, *ES* 147 alone quotes and elaborates on it. The "Telephian" land is Mysia. According to some versions of his legend, Telephus, son of Hercules and the Tegean princess Auge, reached Mysia after Aleus, King of Tegea, had expelled his daughter and her son from his realm. See further Jost, "Telephus" (1), *OCD*[3], pp. 1479–80. "Ausonian" is a poetic term for a native of Italy. From "but the commonplace is true" to the excerpt's end may be Peter's own observation.

F 161 (215 A.D.)

Peter *ES* 148, pp. 262.32–263.2: Antoninus, holding the abuse against him for naught, said, "I know, on the one hand, that these things do not satisfy you. For this reason, however, I have both arms and soldiers, so that I do not have to pay attention to whatever statements you invent."

Xiphil. 335.30–32 (III, p. 716) = Dio LXXVII.20.2 (III, p. 399.16–18): And, in the end, he wrote: "I know, on the one hand, that my actions do not satisfy you. For this reason, however, I have arms and soldiers, in order that I do not have to pay attention to whatever statements you invent."

As Xiphil. 335.26–30 (III, p. 716) = Dio LXXVII.20.1 (III, p. 399.12–26) makes clear, Antoninus' retort was directed against the senate of Antioch, his headquarters from his arrival sometime in May 215 until his departure for Alexandria probably between June and September of the same year.

F 162 (215–216 A.D.)

Peter *ES* 149, p. 263.3–5: Of the Alexandrian contractors, Antoninus, after he had put multitudes to death, wrote to the senate, "It makes no difference how many of you died, for everyone deserved to suffer this."

Xiphil. 336.24–28 (III, p. 717) = Dio LXXVII.22.3 (III, p. 400.28–32): And in order that I may bypass the specific disasters which then had oppressed the wretched city, he slaughtered so many that he did not dare speak about the multitude, but he even wrote to the senate that it made no difference how many of them died or who they were, for they all deserved to suffer this.

Caracalla appears to have been in Alexandria from at least September 215 to March or April of 216. The unfortunate contractors of *ES* 149 evidently were locals who had agreed to provide some unspecified services to the emperor. See Herodian IV.8.6–9.10 with the notes in Wittaker's Loeb edition, Vol. I, pp. 419–28, for the most detailed account of Caracalla's stay in Alexandria, though with no mention of contractors.

F 163 (217 A.D.)

Cod. Vat. 1288 *f.* 5^{v} 1– 5^{v} 2 = Dio LXXVIII.20.1–4 (III, pp. 424.8–425.9): The populace,

Peter *ES* 150, p. 263.6–14: Under Macrinus the populace said to Zeus, "As a master you were angry, seeing that it would escape notice in the competition and being more emboldened by their number, shouted loudly in the hippodrome during the birthday celebrations of Diadumenianus, which were on the fourteenth day of September, both lamenting much else and saying that they themselves alone of all men were leaderless and rulerless. And they began to appeal to Zeus that only he alone should lead them, and in particular they made this very statement: "As a master you were angry, as a father take pity on us." Nor would they heed either equestrian or senator ... they kept praising the emperor and Caesar, with the result that ... they said in Greek: "Oh, what a fine day this day is! Oh, what fine sovereigns!" And wished them, too, to be of the same mind with them. But they began to stretch their hands toward heaven and shout: "This is the Romans' Augustus, having him, we have everything." So much, I suppose, is respect for the better and contempt for the worse naturally imbued in men, with the result that they considered both Macrinus and Diadumenianus no longer to exist at all, but, as if they were already dead, they trampled them underfoot.

as a father have mercy on us." And the senators, having arisen, with much pleasure, in truth, cried out, "Ah, what a fine day today is! Ah, what fine sovereigns!" wishing to attract the populace to themselves. And they did not pay any attention to the senate at all, but began to stretch their hands toward heaven <and to shout>, "This is the Romans' Augustus" (intimating God), "having him, we have everything." Thus are humans wont to choose the better and to condemn the worse.

After the death of Caracalla, Macrinus was acclaimed emperor on April 11, 217, and in the same month his son Diadumenianus (born September 14, 208) was named Caesar. In the winter of 217, both were in Antioch, where they remained until the summer of 218. At Rome, where the events described in F 163 occurred and where relief about Caracalla's death had contributed initially to a passive recognition of M. Opellius Macrinus (*PIR*^{2} O 108) and

M. Opellius Diadumenianus (*PIR*[2] O 107), there was increasing dissatisfaction with the new rulers. The parenthetical "intimating God" must be Peter's or the excerptor's addition.

F 164 (217 A.D.)

Cod. Vat. 1288 f. 6v 2 = Dio LXXVIII.24.1–2 (III, pp. 430.18–431.7): An thus did she, after she had been elevated from common stock to greatness and lived during her husband's reign in very extreme sorrow on account of Plautianus, and witnessed the younger of her sons slaughtered in her own bosom and felt malice toward the younger the whole time he was alive until the end and learned that he had been murdered thus, fell from power while living and killed herself besides, with the result that no one, having considered her, could actually regard as happy all those who have come into great power, unless there subsists for them some pleasure of life that is true and pure and good fortune unmixed and enduring. And thus were Julia's affairs, ...

Peter *ES* 151, p. 263.15–17: Julia, Severus' wife, after she had been lifted from the meanest to such a height and ended pitiably, showed the uncertainty of human life.

Julia Domna (*PIR*[2] I 663), wife of Septimius Severus and mother of Caracalla and Geta, died in April 217, either in consequence of choosing to starve herself to death or as a result of being unable to eat due to a progressive cancer (*Cod. Vat.* 1288 *f.* 6v 2 = Dio LXXVIII.23.5–6 [III, p. 430.11–17]). For Plautianus, see on F 144, above, and, with special emphasis on Plautianus' dealings with Julia, Xiphil. 313.11–21 (III, p. 700) = Dio LXXV.15.6–7 (III, pp. 354.21–355.11). Early in 212, Caracalla, in order to isolate Geta from protectors, had arranged to have Geta join him in a private meeting with Julia. Caracalla then had some of his centurions kill Geta, who had fled to Julia's arms (Xiphil. 327.9–328.2 [III, p. 710]) = Dio LXXVIII.2.1–6 [III, p. 374.6–31]). Though little is known of Julia's roots in Emesa, both Xiphilinus' "common stock" and Peter's "meanest" are inaccurate. On this point, see Birley, *Septimius Severus*, pp, 117–18, and 297–99. Her father was Julius Bassianus (*PIR*[2] I 202), named only at *Epit. de Caes.* 21.2 and 23.2.

F 165 (221 A.D.)

Cod. Vat. 1288 *f.* 11[r] 1 = Dio LXXIX.1.1 (III, p. 453.3–6): Now Avitus, then Pseudo-Antoninus, then, too, Assyrius or even Sardanapallus and Tiberinus (for, in fact, he received this title, too, when, after he had been slain, his body was thrown into the Tiber) ...

Xiphil. 347.10–12 (III, p. 724): And so then Avitus, then Pseudo-Antoninus, then, too, Assyrius or even Sardanapallus and Tiberinus (for, in fact, he received this title, too, when his body, after he had been slain, was thrown into the Tiber) ...

Peter *ES* 152, p. 263.18–22 = Dio LXXIX.17.1 (III, p. 470.16–19): Pseudo-Antoninus was despised and killed by the soldiers. For whenever certain men – and these having been armed – have become accustomed to despise those in power, they make no limit of the right about doing what they wish, but are armed, too, against the very one who has given this.

The beginning of Dio's formal treatment of Elagabalus' reign clearly opened with a review of his various names, the explanation of one of which – Tiberinus – necessitated an anticipation of the circumstances of his death, for which see Xiphil. 353.30–354.8 (III, 729) = Dio LXXIX.20.1–2 (III, pp. 472.23–473.4). Since the trite moralizing of *ES* 152 is extraneous to Dio's purpose, it may well be Peter's own contribution.

F 166 (218 A.D.)

Peter *ES* 153, p. 263.23–25 = Dio LXXIX.18.4 (III, p. 471.26–28): The same man once said this, "I want no titles from war and blood. For it is enough for me to be called Pious and Blessed by you."

Elagabalus' sentiment is unique to *ES* 153. The context is his communication with Rome from Antioch, which he had entered shortly after the defeat and execution of Macrinus around the middle of 218. Cf. *Codex Vaticanus Graecus* 1288 *ff.* 11[r], 1–3 = Dio LXXIX.1–2.2 (III, pp. 453.6–454.7).

F 167 (218–221? A.D.)

Peter *ES* 154, p. 263.26–28 = Dio LXXIX.18.5 (III, p. 471.29–31): Pseudo-Antoninus, being praised once by the senate, said, "On the one hand, you love me, and, by Zeus, the populace, too, and the armies abroad. But the guardsmen, to whom I give these things, I do not please."

It is impossible to establish the occasion of Elagabalus' alleged remark, for which *ES* 154 is the only evidence.

F 168 (221 A.D.)

Peter *ES* 155, p. 263.29–31 = Dio LXXIX.19.1[a] (III, p. 472.4–7): When some people were speaking with Pseudo-Antoninus and had said that he was fortunate to be a consul with his son, he said, "I shall be more fortunate during the coming year, as I am going to be consul with a legitimate son."

Around June 26, 221, Elagabalus had adopted the son of Gessius Marcianus (*PIR*[2] G 171) and Julia Avita (*PIR*[2] I 649). This youth – the future emperor Alexander Severus – , Elagabalus had, by July 221, made consul designate. About the same time, Elagabalus married Annia Aurelia Faustina (*PIR*[2] A 710). The anticipated product of this union must be the "legitimate son" to whom Elagabalus refers. Since Elagabalus dismissed Aurelia sometime near the end of 221, the unique exchange of *ES* 155 must have happened, if it happened at all, while the marriage was intact. In 222, both Elagabalus and Alexander were consuls.

F 169 (238 A.D.)

Herodian VII.7.1: For while it is a fact that all mobs are quick when it comes to radical changes, the populace of Rome, both through its immense mass and also through the variety of the flotsam of people, has a very easy inclination of disposition.	Peter *ES* 156, p. 264.1–4: For while every mob is quick when it comes to radical changes, the populace of Rome, both through its mass and the variety of the flotsam of people converging in it, is stirred up more easily than the rest and races with abandon toward disorder.

The context is the aftermath of the murder in Rome of Vitalianus (*PIR* V 492), a close friend of Maximinus, by soldiers dispatched for the task by Gordian. A portion of the city's population, acting on the assumption that Maximinus, too, was dead, began to run amok and to vent their hatred of Maximinus on his images. Zonaras' very brief treatment of the rioting in Rome (XII.16 [II, p. 577.12–15]) attributes it to a combination of public revulsion against

Maximinus and the overly slow voyage from Africa to Rome of envoys from Gordian. See further Banchich and Lane, *The* History *of Zonaras*, p. 8, notes 18 and 19. Plut. *Regnum et imperatorum apophthegmata* 201 F has P. Cornelius Scipio Aemilianus characterize the Roman populace in the same words – "flotsam of people" (συγκλύδων ἀνθρώπων) – as do Herodian and Peter.

F 170 (238/240 A.D.)

Peter *ELGR* 9, p. 392.3–31 = F 8 Müller *FHG* IV, pp. 186–87: The Carpi, the nation, envying the subsidies paid annually to the Goths, sent a delegation to Tullius Menophilus arrogantly demanding subsidies. This man was *dux* of Moesia and used to drill the army daily. And since he had learned of their arrogance beforehand, he did not receive them for many days, giving them permission to observe in safety the soldiers being drilled. And during the delay, in order to reduce their presumption, after he had taken a seat on a lofty tribunal and surrounded himself with the most imposing men of the camp, he received them, making no account at all of them, but in the middle of their speaking about the delegation he kept talking continuously about other things, just as if he had other more important business. Those who had been ignored said nothing else except, "Why do the Goths receive such payments from you and we do not receive any?" And he said, "The emperor is master of much wealth, and he shows favor to those who are in need of it." And they proposed, "Let him hold us, too, among those in need and give such things to us. For we are better than them." And Menophilus laughed and said, "I need to inform the emperor about these matters. After four months come here to this spot and discover and receive an answer." Then he departed and again began drilling the soldiers. And the Carpi came after four months, and, when he had made a similar show to them, he devised another delay of three months. And again, in another camp, he received them in the same way and gave them an answer, "So far as a compact goes, the sovereign gives to you absolutely nothing. But if it is a welding you require, after you have departed, throw yourselves face down and implore him and it is probable that you will be hammered." And with irritation they departed, and, with respect to the province of Menophilus, which he had obtained for three years, they kept quiet.

The embassy to the Carpi (Bursian, "Carpi," *BNP* 2 [2002], col. 1125) is otherwise unknown. The claim of the Carpi *vis-à-vis* the Goths and their treatment by Menophilus reflect a new hierarchy of power and reformations of "peoples" among Rome's neighbors along and beyond the Danube. The Goths were now preeminent and would remain so until the advent of the Huns. The prestige of the Carpi, in contrast, was on the wane and doubtless all the more so in consequence of their treatment by Menophilus.

Menophilus is Tullius Menophilus (*PIR*² T 387). Martolini, *L'*Anonymus post Dionem, *Pietro Patrizio e la* Leoquelle, p. 232, n. 360, suspects that the excerpt's δοὺξ is an anachronism with regard to the third century. Regardless of whether Zonaras' attribution (XII.31 [II, p. 613.16]) to Diocletian of the same office reflects what John found in his immediate source or is his own choice of words, it is certain that δοὺξ appears nowhere in what remains of Dexippus and that Peter *ELGR* 9, p. 392.6, is its sole appearance in the *EH*. Indeed, the detail about a tenure of three years suggests that Menophilus' official position was *legatus pro praetore*. Δοὺξ, then, may be Peter's or the excerptor's word. Scardigli, "Menofilo e i Carpi," pp. 173–78, thinks that the arrogance attributed to Menophilus in F 170 stems from a source which preserved a hostility to Menophilus linked to what may have been his *damnatio memoriae* at some later date. For the broader context, see Bichir, *The Archaeology and History of the Carpi*, Vol. I, pp. 167–69, and Wolfram, *History of the Goths*, pp. 43–5.

F 171 (*c.* 253 A.D.)

Peter *ES* 157, p. 264.5–9 = *Anon. Cont.* F 1 Müller *FHG* IV, p. 192: The sovereign of the Persians camped with Mariadnes about twenty stades from Antioch. While the prudent fled the city, the great multitude remained, being well disposed toward Mariadnes and also favoring changes, exactly as usually happens as a result of lack of understanding.

The ancient sources variously refer to the Mariadnes of *ES* 157 – probably a mistake of Peter, his source, or the Constantinian excerptor – as Mareades, Mariades, and Cyriades. For translations of the few literary sources which mention or allude to Mariadnes and for the date of the events described in F 171, see Dodgeon and Lieu, pp. 51–3 and pp. 363–64, n. 23, Banchich, "Mareades/Mariades/Mariadnes/Cyriades," and Martolini, *L'*Anonymus post Dionem, *Pietro Patrizio e la* Leoquelle, pp. 203 and 234–47. On the basis of *ES* 157's testimony about Mariadnes' alleged broad following, some – e.g., Ball, *Rome in the East*, pp. 152–53 – see him as the head of an Antiochene pro-Iranian or anti-Roman faction. Against this position, see Millar, *The Roman Near East*, p. 161.

F 172 (253 A.D.)

Peter *ES* 158, p. 264.10–12 = *Anon. Cont.* F 2 Müller *FHG* IV, p. 193: After he had been acclaimed sovereign, Aemilianus wrote to the senate: "I leave the realm to you, and I strive in every way as your general."

Zonar. XII.22 (II, p. 591.9–13): After he had thus been proclaimed emperor, Aemilianus wrote to the senate, promising that he would rid Thrace of barbarians, that he would campaign against Persia, and that, having turned the realm over to the senate, he would do everything and fight as their general.

On Aemilianus (*PIR*[2] A 330), see Banchich, "Marcus Aemilius Aemilianus." Baldini, *Storie Perdute*, pp. 111–14, thinks that *ES* 158 reflects the Constantinian excerptor's compression of his exemplar and warns against attributing to Peter or his source a view of Aemilianus distinct from that in Zonaras and so reflective of separate strands of source traditions. See further Martolini, *L'*Anonymus post Dionem, *Pietro Patrizio e la* Leoquelle, pp. 203 and 234–52.

F 173 (260 A.D.)

Peter *ELRG* 1, p. 3.4–10 = F 9 Müller *FHG* IV, p. 187: Valerian, circumspect about the Persians' offensive – for his army was suffering from plague, and especially the Moors – , having collected an untold amount of gold, sent envoys to Sapor, wishing to end the war through immense gifts. And he, when he had learned about the plague and become more elated by the request of Valerian, after he had put off the envoys, having dismissed them having accomplished nothing, immediately began to follow close behind.

Zos. 1.36.1–2 (Paschoud I, p. 34.13–22): When plague had struck his bases and had destroyed the greater portion of them, Sapor, attacking the east, began to turn everything upside down. And when Valerian, through both the softness and submissiveness of his manner of life, on the one hand, had abandoned hope of rescuing the matters which had come to an extreme and was wishing to end the war by a gift of money, Sapor, on the one hand, dismissed the ambassadors who had been sent about this, having accomplished nothing, and was demanding that the sovereign himself come to him for discussions about what he considered urgent matters.

The events described in F 173, attested elsewhere by Zosimus alone, should probably be set at or near Edessa. Müller (*FHG* IV, p. 187) emended the transmitted ἐλίμωξε ("was suffering from famine") to ἐλοίμωξε ("was suffering from plague"). Since all extant manuscripts of the *ELRG* read ἐλίμωξε, the error almost certainly originated with the copyist of their lost archetype. For these manuscripts, see Németh, *Imperial Systematization of the Past*, pp. 135–41. The trilingual *Res Gestae* of Sapor (Greek, lines 21 and 23 = Dodgeon and Lieu, p. 57) twice mentions Mauretanians among Valerian's army. Dodgeon and Lieu, pp. 58–67, translate most of the sources for Sapor's campaign of 260. See, too, Dignas and Winter, *Rome and Persia in Late Antiquity*, pp. 80–2, and, above all, Potter, *Prophecy and History*, pp. 313–14 and 331–41, and Martolini, *L'*Anonymus post Dionem, *Pietro Patrizio e la* Leoquelle, pp. 85–110, especially pp. 93–100.

F 174 (260 A.D.)

Peter *ES* 159, p. 264.13–25 = *Anon. Cont.* F 3 Müller *FHG* IV, p. 193: Macrinus, Count of the Treasuries and Supervisor of the Stock of Rations, because he had been crippled in one foot, was not to be found in the battle, but in Samosata he received and revived the troops. Sapor sent Cledonius, a man who ushered litigants before the sovereign. He encouraged Macrinus to come to Valerian. He would not consent to depart, saying, "Who is so mad willingly to become a slave and captive in place of a free man? Moreover, those who command me to depart are not my lords. For one is an enemy, the other neither his own master nor ours." And he advised Cledonius to stay and not to return to Valerian. But the latter said that he would not betray the trust of the man who had been his master. And after he had returned, he was held with the captives.

On Macrinus (= Fulvius Macrianus *PIR*^{2} F 549 and Fulvius Macrianus 2, *PLRE* I, p. 528), see Banchich and Lane, *The* History *of Zonaras*, pp. 112–13, n. 76, and Körner, "Usurpers under Gallienus." Cledonius was either *ab admissionibus* (1, *PLRE* I, p. 258) or *a cognitionibus Augusti* (*PIR*^{2} C 1133). *ES* 159's "Supervisor of the Stock of Rations" (ἐφεστὼς τῇ ἀγορᾷ τοῦ σίτου) is the Greek translation of *praepositus annonae*. "Count of the Treasuries" (κόμης τῶν θησαυρῶν) is a translation of *comes largitionum*, though here with a narrow application to the official in charge of the funds Gallienus had with him on this specific campaign. See further Bleckmann, *Reichskrise*, p. 253, n. 122, and Martolini, *L'*Anonymus post Dionem, *Pietro Patrizio e la* Leoquelle, pp. 255–58. The translations are not necessarily Peter's from an immediate Latin source, though on the basis of this fragment alone the possibility cannot be ruled out.

F 175 (*c.* 260–261 A.D.)

Peter *ELRG* 2, p. 3.11–21 = F 10 Müller *FHG* IV, p. 187: Odenathus gave Sapor much attention, viewing him as having for the most part surpassed the Romans. And, wishing to gain influence with him, he sends magnificent gifts and other wares, having loaded them on camels. And he sends letters that had the force of an entreaty and [stated] that he himself did nothing in opposition to Persians. And after he [Sapor] had received the gifts, he ordered his servants to throw them in the river, and, when he had torn up the letters, he crushed them and declared, "Who is he and on what basis does he dare write his own master? Now if he wishes to gain lighter punishment, after he has bound his hands behind him, let him prostrate himself. And if not, let him know that I shall destroy him, his race, and his fatherland."

Sapor's purported response is yet another example of the theme of barbarian haughtiness in general and of Sapor's haughtiness in particular. Though the position of the excerpt suggests a date shortly after the defeat of Valerian for Odenathus' attempt to court Sapor's favor, the content of F 175, whether historical reality or *post factum* invention, may be the beginning of an elucidation of a sequence of events which resulted in Odenathus' offensive against the Persians in the aftermath of the collapse of Roman power *c.* 260. Indeed, as Dodgeon and Lieu observe (p. 369, n. 3), Odenathus "could have come to realize the precarious position of Rome after the fall of Ana in 253 and of Dura in 256" and then attempted to cultivate ties between Palmyra and Persia in order to protect Palmyra's trade routes.

On the other hand, to set Odenathus' overture after 260 creates a series of complex problems, none of which is close to soluble without a mix-and-match selection of details from testimonies otherwise mutually irreconcilable and often, when approached individually, replete with patently absurd specifics. For example, John Malalas (*Chronographia* XII, pp. 296.4–297.18 Dindorf = XII.26, pp. 228–29 Thurn) says that a Domninus (Janiszewski, *The Missing Link*, pp. 282–91) and a Philostratus (*PLRE* I, p. 698; Jacoby *FgrH* 99 F 2) gave discrepant accounts of the campaign of Sapor during which Antioch was sacked. Each sets Sapor's field of operations in different areas, thereby confronting modern scholars with alternative or complementary possibilities, but possibilities nonetheless. Each, too, describes in detail mutually irreconcilable versions of Sapor's death, both baseless, for Sapor died over a decade later and certainly not under circumstances remotely like either of the scenarios attributed by Malalas to Domninus and Philostratus. Yet, because Philostratus names some of the locations also noted in Sapor's *Res Gestae* and because John Zonaras explicitly notes two versions of Valerian's fate, Philostratus has been championed as Zonaras' indirect source via Peter, and F 175, when compared with Philostratus F 1, offered as evidence of

Peter's dependence. Cf., for example, Potter, *Prophecy and History*, pp. 92–4, on Philostratus as a source of Peter and Peter as a source for Zonaras, and Janiszewski, *The Missing Link*, pp. 97–109. But all this becomes an issue with respect to F 175 only if the actions of Odenathus and Sapor described therein are set in or shortly after 260, and this there is no compelling reason to do. See further Kettenhofen, *Die römisch-persischen Kriege*, pp. 72–3 together with his accompanying maps.

F 176 (261 A.D.)

Peter *ELGR* 10, pp. 392.32–393.6 = F 11 Müller *FHG* IV, pp. 187–88: And when Sapor, the Persians' sovereign, had crossed the Euphrates with his personal army, they began to rejoice together and to celebrate, reckoning that they had escaped from great danger. And he sends word to the soldiers in Edessa, having promised to give them all the Syrian money that he has with him, in order that they allow him to pass through undisturbed and not choose an action which would lead to an attack on two fronts and procure for him trouble and a slow-down. For, he said, he did not offer them these things because he feared them, but because he was eager to hold the festival in his own parts and did not wish the delay and postponement for his journey. And the soldiers chose to receive the money without risk and to permit them to pass through.

The alleged attempt to bribe the garrison of Edessa is otherwise unrecorded. Though Sapor had crossed the Euphrates, he remained in Roman territory and, if he moved along the road from Edessa toward Nisibis, it would probably be at least a week before he would be in his own realm. The "two fronts" must refer both to Sapor's own contingent and to other Persian forces beyond Edessa, perhaps waiting to rendezvous with their king. The festival which so concerned Sapor may have been Nô Rôz, the Zoroastrian New Year celebration, which in 261 would have fallen around or just after the middle of September (Bickerman, "Time-Reckoning," *CHI* III.2, p. 791, and Boyce, "Iranian Festivals," *CHI* III.2, pp. 794–800), or Frawardigan, the annual run-up to Nô Rôz. Whether or not this factor stood in Peter's source, festivals and celebrations were an element of international diplomacy of which he was well aware. *De Cerimoniis* I.90 (Reiske, pp. 409.15–410.3), drawn from Peter, advises with regard to the treatment of ambassadors: "If there should be perfect friendship between the states, it is necessary for the sovereign to send inquiries and constantly to consider him [the ambassador in question] and to learn how he fared and to send portions to him and provisions both on our festival days and his days which are significant and to tend to him in diverse ways." Men. *ELRG* 5, p. 189.3–15 = F 15 Müller *FHG* 4, p. 220 = F 9.1.16–29 Blockley, *Men.*, pp. 96–9, with Blockley's note 102, pp.

261–62, relates how, in 567, John (Ioannes 81, *PLRE* III A, pp. 672–74), an ambassador of Justinian, had to wait ten days at Dara before being received at Nisibis because of Frawardigan. See further Kettenhofen, *Die römisch-persischen Kriege*, pp. 122–26.

F 177 (*c.* 262 A.D.)

Peter *ES* 160, p. 264.26–34 = *Anon. Cont.* F 4 Müller *FHG* IV, pp. 193–94: After he had been dispatched to collect supplies, Memor, a Moor, became desirous of a new state of affairs and was immediately killed by the soldiers. The commanders began to complain that he had been unjustly slain. Theodotus, when he had been called upon to give an explanation, said, "Memor was not worthy of much contempt because, possessing the compass and power of such commanders, he undertook the impossible, but because he and those with him failed to achieve their aim through my zeal and through sovereign providence." And the sovereign was pleased with the defense and decreed that no one be prosecuted on Memor's account.

Zos. I.38.1 also mentions Memor's (*PIR*² M 490) rebellion against Gallienus and names an Auriolus (= Aureolus, *PIR*² A 1672 and *PLRE* I, p. 138) and an Antoninus (*PIR*² A 790 = Antoninus 1, *PLRE* I, p. 74) among many others who revolted. Peter's Theodotus (*PIR* T 120) may be Aurelius Theodotus (*PIR*² A 1617 = Theodotus 4, *PLRE* I, p. 906). The relative position of the excerpt suggests that Peter dealt with Memor in connection with events we would place in 260, and this may be correct. However, modern scholars have argued for *c.* 262 or 268 as the actual date of Memor's uprising and death. Cf. Martolini, *L'*Anonymus post Dionem, *Pietro Patrizio e la* Leoquelle, pp. 204–5 and 258–59.

F 178 (*c.* 262 A.D.)

Peter *ES* 161, p. 265.1–3 = *Anon. Cont.* F 4 Müller *FHG* IV, p. 194: Men who have been thoughtlessly promoted are not accustomed to guard friendships carefully, but they change them for minor reasons.

Unless *ES* 161 comes from a speech, it is probably Peter's moralizing comment on the events he has just treated, i.e., the quashing of Memor's rebellion, though, perhaps, with a broader application. Cf. Bleckmann, *Reichskrise*, pp. 261–63.

F 179 (*c.* 259 A.D.)

Peter *ES* 162, p. 265.4–12 = *Anon. Cont.* F 5.1, Müller *FHG* IV, p. 194: The wife of the sovereign Gallienus was offended by the demeanor of Ingenuus, and, when she had summoned Valentinus, said to him, "I know your reputation, and, while I praise the sovereign with respect to your selection, I do not praise him with respect to that of Ingenuus, for I am very suspicious of him. But I am unable to act in opposition to the sovereign. But you keep an eye on the man." Valentinus answered, "Would that Ingenuus be viewed sincere with respect to your service, since, as much as is in me, I could not be at all neglectful of those who see to the favor of your house."

Cornelia Salonina Chrysogene (*PLRE* I, p. 799) was the wife of Gallienus, son of the ill-fated emperor Valerian. Since 253, both father and son had held the title Augustus. Valentinus (*PIR* V 10; 1, *PLRE* I, p. 935), though obviously an appointee of Gallienus and a man trusted by Cornelia, is otherwise unknown. While Gallienus was in Gaul to counter threats from across the Rhine, either barbarian activity along the Danube in 259 or Sapor's capture of Valerian in 260 prompted Roman soldiery in Moesia to acclaim Ingenuus (*PIR*[2] I 23; 1, *PLRE* I, p. 457), governor of Pannonia, Augustus. By the summer of 260, Gallienus had eliminated Ingenuus and established himself in Milan. For context and narrative, see John Drinkwater, "Maximinus to Diocletian and the 'Crisis,'" *CAH*[2] XII, pp. 42–4. Martolini, *L'*Anonymus post Dionem, *Pietro Patrizio e la* Leoquelle, p. 261, distinguishes from a more positive tradition reflected in Zonaras the tendency of Latin sources to denigrate Gallienus' character partly by contrasting him to strong women. For the hostile tradition, see Aurelius Victor *De Caes.* 33, for the positive, Zonar. XII.24–25 (II, pp. 596.15–602.18).

F 180 (260 A.D.)

Peter *ES* 163, p. 265.13–21 = *Anon. Cont.* F 5.2 Müller *FHG* IV, p. 194: In the war against Ingenuus, many children, parents, and siblings perished, to such a degree that a certain fellow brought his own brother before Gallienus as a captive and said, "Sovereign, this is my own brother, and I captured him in the war". He considered the matter, resolved that he be pardoned, dismissed and commended him, and undertook to give him many rewards and to absolve the sin of the usurpation. And he said, "It is not proper that a man live who once took up arms against a sovereign!" And he killed him with his sword. Gallienus was displeased, but he acquiesced in light of the unexpectedness of the events.

The incident is otherwise unrecorded. It may be that the alleged episode is supposed to reflect a broader view of Gallienus as an ineffectual ruler, helpless in the face of events. Cf. on F 179, above, and Martolini, *L'*Anonymus post Dionem, *Pietro Patrizio e la* Leoquelle, pp. 262–65.

F 181 (reign of Gallienus)

Peter *ES* 164, p. 265.22–31 = *Anon. Cont.* F 5.3 Müller *FHG* IV, p. 194: Claudius happened to have been wounded in the ankle, and the sovereign was inquiring about him with great concern. Then one of the soldiers said that, like Achilles, he had been wounded while fighting nobly and that he was being cared for in his tent. As a result, the sovereign said, "Fittingly, he, too, was wounded in the ankle."

The alleged incident is otherwise unknown. Aurelius Victor *De Caes.* 33.28 says that at the time of Gallienus' death (*c.* September 268) Claudius held the rank of *tribunus* at Ticinum. Zonar. XII.26 (II, p. 604.8) says that he had been a cavalry commander (ἵππαρχος) before becoming emperor. Some sources implicate Claudius in Gallienus' death. If Peter depended on that tradition – and certainty here is impossible – , then F 181 might reflect negatively on Gallienus. On Claudius' alleged classical allusion, see Martolini, *L'*Anonymus post Dionem, *Pietro Patrizio e la* Leoquelle, pp. 265–67.

F 182 (260 A.D.)

Peter *ES* 165, pp. 265.32–266.9 = *Anon. Cont.* F 6 Müller *FHG* IV, pp. 194–95: Gallienus the sovereign sent ambassadors to Postumus, who had been acclaimed emperor, to learn what he had done and to tell him that those who had seized the strongpoints ought to maintain peace, saying to him, "Allow them to come to me in order that we contend in war. And let the stronger be sovereign." He, in turn, replied, "I neither allow you ever, of your own volition, to cross the Alps, nor do I pray that I come to such an impasse to make war on Romans." Gallienus responded, "Then let us both fight one-on-one in order that Romans not perish." He, in turn, responded, "I am not a one-on-one fighter, nor have I ever been. But when those provinces you assigned to me were being ruined, I saved them. I have been acclaimed sovereign by the Gauls, and I am content to rule those who have willingly chosen me. If there is anything I can accomplish, through my counsel and power I shall assist them."

The purported exchange is without parallel. Postumus (*PIR*[2] C 466) had been acclaimed emperor in Gaul in *c.* May or July of 260 and would rule the so-called *Imperium Galliarum* until murdered in Mainz by his own troops in May or June of 269. The content of F 182 appears to be an exchange with Gallienus (*PIR*[2] L 197, emperor September/October 253–*c.* September 268) shortly after Postumus' acclamation. It is impossible to tell how close Peter's version of hostilities between Postumus and Gallienus was to that of Zonaras, who writes of almost immediate clashes between the two (Zonar. XII.24 [pp. 597.14–598.18]), though some scholars maintain that Gallienus did not actively campaign against Postumus in Gaul until 265. Cf. Christol, *L'Empire Romain du III*[e] *Siècle*, pp. 139–47, who favors clashes between the rivals as early as 261, and Potter, *The Roman Empire at Bay*[2], pp. 256–57 and 259–62.

F 183 (*c.* 266/267 A.D.)

Peter *ES* 166, p. 266.10–24 = *Anon. Cont.* F 7 Müller *FHG* IV, p. 194: Rufinus executed the old Odenathus on the grounds that he was engaged in revolutionary activities. And the younger Odenathus was accusing Rufinus on the grounds that he had murdered his father. The sovereign asked Rufinus why he had done these things. And he said he had done this with justice. "For he was engaged in novel activities. And would that you now were commanding me to kill this Odenathus, his son, too, and that I did this forthwith." Rufinus was suffering from gout in his feet and hands, being totally unable to move. And the sovereign kept saying to him, "Relying on what sort of power and what sort of body do you say these things." And he kept saying, "Not even if I happened to be healthy, more so than in my youth, would I, through my body, ever be capable of doing anything to him. But, giving commands and making dispositions with your assurance, I would set all in order. For even you yourself, o sovereign, being strong in your body, do not do the things which you do, but you do them by giving commands to your soldiers." And Gallienus praised his words.

The position of *ES* 166 between excerpts whose setting is 260–261 A.D. seems to confirm that the action it describes is set in Gallienus' reign and shortly after Valerian's capture. However, this is impossible if Rufinus' victim was the Odenathus who attacked the victorious Persians as they headed east, for which see on F 175, above. That Odenathus (*PIR* S 339 and *PLRE* I, pp. 638–39) almost certainly died in 266/267 at the hands of one or more of his relatives. Control of Palmyra then passed to his wife, Zenobia, and their son, Vaballathus (*PIR* S 347 and *PLRE* I, p. 122, *s.v.* L. Iulius Aurelius Septimius Vaballathus Athenodorus 2; cf. Gawlikowski, "Les princes de Palmyre," pp. 251–61). Consequently, Mommsen, *The Provinces of the Roman Empire from Caesar to Diocletian*, Vol. II, p. 115, n. 2, set the dramatic date of *ES* 166 in Gallienus' reign, the end of which (*c.* September 268) would then provide a *terminus ante quem* for what *ES* 166 describes. The "old Odendathus" he took to be Zenobia's husband and the "young Odenathus" to be their son Vaballathus, whom the excerptor had mistakenly called Odenathus.

But to accept this view seems to require an admission that *ES* 166's presentation of Odenathus' death was very different from the scenario described by Zonar. XII.24 (II, p. 600.10–23), whose *Epitome of Histories* often corresponds closely to Peter's fragments. For some scholars, this is a compelling reason to distinguish the fragments of the so-called Anonymous Continuer, of which *ES* 166 is one, from the from those of Peter. The story of Rufinus and Odenathus is not in Zonaras because Zonaras used Peter, and the Anonymous and Peter were not one-and-the-same. Of course, this perceived problem and its solution derive from the hypothesis of Zonaras' close dependence on Peter. Furthermore, they require an explanation of why an excerpt which describes events of 266/267 is bordered by excerpts devoted to events of 260 and 261 and of how Vaballathus (b. *c.* 260 and therefore seven years old at the most) would have been in a position to bring murder charges against Rufinus even in the unlikely event that it took seven years to do so?

To maintain the chronological order of material in the *EH* – an order which reflects what the excerptors found in the works from which they drew rather than any organizational principle of their own which they imposed on those works – , it would be necessary to take "the young Odenathus" to be Odenathus, the husband of Zenobia, and his father to have been "the old Odenathus." This would allow the content of the fragment to fall in 260 or 261. At the same time, it would permit the identification of Peter with the Anonymous through the removal of the need to explain why Zonaras' account of the death of Odenathus, the husband of Zenobia, contradicts the account of the death of "the old Odenathus" in *ES* 166 – a neat and simple solution except that the father of Odenathus and the husband of Zenobia is probably to be identified with Septimius Haeranes (*PIR* S 329), not with an Odenathus.

Since Gallienus was never in the East during his reign, any charge against Rufinus brought by "the young Odenathus," whether Zenobia's husband or the son of "the old Odenathus" and Zenobia, would have to have been levelled through correspondence or some intermediary. The identity of Aradius Rufinus may provide a clue. If, prior to 266/267, he was in a position in the East to have executed "the old Odenathus," an argument could be made that "the old Odenathus," who is unambiguously called the father of "the young Odenathus," is either a mistake for Haeranes made by someone who did not know the true name of the father of Odenathus, the husband of Zenobia, or reflects a figurative use of the name "Odenathus" employed in an effort to equate the two Odenathi of *ES* 166. After all, Rufinus maintained the pair merited the same punishment. In addition, ὁ παλαιός/"the old" and ὁ νέος/"the young" do not normally distinguish a father and son of the same name in the way ὁ πρεσβύτερος/"the elder" and ὁ νεώτερος/"the younger" do.

Aradius Rufinus almost certainly is Q. Aradius Rufinus Optatus Aelianus (*PIR*[2] A 1013 and 1016, with Rémy, "La carrière de Q. Aradius Rufinus Optatus Aelianus," pp. 458–77, Christol, "À propos des Aradii: Le stemma d'une famille sénatoriale au iiie siècle après J.-C.," pp. 145–50, and Bleckmann, "Zu den Quellen der Vita Gallieni duo," pp. 91–2). In 228–230 this Rufinus had been governor of Syria (*legatus Augusti pro praetore*), which meant that Palmyra was within his purview. We do not know when Haeranes' reign in Palmyra ended or when the reign of Odenathus, husband of Zenobia, began. The year of Odenathus' birth, too, is unknown, though, to reckon back from the earliest date we can associate with him (252, at which time he held the title *exarchos*), it probably was around 220. If Rufinus' execution of "the old Odenathus" occurred during the former's governorship of Syria, Odenathus would have assumed control of Palmyra at the age of between eight and ten, about thirty years before the first extant reference to him as ruler of Palmyra. The synchronism of Rufinus' governorship and the death of "the old Odenathus" would also explain why Gallienus (born *c.* 213, Augustus from September/October 253–*c.* September 268) would have been ignorant of the circumstances surrounding Rufinus' actions.

If *ES* 166 accurately represents Rufinus' motive for executing "the old Odenathus," the years of Rufinus' tenure as legate would provide the perfect context for "revolutionary activities." These were the very years of the first Sasanian incursions into Roman territory and of the coincident appearance of several usurpers who sought to define their positons within a Roman context and of local magnates who saw an opportunity to enhance their power and prestige, not to mention to protect their local interests, through an alignment with and the backing of Persia. Likewise, a date between late-260–261 fits the situation described in *ES* 166. After several successes against the Persians, Odenathus was powerful, confident, and the recipient of several impressive honorific titles, some perhaps bestowed on him by Gallienus, others – "King of Kings," for instance – deriving from Odenathus' own initiative. By the time Gallienus had returned victorious from his campaigns against the Alamanni to Rome itself, where an encounter with the aged Rufinus would most likely have occurred, he would have only begun to assess how best to balance Odenathus' important contribution to the defense of the East against the Palmyrene ruler's ambition and his potential to become an independent agent who would accept from Rome a formal recognition of that status (cf. Southern, *The Roman Empire from Severus to Constantine*, p. 101). The moment was right for "the new Odenathus" to think he could elicit from Gallienus punishment of Rufinus for the killing of "the old Odenathus," i.e., Haerenus, for Rufinus to work himself into a state of high dudgeon when questioned about his actions, for Gallienus to broach the matter with Rufinus, and, in the process, for someone – whether Rufinus, the author of *ES* 166, or his source – to make a point which, *c.* 261, would not have been lost on Gallienus through the rhetorical equation of Haerenus as "the old Odenathus" and the increasingly problematic Septimius Odenathus, "the new Odenathus."

This interpretation of *ES* 166 explains its position within the chronologically arranged excerpts of the *ES*, admits the "the old Odenathus" to have been the father of "the new Odenathus," takes note of the odd ὁ παλαιός and ὁ νέος, and fits what we know of the whereabouts and circumstances of Septimius Odenathus and Gallienus. If accepted, it would place the death of Haeranes and the beginning of Odenathus' reign between 228–230, add valuable information to what little we know of Roman and Palmyrene reactions to early Sasanian forays westward, and offer a motive in addition to Persian success for the overture of Odenathus described in F 175. It is important, too, for historiographical matters in its reflection of a rich source tradition about Palmyra somehow available to Peter and perhaps extending through an intermediate source or intermediate sources back to lost portions of Dio (cf. Bleckmann, "Zu den Quellen der Vita Gallieni duo," pp. 98–100). Finally, it means that *ES* 166 does not preclude the identification of the Anonymous with Peter. Indeed, it actually meshes well with what Peter and Zonaras maintain transpired with respect to Roman, Persian, and Palmyrene affairs between 230–267, for which see Dodgeon and Lieu, pp. 10–23, along with Frye, "The Sassanians," *CAH*² XII, pp. 464–68, and Sartre, "The Arabs and the Desert Peoples," *CAH*² XII, pp. 512–15.

F 184 (261 A.D.)

Peter *ES* 167, p. 266.25–29 = *Anon. Cont.* F 8.1 Müller *FHG* IV, p. 195: Cyntus, the son of Macrianus, began immediately situating the palace, too, in Emise. And Odenathus arrived with a multitude of barbarians and made it clear to them: "Surrender yourselves or fight." And they were saying that they were content to endure anything whatsoever than to surrender themselves to a barbarian."

Zonar. XII.24 (II, pp. 599.23–600.9): To be sure, Quintus, the younger son of Macrinus, was in the east with Ballista, and had made almost all of it subject to himself. Against them Gallienus sent Odenathus, who was in command of the Palmyrenes. When the defeat of the Macrini that had occurred in Pannonia was announced to Quintus and Ballista, many of the cities under them rebelled. They were quartered in Emesa. When he arrived there, Odenathus attacked them, was victorious, and himself executed Ballista. But the people of the city executed Quintus. The sovereign, repaying Odenathus for his courage, appointed him general of the entire east.

Peter and Zonaras alone recount Quietus' death. Macrianus – Zonaras' Macrinus – , for whom see F 174, and his son of the same name had been murdered by their troops in Pannonia after most of their army had surrendered to Aureolus, one of Gallienus' commanders (*PLRE* I, p. 138/*PIR*² A 1672). After Valerian's capture, some of his soldiers had recognized as emperor the younger Macrianus, whose usurpation Ballista (*PLRE* I, p. 146/*PIR*² B 41) had helped foment. Martolini, *L'*Anonymus post Dionem, *Pietro Patrizio e la* Leoquelle, p. 275, notes the emphasis Peter places on the barbarity of Odenathus. Boissevain (*ES*, p. 266, apparatus) suspected "began immediately situating the palace, too, in Emise" to be corrupt or defective. See Dodgeon and Lieu, pp. 74–7, for translations of additional sources.

F 185 (261 A.D.)

Peter *ES* 168, pp. 266.30–267.6 = *Anon. Cont.* F 8.2 Müller *FHG* IV, p. 195: Cyrinus was distressed when Odenathus appropriated the Romans' war. And when he had learned this, he [Odenathus] ordered him to be killed. Yet he lavished on his funeral many of his personal possessions, which he even showed him while he was still alive. And he [Cyrinus] laughed and said that the man was filled with much ignorance and stupidity – with ignorance, on the one hand, because we kill our enemies but favor our friends – and that he himself [Odenathus] did not know whether he should assign him to friends or to enemies – on the other hand, with stupidity, because he [Odenathus] wishes to pain him and murder him when he exists and is sensate but to honor him with gifts when he is dead and insensate. Yet such good fortune had a swift change.

This particular incident is otherwise unattested. Cyrinus may be Aurelius Quirinius (*PLRE* I, p. 760/*PIR*² A 1593), an official in Egypt under Valerian. Cf. Martolini, *L'*Anonymus post Dionem, *Pietro Patrizio e la* Leoquelle, p. 275. For Odenathus' position as *corrector totius orientis*, see Potter, *The Roman Empire at Bay*², pp. 255–56. For Peter's portrayal of Odenathus' character, see on F 184 and Martolini, *L'*Anonymus post Dionem, *Pietro Patrizio e la* Leoquelle, pp. 275–76.

F 186 (268/9 A.D.)

Peter *ES* 169, p. 267.1–13 = *Anon. Cont.* F 9.1 Müller *FHG* IV, p. 196: During Claudius' reign, when the Scythians had taken Athens and had collected all the books and decided to burn them, one among them considered to be intelligent stopped them, saying, "The Romans, devoting their leisure time to these, neglect war." But how ignorantly he spoke! For, if he had known the virtues of the Athenians and Romans, who were esteemed in words and in wars, he would not have said this.

Sym. *Chronicon* 81, p. 102 Wahlgren: Claudius reigned one year. He was the grandfather of the father of Constantine the Holy. Under him, the Scythians, who had broken through, who had gone off to Athens, took her, and, having gathered all the books, were planning to burn them. But one of them, since he was intelligent, hindered them, when he said, "The Romans, spending their leisure on these, are neglectful of wars."

Ced. I, p. 454.11–22: Claudius reigned two years. He was the grandfather of the father of Constantine the Holy and Great. Under him, the Scythians, when they had broken through and looted the cities and had also taken Athens, gathered all the books and were planning to burn them, except that one of them, more powerful by far in intelligence than the others, hindered them, saying, "The Romans, spending their leisure on these, are neglectful of wars."

Zonar. XII.26 (II, 604.20–605.6): The barbarians overran many areas, and, in fact, besieged Thessalonica, which in the old days is said to have been called Emathia but had its name changed to Thessalonica, from Thessalonica, the daughter of Philip and wife of Cassander. But they were repulsed from that city and, having attacked Athens, captured her. When they had collected all the books in the city, they were planning to burn them. But one of those who among them seemed to be wise dissuaded his tribesmen from their undertaking, saying, "Since they devote their leisure to these, the Greeks are unconcerned with military matters and, thus, become very easily controllable."

The Goths probably occupied Athens in 268. The parallels in Symeon, Cedrenus, and Zonaras suggest that the indignant conclusion of *ES* 169 is Peter's sentiment, though perhaps prompted by something in Dexippus, who was probably the ultimate source about the supposed incident. See, too, Martolini, *L'*Anonymus post Dionem, *Pietro Patrizio e la* Leoquelle, pp. 276–78.

F 187 (268/9 A.D.)

Peter *ES* 170, p. 267.14–18 = *Anon. Cont.* F 9.2 Müller *FHG* IV, p. 196: The Scythians were shouting in derision to those who had shut themselves in the cities, "These men do not live a human life but a life of birds who have perched on high in barns," and "Having abandoned the nurturing earth, they choose these barren cities," and, "They had more confidence in inanimate objects than in themselves."

The context must be the Gothic incursion of 268. No other source records the alleged taunts. Martolini, *L'*Anonymus post Dionem, *Pietro Patrizio e la* Leoquelle, pp. 278–79, notes Tac. *Germ.* 16 and *Hist.* IV.64, along with Amm. Marc. XVI.2.12, as examples of the topos of barbarian disdain for cities.

F 188 (269 A.D.)

Peter *ES* 171, p. 267.19–26 = *Anon. Cont.* F 9.3 Müller *FHG* IV, p. 196: There was a certain Andonnoballus, who fled from the Heruli to the Romans. And he had words with *Bibulus the sovereign* of the Romans, for he [Bibulus] was exhorting him to give himself to the Emperor. And he [Andonnoballus] was calling him a despot-loving slave and less than a belly and saying that he traded freedom for food and dress. And he responded to him, "I am a free man. For I am indeed friend of so great a sovereign and no good thing does he deny to me. But you are well off neither in dress nor food."

The alleged exchange recalls that attributed at Tacitus *Ann.* II.9 to Arminius (*PIR*^{2} A 1063) and Flavus (*PIR*^{2} F 450). The name "Bibulus" is suspect and, if it is the corruption of a proper name, some qualifier appears to be missing before "to the sovereign of the Romans," i.e., to Claudius. Müller (*FHG* IV, p. 196), suggested "eunuch," "slave," or "tribune." Boissevain (Vol. III, p. 745, apparatus) thought "Bibulus" must refer to some German. In any case, the particulars of the exchange described in *ES* 171 do not support *PLRE* I's suggested identification of Andonnoballus (*PIR*^{2} A 581, *PLRE* I, p. 62) with Naulobatus (*PLRE* I, p. 618). Given so much uncertainty, F 188 does not lend much support to Bleckmann's view (*Reichskrise*, p. 212) of Andonnoballus (*PIR*^{2} A 581; *PLRE* I, p. 62), Bibulus, and Naulobatus (*PLRE* I, p. 618) as precursors of later barbarian *magistri militum*. Cf. Martolini, *L'*Anonymus post Dionem, *Pietro Patrizio e la* Leoquelle, pp. 279–80.

F 189 (269 A.D.)

Peter *ES* 172, pp. 267.27–268.4 = *Anon. Cont.* F 9.4 Müller *FHG* IV, p. 197: After the victory over the Scythians, while the sovereign was celebrating and feasting, Andonnoballus came before everyone and said, "I wish at some point to ask a favor of you." And since he thought that at some point he was going to request something great, he granted him a request. And Andonnoballus said, "Give me some fine wine, that I may summon all of my household and celebrate with them." And the sovereign laughed and commanded that wine be given him. And he gave to him many other gifts, too.

For the broader context of Claudius' victory at Naïssus in 269, see Drinkwater, "Maximinus to Diocletian," *CAH*² XII, pp. 48–9. The Andonnoballus of F 188 seems to see things quite differently from the Andonnoballus of F 189.

F 190 (271 A.D.)

Peter *ES* 173, p. 268.5–12 = *Anon. Cont.* F 10.1 Müller *FHG* IV, p. 197: After he had become sovereign and gathered all those in repute in Ravenna as a council, Aurelian was considering how he ought to rule them. For he was hoping from what he had accomplished after the death of Claudius to appear greater than him. And one from the assemblage said to him, "If you want to rule nobly, fortify yourself with gold and iron, the iron against those who discomfit you, the gold for those who do you service." And he who had recommended this base advice was the first banished.

Zonar. XII.27 (II, p. 606.7–13): Aurelian, after he had assumed the leadership of the Romans, asked those in office how he ought to rule. One of them said to him, "If you want to rule nobly, you must ring yourself with gold and iron, employing the iron against those who cause you discomfort, repaying with gold the very men who do you service." He first, so it is said, had the benefit of his own advice, since he felt the iron not soon thereafter.

Aurelian, formerly Claudius' cavalry commander, became emperor in September 270 after Claudius had succumbed to plague. Zonaras affords the sole parallel to Peter.

F 191 (271 A.D.)

Peter *ELGR* 11, p. 393.7–9 = F 12 Müller *FHG* IV, p. 188: The Vandals, when they had been defeated, sent a delegation to Aurelian, appealing for peace. And Aurelian happily received them.

Dexippus *ELGR* 2, p. 385.21–26 = F 24 Müller *FHG* III, p. 685 = Jacoby *FgrH* 100 F 7.1: Under Aurelian, the Vandals, when they had been bested by force by the Romans, sent an embassy to the

And having come to terms with them, he retired.

Romans about an end of war and a treaty. And when both parties, the sovereign and the barbarians, had said much between themselves, the parlay was dissolved and, in the aftermath, the main body of the Roman soldiers was again regrouped ...

Upon his elevation after the death of Claudius at Sirmium, Aurelian had moved from toward Aquilia to deal with Claudius' brother Quintillus, who either was killed by his own troops or committed suicide. The Vandals saw this as an opportune moment to cross the Danube. They quickly met defeat at Aurelian's hands. F 191 treats their subsequent effort to secure a peace. Aurelian granted them safe passage out of the empire in exchange for hostages, the supply of a contingent of cavalry to serve in the Roman army, and recognition of Roman supervision of restricted trade routes (Dexippus *ELGR* 2, pp. 385.26–386.17 = F 24 Müller *FHG* III, pp. 685–86 = Jacoby *FgrH* 100 F 7.2–3). Watson, *Aurelian and the Third Century*, pp. 48–50, provides the broader context. Niebuhr (p. 126.17 and apparatus) emended the transmitted "they retired" to "he retired."

F 192 (271 A.D.)

Peter *ES* 174, p. 268.13–17 = *Anon. Cont.* F 10.2 Müller *FHG* IV, p. 197: Albinus, being an old man, was critically ill. And someone came to him and asked how he was. And he said, "If the fatherland is safe, terrible, for undoubtedly I shall die. But if it is not safe, fine. For I sooner would die before learning of the destruction of the fatherland. And a greater good than this I do not seek."

The anecdote is unparalleled. Albinus may be Nummius Ceionius Albinus (9, *PLRE* I, p. 35), who had been both a consul and urban prefect of Rome in 263. For what he is worth, the author of *SHA Aurel.* 9.2 quotes from what he claims was a letter from the emperor Valerian to an urban prefect named Ceionius Albinus.

F 193 (271 A.D.)

Peter *ES* 175, p. 268.18–23 = *Anon. Cont.* F 10.3 Müller *FHG* IV, p. 197: Aurelian, when he had learned that a detachment of barbarians was in Placentia, declared to them, "If you wish to do battle, behold! I am ready. But if you reckon the better course to surrender yourselves, I receive you as your master." And they declared in turn, "We have no master. On the morrow, prepare yourself, and learn that you fight against free men."

The barbarians in question probably are Juthungi who had seized the opportunity presented them by Aurelian's campaigns in Pannonia to invade Italy. Despite the testimony of *Epit. de Caes.* 35.2 to the contrary, the engagement at Placentia appears to have been a defeat for Aurelian. See Saunders, "Aurelian's 'Two' Iuthungian Wars," pp. 311–27, especially pp. 323–24, on Placentia and, for the broader historical context, see Watson, *Aurelian and the Third Century*, pp. 48–52.

F 194 (272 A.D.)

Peter *ES* 176, pp. 268.24–269.5 = *Anon. Cont.* F 10.4 Müller *FHG* IV, p. 197: Aurelian, in the siege of Tyana, said to the troops, "If we get inside, do not spare a dog." But after the capture he ordered the troops neither to slaughter nor pillage. Then the troops, being angry, said to him, "Those things which you commanded, allow us to do." And he said to them, "It is true that I said, 'Depart, let not a dog be found in this city, but slaughter all.'" And he sent forth both the tribunes and the troops to slaughter all the dogs, in consequence of which the anger of the army was dispelled in laughter. And after this he assembled them and said, "We waged war to free these cities. If we pillage them, they will never trust us. But instead let us seek the spoil of the barbarians and spare these as our own."

SHA Aurel. 22.5–23.3: For when he had come to Tyana and found it sealed, it is said that he, having become angry, said, "I shall not leave a dog behind in this city." Then, when the soldiers pressed on more ardently in the hope of spoils and a certain Heraclammon, in fear lest he be killed along with the others, betrayed his hometown, the city was captured. But from the imperial intellect Aurelian at once displayed two examples of excellence, one that exhibited severity, the other leniency. For the wise victor killed Heraclammon, betrayer of his own hometown and, when the soldiers began demanding the destruction of the city in accordance with that statement in which he denied he would leave a dog in Tyana, he replied to them, "I did deny" he said, "that I would leave a dog behind in this city. Kill all the dogs!" Grand was the emperor's statement, by which plunder was being denied, grander the soldiers' action. For the whole army, just as if it had been enriched, accepted the *princeps'* jest, by which plunder was denied, the city preserved.

The aftermath of the death of Odenathus of Palmyra (*PIR* S 339/*PLRE* I, pp. 638–39, killed after August 29, 267, dead by the spring of 268) saw the rise in power of his widow Zenobia and the extension of Palmyrene influence throughout the Roman east. At the time, the focus of the emperor Claudius' concerns had been various western barbarians and Postumus, ruler of the so-called *Imperium Galliarum*. After Claudius' death (September 270), Quintillus, his brother, reigned briefly until his murder by his own troops or his suicide at the approach of Aurelian, whom elements of Claudius' armies had recognized as emperor. While Aurelian consolidated his hold on the throne and tended to the threat of various western barbarians, Zenobia's forces invaded Egypt. In 272, Aurelian moved against her. Zenobia seems to have countered with attempts to associate her son Vaballathus and herself with Aurelian as mutually recognized holders of legitimate power in the east. This did not deter Aurelian, who, in the course of his advance against her, invested Tyana and, after its capture or capitulation, spared the city from the depredations of his troops. Only *SHA Aurel.* names Heraclammon (*PIR*[2] H 85) as Tyana's betrayer. For a narrative context, see Potter, *The Roman Empire at Bay*[2], pp. 264–68. For ancient sources in translation, see Dodgeon and Lieu, pp. 68–110.

F 195 (272 A.D.)

Peter *ES* 177, p. 269.6–9 = *Anon. Cont.* F 10.5 Müller *FHG* IV, p. 197: Aurelian sent ambassadors to Zenobia, urging that she concede to pay tribute under him. And she declared in turn, "I was not greatly harmed. For those having fallen in the war are nearly all Romans."

Zenobia is evidently referring to the outcome of a major engagement fought near Emesa, which was, in fact a Roman victory, albeit a costly one. Zenobia had subsequently withdrawn to what she mistakenly judged to be the security of Palmyra. For these events, see Zos. I.52–54 and Watson, *Aurelian and the Third Century*, pp. 75–6. A purported exchange of letters between Aurelian and Zenobia quoted verbatim at *SHA Aurel.* 26.7–27.6, allegedly translated from her Syrian by a certain Nicomachus (cf. Peter *HRR* II, pp. 151–52 = Jacoby *FgrH* 215 F 1), bears a superficial similarity to *ES* 177. However, *ES* 177 makes Zenobia respond to ambassadors rather than address a letter to Aurelian. Furthermore, the words attributed to the Palmyrene queen in *ES* 177, while equaling the haughtiness of the "letter" in the *Historia Augusta*, have no parallel therein. Martolini, *L'*Anonymus post Dionem, *Pietro Patrizio e la* Leoquelle, pp. 286–88.

F 196 (?)

Peter *ES* 178, p. 269.10–16 = *Anon. Cont.* F 10.6 Müller *FHG* IV, p. 197: Aurelian once learned of a military mutiny and said that the troops were mistaken if they supposed that the fates of the emperors were in their hands. For he said that God had bestowed the purple (and this he displayed in his right hand) and had totally determined the duration of his reign. And he did not depart before he had punished about fifty instigators of the revolt.

It is impossible to pinpoint the occasion of the mutiny in question. Watson, *Aurelian and the Third Century*, pp. 186–87, links F 196 to the iconography of some of Aurelian's coinage in that Roman soldiers owed allegiance to Aurelian "precisely because he was god's chosen one on earth." Rostovtzeff, *Social and Economic History of the Roman Empire*[2], Vol. I, p. 461 and Vol. II, p. 737, n. 37, suggests on the basis of similar sentiments attributed to Marcus Aurelius by Dio/Ziphilinus (cf. Peter F 126, above) that Aurelian may have taken a cue from his predecessor or that, given the closeness of Aurelius to Aurelianus, Peter may have here confused the latter with the former.

F 197 (282 A.D.)

Peter *ES* 179, p. 269.17–22 = *Anon. Cont.* F 11 Müller *FHG* IV, p. 198: When Carus had moved toward insurrection, Probus was considering what needed to be done about him. When all were silent, a certain Martinianus, a corps commander, spoke very pointedly, enjoined him that matters were being ruined as a result of his hesitation, and encouraged him to act immediately, to declare war, and to oppose the tyrant.

Probus (*PIR*[2] A 1583) and his praetorian prefect Carus (*PIR*[2] A 1475) were both at Sirmium at the moment of the latter's coup (between August 29 and September 13, 282). Latinius Martinianus (*PIR*[2] L 124) is otherwise known only through a single inscription from modern Aime, France (*ILS* 605, Dessau, Vol. I, p. 138), which calls him a *vir egregius* and *procurator Augusti*. The "corps commander" of F 197 renders χιλίαρχος, which, while common in the *EH* – see, for example, the instances from John of Antioch listed by Roberto, *Ioannis Antiocheni Fragmenta ex Historia Chronica*, p. 616, glossing χιλίαρχος as *tribunus militaris* – appears only here in Peter. For various modern takes on Peter's portrayal of Martinianus, see Martolini, *L'*Anonymus post Dionem, *Pietro Patrizio e la* Leoquelle, p. 291. On Probus' reign (276–282), see Potter, *The Roman Empire at Bay*[2], pp. 271–76.

F 198 (282 A.D.)

Peter *ES* 180, p. 269.23–24 = *Anon. Cont.* F 12 Müller *FHG* IV, p. 198: On the occasion of his proclamation, they say that Carus declared that he had come to the throne for the ill of the Persians.

Zonar. XII.30 (II, pp. 610.20–611.1): When he had come into control of the realm, Carus crowned his own two sons, Carinus and Numerianus, with an imperial diadem. Together with one of the boys, Numerianus, he immediately marched against the Persians, and captured Ctesiphon and Seleucia.

The extant literary testimony about Carus is almost uniformly hostile. The *Historia Augusta*, however, is a notable exception in its praise of his character and emphasis on his commitment to victory over the Persians in a war initiated by Probus, his predecessor (*Carus, Carinus, and Numerian* 7–8). Indeed, Carus may have gained control of Ctesiphon. Cf. Dignas and Winter, *Rome and Persia in Late Antiquity*, pp. 25–6, Potter, *The Roman Empire at Bay*[2], p. 275, and, with translations of most of the ancient evidence, Dodgeon and Lieu, pp. 111–16.

F 199 (285 A.D.)

Peter *ES* 181, p. 269.25–27 = *Anon. Cont.* F 13.1 Müller *FHG* IV, p. 198: In his own proclamation itself, Diocletian, swearing to the deities then revered, said that he had killed Carinus not to gain the throne, but through pity for the state.

Zonar. XII.30 (II, 612.3–7): Carinus, of course, the other of Carus' sons, living in Rome, presented a threat to the Romans, since he had become brutal, cruel, and vindictive. He was killed by Diocletian, who had gone to Rome.

The opening of *ES* 181 seems to be the excerptor's notice, added to distinguish Diocletian's "proclamation" (ἀναγόρευσις) from the "proclamation" of Carus, the subject of *ES* 180. The excerptor, too, is more likely than Peter to be responsible for "swearing to the deities then revered." If so, the notice suggests that Peter's text had included some account of Diocletian's pledge to the old gods. Since Carinus (d. August or September, 285) was already dead, the sentiment of *ES* 181, if it actually reflects Diocletian's explanation, was most likely meant for public and senatorial consumption. The setting could be Nicomedia, the site of Diocletian's proclamation as Augustus (November 20, 284) or during the real or fictive visit to Rome (summer of 285?) uniquely ascribed to Diocletian by Zonaras.

F 200 (286/303/305 A.D.)

Peter *ES* 182, p. 269.28–29 = *Anon. Cont.* F 13.2 Müller *FHG* IV, p. 198: Excessive action is the cause of corresponding perils and of many risks.

Because *ES* 181 = F 199 unambiguously deals with Diocletian's accession, it is reasonable to assume that the setting of *ES* 182 likewise fell within Peter's treatment of that emperor's reign. On the basis of the similarity of *ES* 182's ἀντικλιματήρων – a *hapax legomenon* – , the κλιμακτήρων of Ced. I, p. 464.1–2, and the Bonn text of Leo Grammaticus *Chronographia*, p. 80.19–21, where Victorinus requests of Probus to be excused from any future positions of importance "for every office was full of risks and hazards" (κλιμακτήρων), Patzig, "Die römische Quellen des salmasischen Johannes Antiochenus," p. 17, argued that *ES* 181–183 "gave the impression of a collection of maxims which were dragged together from different places" and that *ES* 182's original context had been the exchange between Probus and Victorinus recounted by Leo. In contrast, Bleckmann, *Reichskrise*, p. 50, n. 210, thought that the *Anonymus post Dionem* adapted the aphorism, which he had found in the Probus portion of his sources – the so-called *Leoquelle* – for use in the description of Diocletian's selection of Maximian as a colleague, whether with the rank of Caesar (between the end of October and the beginning of December in 285) or as an Augustus (April 1, 286). Martolini, *L'*Anonymus post Dionem, *Pietro Patrizio e la* Leoquelle, p. 295, on the other hand, took F182, 183, and 184 together to refer either to the joint triumph of Diocletian and Maximian in 303 or to their resignation from their positions as Augusti in 305. Note that Wahlgren, in his edition of Symeon Magister (p. 103 on *Chronicon* 84.3) relegates the passage from Leo to the *apparatus criticus*. For translations of the passages in question, see Banchich and Lane, *The History of Zonaras*, pp. 128–29.

F 201 (298 A.D.)

Peter *ELGR* 12, pp. 393.10–394.17 = F 13 Müller *FHG* IV, pp. 188–89: Aphpharban, being dearest above all to Narseus, the sovereign of Persians, having been dispatched on an embassy, met Galerius with supplication. After he had received license to speak, he said, "It is obvious to the race of mankind that the Roman and the Persian realms are, as it were, two lamps. And it is right that, just as eyes, the one be adorned by the brightness of the other and they not ever, toward their own destruction, alternately exhibit anger. For this is not excellence, but rather is considered levity or softness. For, thinking that the later generations are not able to aid them, they are eager to destroy those who have arrayed themselves against them. Moreover, it is not right that Narseus be considered weaker than all the other sovereigns but that Galerius surpass the other sovereigns to such a degree that Narseus himself justly yields to him alone, and yet not having become inferior to the worthiness of his forebears. In addition to this, Aphpharban was saying that it had been commanded to him by Narseus, who was counting on them to be fair, to entrust the right of his own realm to the philanthropy of Romans. Accordingly, he was not conveying the oaths upon which it was proper that the peace come to pass but had entrusted the entirety to the judgment of the sovereign, except that he was appealing that his children alone and his wives be restored to him, saying that, through their restoration, he would be bound by good deeds rather than out-maneuvered by arms. And he was not able now to express adequately gratitude that, when they had come into captivity, they had not experienced outrage there, but had not been handled in such a way that they could not yet be restored to their own nobility. In this, he brought to mind the mutability of human affairs. And Galerius, after he had appeared angered at this, when he had contorted his body, replied, saying he did not reckon with favor that Persians remind others of the mutability of human affairs, when they themselves, having espied an opportunity, did not abstain from visiting misfortunes on mankind. "For you did not observe the measure of victory in the case of Valerian, you who, after you had tricked him with deceptions, held him to extreme old age and did not spare him a dishonorable end, then, after death, by some abominable art, having preserved his skin, perpetrated an immortal outrage on a mortal body." When he had gone over these matters, the sovereign, after he had said, too, that he himself had not been swayed by what the Persians spoke of via the embassy – that it was mandatory to keep human fortunes in view – , for, through this, it would have been right to be moved even more to anger, if one had been attentive to what the Persians had done, but that he followed the footsteps of his ancestors, for whom it was a habit, on the one hand, to show mercy to the vanquished, on the other hand, to pronounce sentence upon those who arrayed themselves in opposition, ordered the man who had been dispatched as an envoy to report to his own sovereign the goodness of the Romans whose virtue he made trial of and to be hopeful that not much later envoys would come to him, according to the inclination of the sovereign.

F 201 is the only account we have of the exchange between Galerius and Aphpharban, though F 202 also mentions the latter. The rich detail in those two fragments may reflect Peter's personal interest in such matters as a result of his participation in negotiations between Justinian and Chosroes (cf. above, T 8–10). If so, this suggests a *terminus post quem* of 561 for the composition of the *History*. Dignas and Winter, pp. 122–23, suggest that Peter drew from archival material and that Theophyact of Simocatta's wording at IV.11.1–2 must be based on Peter's. Whitby and Whitby, *The History of Theophyact of Simocatta*, p. 117, n. 40, are more cautious, noting the verbal similarity here between Theophylact and Peter but suggesting the possibility that Peter's wording is anachronistic rather than reflective of an official record. With this, cf. Canepa, *The Two Eyes of the Earth*, p. 122, who is noncommittal. Whatever the case, Aphpharban's alleged use of "sovereign" (βασιλεύς) to describe both Narses and Galerius – the latter then a Caesar – and either Peter's or the excerptor's use of the same word to designate Galerius – "the sovereign ... ordered the man" – would require explanation. Vergil *Aen.* VI.853 lies behind Galerius' "to show mercy to the vanquished." For Galerius' victory over Narses at Satala in Armenia, the prelude to the negotiations of 298, see Dignas and Winter, pp. 84–8. Dodgeon and Lieu, pp. 124–32, translate most of the sources for Roman clashes with Persia between 293–298. See too, Potter, *The Roman Empire at Bay*², pp. 286–90, and below, F 202.

F 202 (298 or 299 A.D.)

Peter *ELRG* 3, pp. 3.22–4.20 = F 14 Müller *FHG* IV, p. 189: Galerius and Diocletian met at Nisibis, where, after they had deliberated, in common they sent an envoy to Persia, Sicorius Probus, Secretary of Official Correspondence. Narseus received him warmly in the hope of what had been offered. But Narseus also employed a certain delay, for, on the grounds that he was wishing, so he pretended, that the envoys with Sicorius recover, ostensibly because they had been exhausted, he diverted Sicorius, who was not ignorant about what was going on, as far as around the Asprudis River of the Median [area?], until those who had been scattered here and there on account of the war regrouped. Then, deep within the palace, after he had separated all the others and been satisfied with the presence of Aphphapharban and Archatepus and Barsaborsus, of whom the one of the two was prefect of the praetorians and the other held the governorship of Symius, he commanded Probus to rehearse the embassy in detail. The headings of the embassy were these: that with respect to the eastern region, the Romans hold Intelene with Sophene and Arzanene with Cardyenae and Zabdicene; and that the Tigris River be a boundary of each of the two states; and that, with respect to Armenia, Zintha, the base situated in a border zone of Media, mark the boundary; and that the sovereign of Iberia owe to Rome the insignia of his own realm; and that Nisibis – the city situated beside the Tigris – be a spot of their transactions.

When he heard these things, since his present fortune kept him from rejecting any of these things, Narseus was agreeing to them all, except – lest he seem to do everything by necessity – he rejected only "Nisibis be a spot of their transactions." And Sicorius [replied], "You are obliged to yield to this. For the embassy is not fully empowered, and no leeway has been granted about this from the sovereigns." Then, when these things had been agreed, to

Narseus were returned both his wives and his children, their chastity having been preserved for them with the help of the sovereign's love of honor.

The headings of the treaty preserved in F 202 – variously referred to in modern scholarship as the Treaty of Nisibis, the Treaty of 298, or the Treaty of 299 – are exceptionally important evidence for the place of diplomacy in Roman and Persian international affairs. See, e.g., Blockley, "The Romano-Persian Peace Treaties of A.D. 299 and 363," pp. 28–49, and Dignas and Winter, *Rome and Persia*, pp. 122–30 and 195–207. For translations of the literary sources, see Dodgeon and Lieu, pp. 125–36.

The Battle of Satala and Galerius' subsequent capture of Narses' wives and children during Narses' retreat occurred in 298. His pursuit of the Persian king had taken Galerius deep into Mesopotamia, from which he returned to Nisibis, but not before he had had the exchange with Aphpharban described in F 201 (Barnes, *New Empire*, p. 63). Galerius and Diocletian would have met there late in 298. It is impossible to judge how much, if any, significance should be placed on Peter's comment that the Caesar and the Augustus dispatched the embassy "in common." However, it is clear that, once the conditions to be presented to Narses were set, matters proceeded quickly. There is a good chance, then, that the return of Narses' family happened in 298 and, of course, this was contingent on Narses' acceptance of Galerius and Diocletian's terms. Consequently, though the implementation of non-negotiable points presented to Narses probably would have occurred in 299, the settlement is here referred to as the Treaty of 298.

Sicorius Probus is otherwise unknown. Peter labels him ἀντιγραφεὺς τῆς μνήμης (Secretary of Official Correspondence), the Greek term for *magister memoriae*, for which see Peachin, "The Office of the Memory," pp. 168–208. For "what had been offered," see F 201.

Narses received Probus and his unnamed associates in a palace, and there is nothing against the spot being Ctesiphon. Peter's reference to an Asprudis River in Media, if he meant to be taken literally, creates minor difficulties, for no river of that name is known in Media or elsewhere. Furthermore, if Probus' embassy had headed south from Nisibis to Ctesiphon or any palace between Nisibis and Ctesiphon, it would not have been close to Media proper. In addition, *ELRG* 3 contradictorily implies that the Asprudis was both near the palace but far from the formal accommodations of the Roman embassy. To remove the first two of these obstacles, one need understand Peter's or the excerptor's τῆς Μηδικῆς as a synonym for Persian territory, as it is regularly employed (e.g. Men. *ELRG* 3, p. 178.23–24 = F 11 Müller *FHG* IV, p. 211 = F 6.1.263 Blockley *Men.*, p. 68, and *ELRG* 3, p. 180.9–10 = F 11 Müller *FHG* IV, p. 212 = F 6.1.319 Blockley *Men.*, p. 70), rather than a designation of one of several areas within the Persian realm which could be called "Media" in a narrower sense, and to assume the Asprudis to be but one of many ancient rivers whose existence is unattested under names we now recognize.

The third obstacle remains. P. Paul Peeters, "L'intervention politique de Constance II dans la Grande Arménie en 338," pp. 25–6, may inadvertently provide a solution. He proposed that Peter's Asprudis masks the Pahlavi Asp-rôdh, i.e., "River of the Horse." From "River of the Horse," he moved to the Greek *Hippos* and noted the existence of a Hippos River that marked the eastern border of the territory Bedia (cf. Greatrex and Lieu, *The Roman Eastern Frontier and the Persian Wars*, Part II, Map 4, p. xxxi, and *The Barrington Atlas*, Maps 87, H 2 and 88, A 2). Bedia, in turn, he identified with a Madia mentioned by Ptolemy (*Geog.* V.9, p. 925.7 Müller). The name Asprudis, then, which Sicorius Probus or his interpreter heard was undoubtedly the Pahlavi translation of a local name, Georgian or Laz. "Media," on the other hand, was Peter's own misunderstanding of his documentary source's "Bedia" or "Madia."

Of course, if Peter's ingenuous etymological argument is correct, Probus' embassy would have met Narses somewhere in what is now Georgia, and this seems close to impossible. But taken figuratively *ELRG* 3's "as far as around the Asprudis River of the Median (area)" would be a hyperbolic equivalent of "a very, very great distance." If the Asprudis is the Hippos – and, given what we know of the process of translation and re-translation between Romans and Persians in the course of diplomatic exchanges and the drafting of agreements (cf. Men. *ELRG* 3, pp. 179.30–180.5 = F 11 Müller *FHG* IV, pp. 211–12 = F 6.1.304–313 Blockley *Men.*, p. 70, and *ELRG* 3, pp. 182.29–183.9 = F 11 Müller *FHG* IV, pp. 213–14 = F 6.1.408–423 Blockley *Men.*, p. 76), this is well within the realm of possibility. In fact, Peter was probably aware of its remoteness, for in 561 or 562 he led an embassy to Persia in order to negotiate a treaty made possible by an earlier cessation of hostilities (*c.* 557) in Colchis and Lazica. On this count, he would also have known the difference between "Bedia" and "Media," the confusion of which in *ELRG* 3 would then be the fault of the excerptor rather than of Peter. Finally, since this figurative language would work only among readers familiar with the erroneous Asprudis appellation, "as far as around the Asprudis River of the Median (area)" = "a very, very great distance" might point to the late 550s or early 560s as a *terminus post quem* for Peter's composition of at least this portion of the *History*, though Menander's comment (*ELRG* 4, p. 188.11–16 = Müller F 13 *FHG* IV, p. 218 = F 6.3.1–6 Blockley *Men.*, pp. 88–90) that Peter died soon after his return from this embassy gives pause.

The related issues of misunderstandings of translation and transcription figure, too, in the names of Persians present at Narses' meeting with Probus. *ELRG* 3 names three Persians – Aphphapharban and Archatepus and Barsaborsus – but then notes that "the one of the two was prefect of the praetorians and the other held the governorship of Symius." One explanation (Peeters, "L'intervention politique," p. 27) has been to see the name Archapetus as a mistake for the Persian title *argabêdh* or *argbed*, on which see Chaumont, "Argbed," *Encyclopedia Iranica*, Vol. II.4, pp. 400–1, though Chaumont confuses Peter with Menander. Certainly "prefect of the praetorians" would be a reasonable Roman equivalent of *argbed*. But is the *argbed* Aphphapharban or Barsaborsus? If Aphphapharban, "dearest above all to Narseus" (F 201), *ELRG* 3's text would have to be understood as a garbled: "Aphphapharban, also *argbed*, and Barsaborsus, of whom the one of the two was prefect of the praetorians and the other [i.e. Barsaborsus] held the governorship of Symius" (cf., e.g., Peeters, "L'intervention politique," p. 27). If Barsaborsus, the alternative would be: "Aphphapharban and an *argbed*, too, Barsaborsus, of whom the one of the two was prefect of the praetorians [Aphphapharban or Barsaborsus?] and the other [– if not Barsaborsus, who? –] held the governorship of Symius" (cf., e.g., Felix, *Antike litterarische Quellen zur Aussenpolitik des Sasanidenstaates*, Vol. I, p. 124, and Dignas and Winter, p. 124). Neither option seems satisfactory. Perhaps, then, "Archapetus" is a hellenized proper name after all (cf., e.g., Dodgeon and Lieu, p. 133). Indeed, Peter's familiarity with Persian titles suggests that he would not have muddled *argbed*. Likewise, he would have been comfortable with rendering the Persian title *dabîrbêth* (Tafażżolī and Rajabzadeh, "*Dabîr*," *Encyclopedia Iranica*, Vol. VI.5, pp. 534–39) into Greek as τὴν τοῦ σημείου εἶχεν ἀρχήν, i.e., "held the office of recorder," which has been reasonably conjectured (Peeters, "L'intervention politique," p. 27) to be what the excerptor thought to refer to an otherwise unattested "Symius" (τὴν τοῦ Συμίου εἶχεν ἀρχήν, i.e., "held the governorship of Symius").

The first of the five headings of the terms advanced by Probus was that "with respect to the eastern region, the Romans hold Intelene with Sophene, and Arzanene with Cardyenae and Zabdicene." Once the transmitted Intelene is corrected to Ingelene, the list as *ELRG* 3 gives it is fairly unproblematic (cf. *The Barrington Atlas*, Map 89, B 2–E 2, with names of modern locations, and Felix, *Antike litterarische Quellen*, Vol. I, p. 124). On Peter's ordering and on the designation Sophene, see Blockley, "The Romano-Persian Peace Treaties of A.D. 299 and 363," pp. 31–2, and, on the relationship of Peter's list of regions to those Ammianus Marcellinus and Zosimus provide (XXXV.7.9 and III.31.1, respectively) in their descriptions of the terms of Jovian's treaty with Sapor in 363, see Paschoud's annotation to Zos. III.31 (Zosime, *Histoire Nouvelle*, II.1, n. 91, pp. 217–20). On discrepancies between Peter and Ammianus in particular, see Felix, *Antike litterarische Quellen*, Vol. I, pp. 124–25.

After the Treaty of 298, it was Armenia, not Rome, which controlled directly or through vassals the five regions referred to in *ELRG* 3 (Lightfoot, "Armenia and the Eastern Marches," *CAH*[2] XII, pp. 489–95). Perhaps this explains the wording ἔχειν ("hold" or "have") rather than ἄρχειν ("rule," "control," or "govern"), i.e., Rome would have control of the regions in question through her Armenian proxy. This interpretation has the added virtue of helping to explain the seemingly contradictory proviso that "with respect to the eastern region, ... the Tigris River be a boundary (ὁροθεσίον) of each of the two states," for that provision cannot have applied in any broad, literal sense. Rather, with respect to Persia, it must refer to a stretch of the Tigris below the southernmost limit of the areas to be administered by Armenia but above some point certainly defined in the treaty but probably omitted (with Rehimena?) by the excerptor. The same narrow application would apply, too, to Rome.

The term ὁροθεσίον is, in fact, unusual in the context of political geography and diplomacy, where, apart from Peter, it appears only in his contemporary Menander Protector. Just as in Peter, in Menander (*ELRG* 3, p. 181.13 = F 11 Müller *FHG* IV, p. 212 = F 6.1.356 Blockley *Men.*, p. 72, and *ELGR* 23, p. 464.24 = F 46 Müller *FHG* IV, p. 248 = F 20.1.43 Blockley *Men.*, p. 180), the context is descriptions of treaty negotiations between the Romans and Persians, one involving Peter himself (*ELRG* 3, p. 179.34 = F 46 Müller *FHG* IV, p. 212 = F 6.1.308 Blockley Men., p. 70), the other (*ELGR* 23, p. 464.4 = F 46 Müller *FHG* IV, p. 248 = F 20.1.19 Blockley *Men.*, p. 180) Peter's son Theodorus (34, *PLRE* III, pp. 1255–56). As was the case with F 201, this raises the question of whether F 202 reflects continuity in the vocabulary of international relations between the reigns of Diocletian and Justinian or the anachronistic application by Peter of terminology of his own day to an account of a treaty negotiated in 298.

The application of the Latinism κάστρον/*castrum* ("base") to Zintha involves the same issue. Though common in the periods of Diocletian and of Constantine Porphyrogenitus, κάστρον occurs only here in the *EH*, never in Procopius, and only twice in John Lydus. Zintha's precise location is unknown. However, the Media in question must be Media Atropatene. Zintha, then, would serve as a marker between Armenia and Persia in a border zone stretching from Lake Van to the Caspian (*The Barrington Atlas*, Maps 89 and 90). From the perspective of Armenia, these two provisions would have, at least *de iure*, set its eastern frontier with Persia from the Caspian to the Tigris, and with Rome up the Tigris at least from Zabdicene, while the proviso that the legitimacy of the ruler of Iberia derive from Roman recognition would have gone far toward eliminating any worries Armenia had about her neighbor to the north.

The treaty's final clause, and the only one to which Narses' delegation took exception, pertained to the designation of Nisibis as a conduit for Roman and Persian imports and exports. A misunderstanding of the Greek of *ELRG* 3 has had serious consequences for our view of the impact of economic forces on the formulation of Rome's foreign policy and military strategy in the east. Peter says the treaty mandated "that Nisibis ... be a spot of their transactions" and that Narses "rejected only 'Nisibis be a spot of transactions.'" However, Narses' complaint is often misread as his rejection of a proposal that Nisibis be the *only* spot of transactions. The reality would have been that, along the ὁροθεσίον between Rome and Persia established by the treaty and distinct from Roman exchanges within that area that did not involve Persians, all business had to be conducted in Nisibis. On the Tigris above that ὁροθεσίον, for example, non-Persian and perhaps Persian traders might move out of Armenian controlled territory or into it from Roman territory along a major road (*The Barrington Atlas*, Map 89, D 3). Below the treaty's ὁροθεσίον, the Tigris would not have been a factor in international exchange, for Rome and Persia did not face one another across that river. So understood, the Nisibis proviso warrants a recalibration of modern analyses of the economic dimensions of the treaty of 298, especially to the degree that such studies emphasize the impact of Nisibis as the sole location approved as an entrepôt for Persian goods headed into Roman territory (e.g., Dignas and Winter, pp. 199–203).

F 203 (303 A.D.?)

Peter *ES* 183, p. 270.1–2 = *Anon. Cont.* F 13.3 Müller *FHG* IV, p. 198: Human nature is more disposed to persevere amidst adversities than to maintain measure amidst good fortune.

Zonar. XII.31 (II, p. 617.7–14): Diocletian, when he had become elated and arrogant as a result, no longer tolerated being addressed by the senate as before, but made it a custom to receive obeisance, adorned his clothing and shoes with gold and precious stones and pearls, and introduced greater extravagance into the imperial insignia. For the previous sovereigns had been honored in the fashion of consuls and had as a sign of their sovereignty only a purple robe.

The context of F 203 may have been a prelude to F 204.

F 204 (306 A.D.)

Peter *ES* 184, p. 270.3–5 = *Anon. Cont.* F 13.4 Müller *FHG* IV, p. 198: Despite the attainment of the rank of an immortal, it was incumbent to keep in mind that he was mortal and not divorced from human circumstances.

F 204 may be a continuation of the theme taken up in F 203. "Attainment of the rank of an immortal" probably refers to Diocletian's earlier assumption on April 1, 286 of the appellation "Jovius" or perhaps to broader and earlier iconographic associations of Diocletian with Jupiter and the attendant *adoratio*, ritual prostration. Note the singular "he" of *ES* 184, which fits nicely the focus on Diocletian alone in the parallel section in Zonaras. It is unnecessary to attribute to Peter or his source any particular authority with regard to the emperors' precise status *vis-à-vis* the gods. On the *-ius signa* "Jovius" and "Herculius", see Rees, "The Emperors' New Names: Diocletian Jovius and Maximian Herculius," *Herakles and Hercules*, pp. 223–39. Though Lactant. *De Mort. Pers.* 52.3 condemns the arrogance of Diocletian and Maximian for assuming the *signa*, the sentiment of *ES* 184 does not necessarily imply a Christian sensibility, but, in fact, in its recognition of "the attainment of the rank of an immortal," strongly suggests just the opposite.

F 205 (303 A.D.)

Peter *ES* 185, p. 270 = *Anon. Cont.* F 13.5 Müller *FHG* IV, p. 198: Lucius Octavius, who had been summoned to a dinner from a triumph and called away, responded that he would not attend the banquet unless the finest portions possible were sent to him.

Zonar. XII.32 (II, p. 618.14–16): Before they abdicated their office, they returned to Rome and celebrated a triumph for the victory over the Persians ... .

The context of *ES* 185 is probably a description of the triumph associated with the *vicennalia* of Diocletian and Maximian, celebrated on November 20, 303, in Rome. The precise identity of Lucius Octavius is uncertain. See further Martolini, *L'*Anonymus post Dionem, *Pietro Patrizio e la* Leoquelle, p. 305.

F 206 (305 A.D.)

Peter *ES* 186, p. 270 = *Anon. Cont.* F 13.6 Müller *FHG* IV, p. 198: Because some sort of apparition had repeatedly troubled him in his dreams to entrust the realm to precisely whom the apparition signified by name, Diocletian suspected this to be the result of witchcraft, and one day he summoned him and to him alone said, "Take the empire that you seek from me every night and do not begrudge the emperor his nourishment from rest."

ES 186 is the sole source for the story of the apparition. Galerius is the unnamed recipient of Diocletian's directive. Diocletian's physical condition and state of mind had been in decline for over a year. In March 305, Galerius arrived at Diocletian's residence in Nicomedia and, after Galerius' attempts to persuade Diocletian to make him an Augustus had given way to predictions of civil war should Diocletian decide otherwise,

Diocletian yielded. On May 1, 305, at Nicomedia, Galerius became Augustus. Constantius Chlorus, then in Gaul, received the same title, while Maximinus Daia and Fl. Valerius Severus – both on Galerius' insistence – became Caesars. Lactant. *De Mort. Pers.* 17–18, with Creed's annotations, pp. 96–9, is by far the most detailed account of what transpired at Nicomedia.

F 207 (316 A.D.)

Peter *ELGR* 13, p. 394.18–37 = F 15 Müller *FHG* IV, pp. 189–90: Licinius sends an envoy to Constantine, Count Mestrianus. And when Mestrianus had come, the sovereign kept disparaging him for some time. And after this, both taking into account the uncertainty of the war and also, at the same time, because Licinius' men, having launched a clandestine attack, held his baggage together with the royal retinue, he received him. And he began negotiating a peace for the two sovereigns, saying it was not right for the one who had defeated his kinsmen to bring violence down upon them. For whatever might be destroyed, this would be lost for the future to the one who had been victorious, but not to those who had been vanquished. And that "The man who denies peace for one becomes a cause of many internecine wars." And the sovereign, showing the magnitude of his anger in his face and in the movement of his body and having barely emitted a sound, said, "We did not bring things to the present state of affairs nor did we, warring and winning from the ocean as far as the places here, arrive here to be unwilling, on account of his abominations, to have our own relative as a colleague and to renounce the bond of kinship and to admit into the sovereignty with him a no-account slave." Then, this portion of the embassy concluded, he commanded Mestrianus, if he wished to request something else, to speak. And he resolved that Valens was deposed from the sovereignty.

Precisely where Constantine received the embassy is uncertain. Only Peter and the Anonymous Valesianus = *Orig. Const.* 5.18 (Mommsen *MHG AA* IX, p. 9.12) name Mestrianus (*PLRE* I, p. 600). The context is Constantine's campaign against Licinius (Val. Licinianus Licinius 3, *PLRE* I, p. 509) and Valens (Aur. Val. Valens 13, *PLRE* I, p. 931), which prompted Licinius to bind Valens, formerly a border commander (*dux limitis*) in Dacia, to him through his recognition of the latter as either a Caesar or an Augustus. When Constantine appeared to have gained the upper hand in a battle on the Campus Ardiensis, perhaps modern Harmanli in modern Bulgaria (cf. *The Barrington Atlas*, Maps 22 C7 and 51 F1, with König, *Origo Constantini: Anonymus Valesianus*, Teil 1, pp. 128–29), Licinius lost his nerve and dispatched

Mestrianus to Constantine. *Epit. De Caes*. 40.9 makes Licinius responsible for Valens' subsequent execution, while Zos. II.20.1 makes his elimination part of the deal reached by Constantine and Licinius. See further Paschoud, *Zosime*, Vol. I, pp. 209–10, and Barnes, *Constantine: Dynasty, Religion and Power in the Later Roman Empire*, p. 103.

F 208 (Summer, 323 A.D.)

Peter *ES* 187, p. 270.15–20 = *Anon. Cont.* F 14.1 Müller *FHG* IV, p. 199: Licinius did not accept the gold coinage on which Constantine emblazoned his victory against the Sarmatians, but melted it down and converted it to other uses, giving no answer to those who faulted him with regard to this than that he did not wish foreign affairs to have a place in domestic business.

Zonar. XIII.2 (III, p. 13.9–13): When the Sarmatians and Goths had bestirred themselves against territory of Romans and were plundering the Thracian sector, Constantine the Most Great took the field against them. When he had occupied Thrace, he joined battle with the barbarians and set up a most glorious trophy over them.

The Anonymous Valesianus = *Orig. Const.* 5.21 (Mommsen *MGH* AA 9, p. 9.21–24) has Licinius complain that Constantine had campaigned within his territory. For the regions under Licinius' control, see Zos. II.20.1. Zos. II.21–22.3 describes Constantine's offensive against the Sarmatians and his building of a port and fleet at Thessalonica, both intended to give him an advantage in any conflict with Licinius. For coins celebrating Constantine's defeat of the Sarmatians, see Brunn, *Constantine and Licinius*, p. 115, no. 289, p. 135, no. 209, pp. 201–2, no. 429, p. 262, no. 257, and p. 475, no. 48.

F 209 (Summer, 324 A.D.)

Peter *ES* 188, p. 270 = *Anon. Cont.* F 14.2 Müller *FHG* IV, p. 19: The momentous achievements of Crispus, Constantine's son, were patent. And Licinius, often beaten by him, was annoyed and uttered these Homeric lines: "Old man, for certain it is that young warriors distress you, and your strength has been destroyed, and dire senility pursues you."

Zonar. XIII.2 (III, p. 12.9–13): From Fausta, the daughter of Maximian, the sovereign produced three sons – Constantine, Constantius, and Constans – and a daughter Helen, who later married Julian. By a concubine he also had another son, called Crispus, older than his other sons, who distinguished himself often in the war against Licinius.

Licinius quotes Hom. *Il.* VIII.102–103. Soz. *HE* I.7 makes the quotation a response to Licinius of the Oracle of Apollo at Miletus as related by "Hellenes." For additional sources on Crispus' successes, see Barnes, *New Empire*, p. 83. The anonymous concubine is Minervina (*PLRE* I, pp. 602–3), whose actual status is uncertain. See further Barnes, *New Empire*, pp. 42–3.

F 210 (337 A.D.)

Peter *ES* 189, p. 270.26–29 = *Anon. Cont.* F 14.3 Müller *FHG* IV, p. 199: Tiberius moved in the senate that Christ be the thirteenth god. The senate did not accept the motion, with the result that some wit remarked, "You rejected him as thirteenth and he comes in first!"

The broader context of this anecdote is impossible to determine. The suspect tradition that Tiberius had asked the Roman senate to recognize Jesus as a god goes back as far as Tertullian (*Apol.* 5.2), to whom Eusebius refers in his account of the purported request (*HE* II.2). Perhaps F 210 reflects debates about the theological ramifications of the acceptance of the divinity of Jesus famously current in Constantine's day and so central to the concerns of the Council of Nicaea. If so, treatment of this theme strongly suggests a Christian perspective. Is this perhaps an example of Peter's (?) own concerns and interests embedded in a non-Christian narrative on which he depended?

F 211 (337 A.D.)

Peter *ES* 190, p. 271.1–3 = *Anon. Cont.* F 15.1 Müller *FHG* IV, p. 199: Constantine first thought to transfer the government to Sardica, and, loving that city, he often said, "Sardica is my Rome."

Zonar. XIII.3 (III, p. 3.14–17): When, on the basis of a divine oracle, he had resolved to build a city so he might call it after his own name, he first proposed to establish it in Serdica, then in Sigeum (this is the promontory of the Troad), and there they say he laid foundations.

The purported quotation is otherwise unattested. The city had been Constantine's residence between at least December 4, 316 and April 17, 317, from the fall of 319 through at least May 19, 320, during the periods December 17–31 and February 6–27, 321, and on December 18, 322. For the evidence, see Barnes, *New Empire*, pp. 73–8. Regardless of when and if – note Peter's "they say" – Constantine actually did begin to construct his New Rome at Serdica, the context of F 211 in Peter's *History* is clearly his account of the foundation of Constantinople.

F 212 (337 A.D.)

Peter *ES* 191, p. 271.4–8 = *Anon. Cont.* F 15.2 Müller *FHG* IV, p. 199: Because he wished to obscure the achievements of former rulers, Constantine liked to deprecate their virtues in certain nicknames. For he called Octavian Augustus "Fortune's Ornament," Trajan "Wall Vine," Hadrian "Artist's Instrument," and Marcus "Ridiculous," and Severus ...

As is the case with F 211, the context here seems to be Peter's treatment of Constantine's role in the construction of Constantinople. Cf. *Epit. de Caes.* 41.13: "On account of the legends inscribed on many structures, he was accustomed to call Trajan 'Wall Plant.'" and Amm. Marc. XXVII.3.7: "The emperor Trajan is also said to have suffered from this fault, with the result that in jest they nicknamed him 'Wall Plant.'" Due to the loss of leaves discarded from *Vat. Graec.* 73, *ES* 191 ends in mid-sentence. More material drawn from Peter's *History* would have followed. See Boissevain, *ES*, p. 271.8, and his diagram of foliation at p. xii.

F 213 (350 A.D.)

Peter *ELGR* 14, p. 395.1–32 = F 16 Müller *FHG* IV, p. 190: Magnentius and Vetranio sent ambassadors to Constantius. Rufinus and Marcellinus were sent, one being a praetorian prefect, the other a commander, and Nunechius, a senatorial prefect, and, in addition to them, Maximus, in order to suggest to Constantius that he lay aside arms and assume first rank in the realm. And through them Magnentius was promising moreover to give his own daughter to Constantius as a wife and that he would take Constantia, the sister of Constantius. The sovereign, then, received the ambassadors of Vetranio and Magnentius, among whom Rufinus, employing his personal rank, often reminded Constantius of the current state of affairs, saying that there was no	Zonar. XIII.7 (III, pp. 37.2–39.4): Constantius the sovereign secured Nisibis and reinstated her citizens, and he himself, since, at the Persians' initiative, there already was a truce in the east, hastened toward the west. It was reported to him that Vetranio had acted in common with Magnentius. For this man, when he happened to be commander of the troops in Illyricum and had learned of Magnentius' rebellion and the murder of Constans, did not yield to the usurper, but he too, for his part, had attempted usurpation. He wrote a letter to Constantius saying that he was resisting the usurper and urging him to press on toward his destruction. Then Vetranio and Magnentius, who had concluded a truce with one another under specified conditions, both in common sent ambassadors

need for him, when he had already labored in wars, to summon to war against him two sovereigns experienced in military science and of like mind with one another and still fresh; the quality and quantity of these men who, unless he agreed to a peace, would be arrayed against him in the course of a civil war, whether one was alone or both together were at hand, he [Rufinus] did not wish him to learn from anywhere other than their previous accomplishments, when, by their engagements, on his and his family's behalf, triumphs were achieved. And Nunechius straightway began saying in his opening remarks that Magnentius sought peace. When he had heard this embassy, the sovereign was deeply perplexed, and, after he had gone to sleep, saw a vision – that his father, as if descending from the heavens and holding by the hand Constans, whom Magnentius had killed, bringing him to him, seemed to utter these words: "Constantius, behold Constans, the progeny of many sovereigns, my son and your brother, treacherously slain. Therefore, neither suffer to look upon a realm sundered and a constitution overturned nor continence threats, but pay heed to the glory of every enterprise that will henceforth come to be for you and do not see your brother unavenged." After this vision, when he had awakened, Constantius, when all the ambassadors save Rufinus had been placed under arrest ...

to Constantius, demanding that he lay down his arms and retain the first rank. Then indeed, the ambassadors, meeting the emperor near Heraclea of Thrace, delivered their messages to him. As a result, he became worried and, when it was night, he saw a dream of the following sort. It seemed that his father was standing next to him, holding his son Constans firmly by the hand and saying to him, "Constantius, behold Constans, your brother, kinsman of many sovereigns, who was destroyed by a usurper. You must avenge him, you must not overlook the empire being sundered or the state being overturned, you must hasten to quash the usurpation, and not leave your brother with justice undone." After this, when Constantius awoke, he took the ambassadors into custody and sent them to jail. Straightway, with no hesitation, he arrived at Serdica. Vetranio cowered at Constantius' unexpected arrival and received him as one receives a master, having both abandoned his former plans and jettisoned his agreements with Magnentius. Constantius accepted him warmly and made him a companion at his table. For, after he had stripped off the marks of sovereignty, Vetranio, in the garb of a commoner, embraced the sovereign's feet. And he embraced Vetranio, called him "father," and, offering his hand to him and supporting him, since he was elderly, made him his dinner companion. Then Prusa (this is a city in Bithynia) was assigned to him for a residence and the countryside allotted to him for supplying of provisions. Living there in luxury for about six years, he measured out his life.

From September of 337, Constantine the Great's sons Constantine (Fl. Val. Constantinus 3, *PLRE* I, p. 223), Constans (Fl. Iul. Constans 3 *PLRE* I, p. 220), and Constantius (Fl. Iul. Constantius 8, *PLRE* I, p. 226) had shared the title of Augustus and presided over mutually agreed upon portions of the empire. By the beginning of April of 340, the younger Constantine had perished in the course of a war with Constans. On January 18, 350, Flavius Magnentius (*PLRE* I, p. 532) was acclaimed Augustus at Augustodunum (Autun). The fugitive Augustus, Constans, was soon dispatched. On March 1 of the same year, Vetranio (1, *PLRE* I, p. 954), Constantius' *magister peditum,* took the purple in Sirmium, perhaps in an attempt to protect the Balkans from Magnentius on behalf of Constantius, who was then engaged in a campaign against Sapor.

In 350, Vulcacius Rufinus (25, *PLRE* I, pp. 782–83) was probably praetorian prefect in Illyricum. On the basis of F 213's possibly anachronistic στρατηλάτης (translated above as "commander"), Marcellinus (9, *PLRE* I, p. 546) is thought to have been Magnentius' *magister militum*. Both he and F 213's Maximus (12, *PLRE* I, p. 581, unless he is to be indentified with Vulcacius Rufinus' nephew Maximus [17, *PLRE* I, p. 582]), are otherwise unknown. The same is true of Nunechius (*PLRE* I, p. 635) and of his characterization in F 213 as "a senatorial prefect" (συγκλητικὸς ὕπαρχος). Constantia is Constantina 2 (*PLRE* I, p. 222), who supposedly had encouraged Vetranio's usurpation and whom Constantius would in 351 wed to Gallus (Flavius Claudius Constantius Gallus 4, *PLRE* I, pp. 224–25). Magnentius' daughter = Anonyma 3, *PLRE* I, p. 1038.

The embassy and Constantius' dream are unique to Peter and Zonaras, Vetranio's six years in Prusa is unique to Zonaras. Philostorgius *HE* III.22, Socrates *HE* II.28, and Sozomenus *HE* IV.4.2–4, all give more detailed accounts of Vetranio's meeting with Constantius late in 350 and its aftermath. Magnentius eventually committed suicide in Lyon on August 10, 353.

F 214 (357/358 A.D.)

Peter *ELGR* 15, pp. 395.33–396.2 = F 17 Müller *FHG* IV, p. 190: Envoys of Persia came before Constantius. And the head of the embassy, Narseus, when he had mixed the harshness of the letter he was bearing with the mildness of his own manners, presented it to be read.

Zonar. XIII.9 (III, p. 48.5–19): Now then, ambassadors from Persia who had been sent by Sapor, who was demanding that Mesopotamia and Armenia be ceded to Persia in order that the Persians thus cease hostilities against the Romans, met with Constantius near Sirmium as he was moving from the west and returning to Byzantium. For from the remote days of their ancestors these territories had belonged to them. If he did not agree, he made it clear to the emperor that the pursuit of the discussion would be made with Ares as adjudicator. To this, Constantius responded to him that he was amazed that, if he had forgotten, Persians were slaves to the Macedonians and that, since Macedonians were subordinate to Romans, those who were slaves to them were also subjects to Romans. Sapor was enraged by this and looked toward war. He again settled himself down to a siege of Nisibis. Since he was making no headway against it, he withdrew and made trial of other places. Because he was repulsed from these too he arrived at Amida and captured it.

The Persian embassy of F 214 is probably that dispatched by Sapor in 357. It arrived in Constantinople on February 23, 358. Peter alone names Narses (*PLRE* I, p. 617. *s.v.* Narseus) as its leader. See further Banchich and Lane, *The* History *of Zonaras*, p. 220, n. 76, and Dodgeon and Lieu, pp. 211–12 and p. 228:

F 215 (358 A.D.)

Eunapius *ELGR* 1, pp. 591.7–592.1 = F 12 Müller *FHG* IV, pp. 17–18 = F 18.6 Blockley *FCH*, Vol. II, pp. 24–7: When Julian was advancing into enemy territory and the Chamavi were imploring him to spare even this as his own, Julian was acquiescing and, having ordered their sovereign to come forward, when he came forward and saw him standing on the bank, having boarded a boat (the boat, then, being out of bowshot), having an interpreter, he began to converse with the barbarians. And when they were prepared to do everything, seeing that peace was attractive and at the same time necessary for himself (for, when the Chamavi are unwilling, it is impossible that the grain shipment from the island of Britain be conveyed to the Roman garrisons), bowing under the need, he agreeably offers peace, and he begins to request to receive hostages as a token of faith. And when they were saying the prisoners of war were enough, he was declaring that war had given those to him, for he had not received them according to an agreement, and that right now he seeks from them the best, if they are not scheming about the peace. And with them imploring and consenting that he say whom he wants, having already gained possession of the son of their sovereign, pretending, he requests whom he has, just as

Peter *ELGR* 16, p. 396.3–15 = F 18 Müller *FHG* IV, p. 191: The barbarians, under Julian the Transgressor, were requesting peace. And he came for the purpose of treating with them and was seeking to receive hostages. And the barbarians were saying that he had many indeed, whom Julian declared he held by the law of war but who had not been given by them, and that now he was seeking pledges of peace, if any among them should be favorable for this. And with them refusing nothing, but agreeing they would give whomever he himself selects, he was requesting to receive the son of the sovereign, on the grounds that he alone was acceptable in place of many. He was holding him as a prisoner of war. And the barbarians, supposing him already dead, at the same time all, along with their sovereign, mourning and moaning, began begging the Caesar not to seek impossible things, requesting those already dead as hostages, and that this was an indication that he did not wish that a truce be made.

though not having him. And then their sovereign and the barbarians, having stretched themselves out facedown, availed themselves of wailing and lamentation aplenty, begging that nothing impossible be imposed, that it is impossible for them to resurrect those who had fallen and to give as hostages those who had met their ends.

For the substantial remainder of Eunapius passage, see *ELGR* 1, pp. 592.1–593.19 = F 12 Müller *FHG* IV, pp. 18–19 = F 18.6.20–70 Blockley *FCH*, Vol. II, pp. 26–29. Zos. III.7.6–7 recounts the same episode. The Nebisgastes (*PLRE* I, p. 619) mentioned by Eunapius at *ELGR* 1, p. 593.16–17, could be the king of the Chamavi, his son, or neither. The "and that this was an indication that he did not wish that a truce be made" with which F 215 concludes but which is not paralleled in Eunapius may be Peter's own contribution or, alternatively, the excerptor of Eunapius may have chosen to omit notice of the alleged suspicion. See further Ochoa, *La transmisión de la* Historia *de Eunapio*, pp. 259–61. Constantius (Fl. Iul. Constantius 8, *PLRE* I, p. 226) had dispatched Julian (Fl. Claudius Julianus 29, *PLRE* I, pp. 477–78) to Gaul with the rank of Caesar. Zos. IV.4–5.2 mentions Julian's efforts to transport grain from Britain to the continent in order to supply former captives of the barbarians. Julian *Ep. ad Ath.* 280B and Amm. Marc. XVII.8.5 deal briefly with operations against the Chamavi, on whom see Klose, "Chamavi," *BNP* 3, cols. 185–86. For context, see Bowersock, *Julian the Apostate*, pp. 33–45, and Hunt, "Julian," *CAH*[2] XIII, pp. 48–56.

BIBLIOGRAPHY

TEXTS AND TRANSLATIONS

Acta Conciliorum Oecumenicorum, Vol. IV.1, ed. E. Schwartz, Reprint of 1928 ed., Berlin: Walter de Gruyter, 1962.

The Acts of the Council of Constantinople of 553, trans. R. Price, 2 vols., *TTH* 51, Liverpool: Liverpool University Press, 2009.

Ammianus Marcellinus, *Ammiani Marcellini Rerum Gestarum*, ed. W. Seyfarth, 2 vols., Leipzig: B. G. Teubner, 1978.

Ammianus Marcellinus, *Res Gestae*, trans. J. C. Rolfe, 3 vols., *LCL*, Reprint of 1935–1939 ed., Cambridge, MA: Harvard University Press, 1964–1971.

Anecdota Graeca e Regia Parisiensi, et e Veneta S. Marci Bibliothecis deprompta, ed. Jean-Baptiste Gaspard d'Ansse de Villoison, Venice: Typis et Sumptibus Fratrum Coleti, 1781.

Anonymous, *Ἀνωνύμου Σύνοψις Χρονική*, ed. K. N. Sathas, *Bibliotheca Graeca Medii Aevi*, Vol. VII, Reprint of 1894 ed., Hildesheim: Georg Olms, 1972.

Anonymous, *Dialogue on Political Science*, trans. P. Bell, *Three Political Voices from the Age of Justinian*, *TTH* 52, Liverpool: Liverpool University Press, 2009, pp. 123–88.

Anonymous, *Excerpta Anonymi Byzantini ex Codice Parisino Suppl. Gr. 607 A*, ed. M. Treu, *Städtisches Gymnasium zu Ohlau 8, Wissenschaftlicher Teil 2*, Ohlau: A. Bial, 1880.

Anonymus post Dionem, *FHG* IV, pp. 191–99.

Basilicorum Libri LX, Series B 1, ed. H. J. Scheltema, Groningen: J. B. Wolters, 1953.

Cassiodorus, *Variae*, ed. T. Mommsen, *Monumenta Germaniae Historica, Auctorum Antiquissimorum*, Vol. XII, Berlin, Weidmann, 1894.

Cassiodorus, *Variae*, trans. S. Barnish, *TTH* 12, Liverpool: Liverpool University Press, 1992.

Cassiodorus, *Variarum libri XII*, ed. M. Accursius, Augsburg: Heinrich Steiner, 1533.

Cassius Dio, *Dionis Cassii Cocceiani Historia Romana*, ed. L. Dindorf, Vol. V, Leipzig: B. G. Teubner, 1865.

Cassius Dio, *Cassii Dionis Cocceiani Historiarum Romanarum Quae Supersunt*, ed. U. Boissevain, 5 vols., Reprint of 1895 ed., Berlin: Weidmann, 1941.

Cassius Dio, *Dionis Cassii Cocceiani Historiae Romanae Libri XLVI*, ed. I. Lenclavius, Frankfurt: Apud Andreae Wecheli heredes, Claudium Marnium & Ioan. Aubrium, 1592.

Cassius Dio, *Roman History*, trans. E. Cary, 9 vols., *LCL*, Cambridge, MA: Harvard University Press, 1914–1927.

Cedrenus, George, *Georgii Cedreni Historiarum Compendium*, ed. I. Bekker, 2 vols., *CSHB*, Bonn: Weber, 1838.

Chronicon Paschale, ed. L. Dindorf, 2 vols., *CSHB*, Bonn: Weber, 1832.

Constantine Porphyrogenitus, *Constantini Porphyrogeniti Imperatoris De Cerimoniis Aulae Byzantinae Libri Duo*, ed. J. Reiske, 3 vols., *CSHB*, Reprint of 1751–1754 ed., Bonn: Weber, 1829.

Constantine Porphyrogenitus, *The Book of Ceremonies*, 2 vols., trans. A. Moffatt and M. Tall, *Byzantina Australiensia* 18, Canberra: Australian Association for Byzantine Studies, 2012.

Corippus, *In Laudem Iustini Augusti Minoris Libri IV*, ed. A. Cameron, London: Athlone Press, 1976.

Dexippi, Eunapii, Petri Patricii, Prisci, Malchi, Menandri Historiarum Quae Supersunt, ed. I. Bekker and B. G. Niebuhr, *CSHB*, Bonn, Weber, 1829.

Dexippus of Athens, *Die Fragmente der griechischen Historiker*, Vol. II A, ed. F. Jacoby, Reprint of 1926 ed., Leiden: Brill, 1961, no. 100, pp. 452–80.

Diogenes Laertius, *Vitae Philosophorum*, ed. H. S. Long, 2 vols., Oxford: Oxford University Press, 1964.

Epigrammatum anthologia Palatina cum Planudeis et appendice nova, ed. E. Cougny, Vol. III, Paris: Didot, 1890.

Epitome de Caesaribus, ed. F. Pichlmayr and R. Gruendel, 2nd ed., Leipzig: B. G. Teubner, 1970.

Epitome de Caesaribus, A Booklet About the Style of Life and the Manners of the Imperatores, trans. T. M. Banchich, 2nd ed., Buffalo, NY: *Canisius College Translated Texts*, 2009, http://www.luc.edu/roman-emperors/epitome.htm.

Eudocia Augusta, *Violarium*, ed. I. Flach, Leipzig: B. G. Teubner, 1880.

Eunapius, *History*, ed. and trans. R. Blockley, *The Fragmentary Classicising Historians of the Later Roman Empire*, Vol. II, Liverpool: Francis Cairns, 1983, pp. 2–150.

Euripides, *Phoeniciae*, ed. J. Diggle, *Euripidis Fabulae*, Vol. III, Oxford: Oxford University Press, 1981.

Eusebius, *Die Kirchengeschichte*, ed. E. Schwartz, T. Mommsen, and F. Winkelmann, 2nd ed., *Eusebius Werke*, Vol.II.1–3, *GCS* N.F. 6.1–3, Berlin: Akademie Verlag, 1999.

Excerpta Historica Iussu Imperatoris Constantini Porphyrogeniti Confecta, ed. U. Boissevain, C. de Boor, T. Büttner-Wobst, and A. Roos, 4 vols., Berlin: Weidmann 1903–1910.

Excerpta de Legationibus Romanorum ad Gentes, ed. C. de Boor, *EH*, Vol. I.1, Berlin: Weidmann, 1903.

Excerpta de Legationibus Gentium ad Romanos, ed. C. de Boor, *EH*, Vol. I.2, Berlin: Weidmann, 1903.

Excerpta de Insidiis, ed. C. de Boor, *EH*, Vol. III, Berlin: Weidmann, 1905.

Excerpta de Sententiis, ed. U. Boissevain, *EH*, Vol. IV, Berlin: Weidmann, 1906.

Excerpta de Virtutibus et Vitiis, ed. A. Roos, *EH*, Vol. II.1–2, Berlin: Weidmann, 1910.

Herodian, ed. C. R. Whittaker, 2 vols., *LCL*, Cambridge, MA: Harvard University Press, 1969–1970.

Historci Graeci Minores, ed. L. Dindorf, 2 vols., Leipzig: B. G. Teubner, 1870–1871.

Homer, *Iliad*, ed. D. B. Munro and T. W. Allen, 2 vols., 3rd ed., Oxford: Oxford University Press, 1920.

Homer, *Odyssey*, ed. T. W. Allen, 2 vols., 2nd ed., Oxford: Oxford University Press, 1917.

Inscriptiones Latinae Selectae, ed. H. Dessau, Vol. I, Berlin: Weidmann, 1892.

Iohannis Antiocheni, Fragmenta Quae Supersunt Omnia, ed. and trans. S. Mariev, *CFHB*, Berlin and New York: Walter de Gruyter, 2008.

John of Antioch, *Ioannis Antiocheni Fragmenta ex Historia Chronica*, ed. and trans. U. Roberto, *Texte und Untersuchungen zur Geschichte der altchristichen Literatur* 154, Berlin and New York: Walter de Gruyter, 2005.

John Lydus, *De Magistratibus Populi Romani*, ed. R. Wünsch, Leipzig: B. G. Teubner, 1903.

John Lydus, *Joannis Laurentii Lydi Philadelpheni De magistratibus reipublicae Romanae libri tres*, ed. J. Dominique Fuss, Paris: J.–M. Eberhart, 1812.

Julian, *Letter to the Athenians, Discours de Julien César* (I–V), ed. J. Bidez, *Oeuvres complètes*, Vol. I.1, Paris: Les Belles Lettres, 1932, pp. 213–35.

Justinian, *Novellae*, ed. R. Schoell and W. Kroll, Reprint of 1954 ed., Berlin: Weidmann, 1972.

Lactantius, *De Mortibus Persecutorum*, ed. and trans. J. L. Creed, Oxford: Oxford University Press, 1984.

Leo the Grammarian, *Leonis Grammatici Chronographia*, ed. I. Bekker, *CSHB*, Bonn: Weber, 1842.

Lexica Segueriana, ed. I. Bekker, *Anecdota Graeca*, Vol. I, Berlin: G. C. Nauck, 1814.

Malalas, John, *Chronographia*, ed. I. Thurn, *CFHB, Series Berolinensis* 35, Berlin: Walter de Gruyter, 2000.

Malalas, John, *The* Chronicle *of John Malalas*, trans. E. Jeffreys, M. Jeffreys, and R. Scott, with B. Croke, J. Ferber, S. Franklin, A. James, D. Kelly, A. Moffat, and A. Nixon, *Byzantina Australiensia* 4, Melbourne: Australian Association for Byzantine Studies, 1986.

Martial, *Epigrammata*, ed. W. M. Lindsay, 2nd ed., Oxford: Oxford University Press, 1929.

Menander, *Reliquiae Selectae*, ed. F. H. Sandbach, Oxford: Oxford University Press, 1990.

Menander Protector, *The* History *of Menander the Guardsman*, ed. and trans. R. Blockley, Liverpool: Francis Cairnes, 1985.

On Sytax, ed. I. Bekker, *Anecdota Graeca*, Vol. I, Berlin: G. C. Nauck, 1814, pp. 117–80.

Origo Constantini, trans. J. Stevenson, *From Constantine to Julian*, ed. S. N. C. Lieu and D. Montserrat, London: Routledge, 1996, pp. 39–62.

Peter the Patrician, *FHG* IV, pp. 181–91.

Philostorgius, *Kirchengeschichte*, ed. J. Bidez and F. Winkelmann, 2nd ed., *GCS*, Berlin: Akademie Verlag, 1972.

Pliny, *Epistolae*, ed. R. C. Kukula, Leipzig: B. G. Teubner, 1923.

Plutarch, *Parallel Lives*, ed. and trans. B. Perrin, 11 vols., *LCL*, Cambridge, MA: Harvard University Press, 1914–1926.

Plutarch, *Regnum et Imperatorum Apophthegmata*, ed. and trans. F. C. Babbit, Vol. III of *Plutarch's Moralia*, *LCL*, Cambridge, MA: Harvard University Press, 1931, pp. 8–194.

Procopius, *Anecdota*, Vol. III.1 of *Procopii Caesariensis opera omnia*, ed. J. Huary and G. Wirth, Reprint of 1906 ed., Munich and Leipzig: K. G. Saur, 2001.

Procopius, *De Bello Gothico*, Vol. II of *Procopii Caesariensis opera omnia*, ed. J. Huary and G. Wirth, Reprint of 1905 ed., Munich and Leipzig: K. G. Saur, 2001.

Psellus, Michael, *Michaelis Pselli Historia Syntomos*, ed. W. J. Aerts, *CFHB, Series Berolinensis* 30, Berlin: Walter de Gruyter, 1990.

Ptolemy, *Geographia*, ed. C. Müller, Paris: Didot, 1901.

Scholia Basilicorum VIII.2.1, ed. H. J. Scheltema, *Basilicorum Libri LX*, Series B 1, Groningen: J. B. Wolters, 1953.

Scholia Platonica, ed. W. C. Greene, Haverford, PA: American Philological Association, 1938.

Scriptores Historiae Augustae, ed. and trans. D. Magie, 3 vols., *LCL*, Cambridge, MA: Harvard University Press, 1921–1932.

Seneca, *Octavia*, ed. R. Ferri, Cambridge: Cambridge University Press, 2003.

Socrates Scholasticus, *Ecclesiastical History*, ed. R. Hussey, Oxford: Oxford University Press, 1878.

Sozomenus, *Kirchengeschichte*, ed. J. Bidez and G. C. Hansen, 2 vols., *GCS*, Berlin: Akademie-Verlag, 1960.

Stephanus of Byzantium, *Ethnica*, ed. M. Billerbeck, J. Felix Gaertner, B. Wyss, and C. Zubler, Vol. I, Berlin: Walter de Gruyter, 2006.

Stephanus of Byzantium, *Stephani Byzantini Ethnicorum Quae Supersunt*, ed. A. Meineke, Vol. I, Berlin: G. Reimer, 1849.

Suda, *Suidae Lexicon*, ed. A. Adler, 5 vols., Leipzig: B. G. Teubner, 1937.

Suetonius, *Lives of the Caesars*, ed. J. C. Rolfe, 2 vols., *LCL*, Reprints of 1951 and 1914 eds., Cambridge, MA: Harvard University Press, 1979.

Symeon Magister, *Symeonis Magistri et Logothetae Chronicon*, ed. S. Wahlgren, *CFHB, Series Berolinensis* 44.1. Berlin: Walter de Gruyter, 2006.

Tacitus, *Annales*, ed. E. Koestermann, Reprint of 1960 ed., Stuttgart: B. G. Teubner, 1971.

Tacitus, *Germania*, ed. H. Furneaux and J. G. C. Anderson, *Opera Minora*, Reprint of 1939 ed., Oxford: Oxford University Press, 1962.

Tacitus, *Historiae*, ed. E. Koestermann, Leipzig: B. G. Teubner, 1969.

Tertullian, *Apologetitus*, ed. and trans. T. R. Glover, *LCL*, Cambridge, MA: Harvard University Press, 1953.

Theodore Scutariotes, *Theodori Scutariotae Chronica*, ed. R. Tocci, *CFHB, Series Berolinensis* 46, Berlin: Walter de Gruyter, forthcoming, 2016.

Theophylact Simocatta, *Historiae*, ed. C. de Boor and P. Wirth, Reprint of 1887 ed., Stuttgart: B. G. Teubner, 1972.

Theophylact Simocatta, *The* History *of Theophylact Simocatta*, trans. M. and M. Whitby, Oxford: Oxford University Press, 1986.

Three Political Voices from the Age of Justinian, trans. P. Bell, *TTH* 52, Liverpool: Liverpool University Press, 2009.

Vergil, *Aeneid*, ed. F. Hirtzel, Oxford: Oxford University Press, 1900.

Vigilius, *Epistulae*, ed. E. Schwartz, *Vigiliusbriefe*, *Sitzungsberichte der Bayerischen Akademie der Wissenschaften*, Philosophisch-Historische Abteilung, Heft 2 (1940), pp. 1–32.

Xiphilinus, John, *Xiphilini Epitome librorum 36–80*, ed. U. Boissevain, *Cassii Dionis Cocceiani Historiarum Romanarum Quae Supersunt*. Vol. III, Appendix 1, Berlin: Weidmann, 1901, pp. 657–730.

Zonaras, John, *Ioannis Zonarae Epitomae Historiarum*, ed. M. Pinder and T. Büttner-Wobst, 3 vols., *CSHB*, Bonn: Weber, 1841–1897.

Zosimus, *New History*, trans. R. T. Ridley, *Byzantina Australiensia* 2, Canberra: Australian Association for Byzantine Studies, 1982.

Zosimus, *Zosime Histoire Nouvelle*, ed. and trans. F. Paschoud, Vol. I, 2nd ed., *Collection Budé*, Paris: "Les Belles Lettres," 2003.

Zosimus, *Zosime Histoire Nouvelle*, ed. F. Paschoud, Vols. II–III, *Collection Budé*, Paris: "Les Belles Lettres," 1971–1989.

Zosimus, *Zosimi Comitis et Exadvocati Fisci Historia Nova*, ed. L. Mendelssohn, Leipzig: B. G. Teubner, 1887.

MODERN SCHOLARSHIP

Ameling, W., "Cleopatra II 12," *BNP*, Vol. II, Leiden: Brill, 2002, cols. 444–45.

Anderson, J. G. C., "The Eastern Frontier from Tiberius to Nero," *CAH*, Vol. X, Cambridge: Cambridge University Press, 1934, pp. 743–80.

Antonopoulos, P., Πέτρος Πατρίκιος. Ὁ βυζαντινός διπλωμάτης, ἀξιωματοῦχος καί συγγραφέας, *Historical Monongraphs* 7, ed. E. K. Chrysos, Athens: S. D. Basilopoulos, 1990.

Badian, E., "Alexander 4," *BNP*, Vol. I, Leiden: Brill, 2002, cols. 469–75.

Badian, E., "Cassander," *BNP*, Vol. II, Leiden: Brill, 2002, cols. 1155–57.

Badian, E., "Philippus I.4," *BNP*, Vol. XI, Leiden: Brill, 2007, cols. 28–33.

Badian, E., "Thessalonica 2," *BNP*, Vol. XIV, Leiden: Brill, 2009, col. 577.

Baldini, A., *Storie Perdute (III secolo d.C), Studi di stori* 6, Bologna: Pátron editore, 2000.

Ball, W., *Rome in the East*, New York and London: Routledge, 2000.

Banchich, T. M., "Marcus Aemilius Aemilianus," *De Imperatoribus Romanis* 2002, http://www.roman-emperors.org/aemaem.htm.

Banchich, T. M., "Mareades/Mariades/Mariadnes/Cyriades," *De Imperatoribus Romanis* 2002, http://luc.edu/www.roman-emperors/mareades.htm.

Banchich, T. M., and Lane, E. N., *The* History *of Zonaras from Alexander Severus to the Death of Theodosius the Great*, corrected 2009 ed., London and New York: Routledge, 2012.

Barnes, T. D., *Constantine: Dynasty, Religion and Power in the Later Roman Empire*, Oxford: Wiley-Blackwell, 2011.

Barnes, T. D., *The New Empire of Diocletian and Constantine*, Cambridge, MA: Harvard University Press, 1982.

Barrett, A., *Agrippina: Sex, Power, and Politics in the Early Empire*, New Haven, CT: Yale University Press, 1996.

Barrett, A., *Caligula: The Abuse of Power*, 2nd ed., London and New York: Routledge, 2015.

Barrett, A., *Livia: First Lady of Imperial Rome*, New Haven, CT: Yale University Press, 2002.

The Barrington Atlas of the Greek and Roman World, ed. R. Talbert, Princeton, NJ: Princeton University Press, 2000.

Bennett, J., *Trajan,* Optimus Princeps, Bloomington and Indianapolis, IN: Indiana University Press, 1997.

Bichir, G., *The Archaeology and History of the Carpi from the Second to the Fourth Century A.D.*, 2 vols., trans. by N. Hampartumian, *British Archaeological Reports, Supplementary Series* 16 (1976).

Bickerman, E., "Time-Reckoning," *CHI*, Vol. III.2, Cambridge: Cambridge University Press, 1983, pp. 778–91.

Birley, A., "Cassius Dio," *BNP*, Vol. II, Leiden: Brill, 2002, cols, 1171–72

Birley, A., *The* Fasti *of Roman Britain*, Oxford: Oxford University Press, 1981,

Birley, A., *Hadrian: The Restless Emperor*, New York: Routledge, 1997.

Birley, A., *Marcus Aurelius*, Boston: Little, Brown, 1966.

Birley, A., *Septimius Severus: The African Emperor*, London: Eyre and Spottiswoode, 1971.

Bleckmann, B., *Die Reichskrise des III. Jahrhunderts in der spätantiken und byzantinischen Geschichtsschreibung, Untersuchungen zu den nachdionischen Quellen der Chronik des Johannes Zonaras*, Munich: Tuduv, 1992.

Bleckmann, B., "Zu den Quellen der Vita Gallieni duo," *Historia Augusta Colloquium Maceratense, Historia Augusta Colloquia* N.S. III, ed. G. Bonamenta and G. Paci, Bari: Edipuglia, 1995, pp. 75–105.

Blockley, R., "The Romano-Persian Peace Treaties of A.D. 299 and 363," *Florilegium* 6 (1984), pp. 28–49.

Boissevain, U., *De Excerptis Planudeis et Constantinianis ab Angelo Maio editis quae vulgo Cassio Dioni attribuunter, Programma voor den Cursus 1884/1885*, Erasmiaansch Gymnasium: Rotterdam: H. A. Kramers & Son, 1884, pp. 13–40.

Boor, C. de, "Römische Kaisergeschichte in byzantinischer Fassung I. Der Anonymus post Dionem," *Byzantinische Zeitschrift* I (1892), pp. 13–33.

Boucher, J-P., *Caius Cornélius Gallus,* Paris: Les Belles Lettres, 1966.

Bowersock, G. W., *Julian the Apostate*, Cambridge, MA: Harvard University Press, 1978.

Boyce, M., "Iranian Festivals," Chapter 21 (b) of *CHI*, Vol. III.2, Cambridge: Cambridge University Press, 1983, pp. 792–815.

Brecht, S., *Die römische Reichskrise von ihrem Ausbruch bis zu ihrem Höhepunkt in der Darstellung byzantinischer Autoren. Althistorische Studien der Universität Würzburg*, Band I, Rahden, Westf.: Verlag Marie Leidorf GmbH, 1999.

Brill's New Jacoby, ed. I. Worthington, Leiden: Brill, 2006–.

Brill's New Pauly, ed. H. Cancik and H. Schneider, Leiden: Brill, 2003–2007.

Bruun, P. M., ed., *Constantine and Licinius, A.D. 313–337*, Vol. VII of *Roman Imperial Coinage*, ed. C. H. V. Sutherland and R. A. G. Carson, London: Spink and Son Ltd., 1966.

The Cambridge Ancient History, Vol. X, ed. S. Cook, F. Adcock, and M. Charlesworth, Cambridge: Cambridge University Press, 1934.

The Cambridge Ancient History, 2nd ed., Vol. X, ed. A. Bowman, E. Champlin, and A. Lintott; Vol. XII, ed. A. Bowman, P. Garnsey, and A. Cameron; Vol. XIII, ed. A. Cameron and P. Garnsey; Vol. XIV, ed. A. Cameron, B. Ward-Perkins, and M. Whitby, Cambridge: Cambridge University Press, 1996–2000.

The Cambridge History of Iran, Vol. III.2, ed. E. Yarsharter, Cambridge: Cambridge University Press, 1983.

Cameron, A., *The Last Pagans of Rome*, New York: Oxford University Press, 2011.

Canepa, M., *The Two Eyes of the Earth*, Berkeley and Los Angeles, CA: University of California Press, 2009.

Chaumont, M. L., "Argbed," *Encyclopedia Iranica*, Vol. II.4, ed. E. Yarshater, London and Boston: Routledge and Kegan Paul, 1986, pp. 400–1; updated online version at http://www.iranicaonline.org/articles/argbed-a-high-ranking-title-in-the-parthian-and-sasanian-periods.

Christol, M., "À propos des Aradii: Le stemma d'une famille sénatoriale au IIIe siècle après J.-C.," *Zeitschrift für Papyroligie und Epigraphik* 28 (1978), pp. 145–50.

Christol, M., *L'Empire Romain du IIIe Siècle*, Paris: Editions Errance, 1997.

Cumont, F., *Testimonia de Astrologis Romanis ex Codice Parisino Suppl. Gr. 607 A, Catalogus Codicum Astrologorum Graecorum 8.4*, Brussels: Lamertin, 1921.

Daly, L. J. and Reiter, W., "The Gallus Affair and Augustus' *lex Iulia maiestas*: a Study in Historical Chronology and Causality," *Studies in Latin Literature and Roman History* I, ed. C. Deroux, *Collection Latomus* 164, Latomus: Brussels, 1979, pp. 289–311.

Dignas, B. and Winter, E., *Rome and Persia in Late Antiquity*, Cambridge: Cambridge University Press, 2007.

Dodgeon, M. H. and Lieu, S. N. C., *The Roman Eastern Frontier and the Persian Wars. A.D. 226–363*, London: Routledge, 1991.

Drinkwater, J., "Maximinus to Diocletian and the 'Crisis,'" *CAH*, 2nd ed., Vol. XII, Cambridge: Cambridge University Press, 2005, pp. 28–66.

Drogula, F., "Controlling Travel," *Classical Quarterly* 62 (2011), pp. 230–66.

Eck, W., "Aurelius Cleander, M.," *BNP*, Vol. II, Leiden: Brill, 2007, col. 384.

Felix, W., *Antike litterarische Quellen zur Aussenpolitik des Sasanidenstaates*, Vol. I, *Sitzungsberichte der Österreichischen Akademie der Wissenschaften, Philosophisch-*

Historische Klasse, Vol. 456, Vienna: Österreichische Akademie der Wissenschaften: 1985, pp. 224–309.

Fragmenta Historicorum Graecorum, ed. C. Müller, 5 vols., Paris: Didot, 1841–1883.

Die Fragmente der griechischen Historiker, ed. F. Jacoby, 15 vols., Leiden, Brill, 1923–1999.

Frigo, T., "Labienus, Q., 2," *BNP*, Vol. VII, Leiden: Brill, 2005, col. 134.

Frye, R. N., "The Sassanians," *CAH*, 2nd ed., Vol. XII, Cambridge: Cambridge University Press, 2005, pp. 460–80.

Fündling, J., "Ventidius, P., I 3," *BNP*, Vol. XV, Leiden: Brill, 2010, cols. 281–83.

Furneaux, H., *The Annals of Tacitus*, 2nd ed., 2 vols., Oxford: Oxford University Press, 1896.

Gawlikowski, M., "Les princes de Palmyre," *Syria* 62 (1985), pp. 251–61.

Ginsburg, J., *Representing Agrippina*, New York: Oxford University Press, 2006.

Görres, F., "Zur Kritik einiger Quellenschriftsteller der spätern römischen Kaiserzeit," *Neue Jahrbücher für Philologie und Paedogogik* 111 (1875), pp. 212–19.

Greatrex, G., and Lieu, S. N. C., *The Roman Eastern Frontier and the Persian Wars, Part II*, London and New York: Routledge, 2002.

Griffin, M., *Nero: The End of a Dynasty*, New Haven, CT: Yale University Press, 1984.

Griffin, M., *Seneca: A Philosopher in Politics*, Oxford: Oxford University Press, 1992.

Historicorum Romanorum Reliquiae, ed. H. Peter, 2 vols., Reprint of 1906 ed., Stuttgart: B. G. Teubner, 1967.

Hunger, H., *Die Hochsprachliche Profane Literatur der Byzantiner*, 2 vols., Munich: C. H. Beck, 1978.

Hunt, D., "Julian," *CAH*, 2nd ed., Vol. XIII, Cambridge: Cambridge University Press, 1998, pp. 44–77.

Hurschmann, R., "Nudity, § C, Everyday Life and Sport," *BNP*, Vol. IX, Leiden: Brill, 2002, col. 874.

Janiszewski, P., *The Missing Link: Greek Pagan Historiography in the Second Half of the Third Century and in the Fourth Century AD*, trans. D. Dzierzbicka, Supplement Vol. VI of *The Journal of Juristic Papyrology*, Warsaw: Warsaw University, Faculty of Law and Administration; Warsaw University, Institute of Archaeology; The Raphael Taubenschlag Foundation, 2006.

Johnson, M., "A Witticism of Antoninus Caracalla?," *Augusto augurio. Rerum humanarum et divinarum commentationes in honorem Jerzy Linderski*, ed. C. F. Konrad, Wiesbaden: Franz Steiner Verlag, 2004, pp. 101–4.

Jost, M., "Telephus" (1), *OCD*, 3rd ed., pp. 1479–80.

Kettenhofen, E., *Die römisch-persischen Kriege des 3. Jahrhunderts n. Chr. nach der Inschrift Šāhpuhrs I. an der Ka'be-ye Zartošt (ŠKZ)*, Beiheft TAVO B 55, Wiesbaden, 1982.

Kienast, D., *Römische Kaisertabelle*, 3rd ed., Darmstadt: Wissenschaftliche Buchgesellschaft, 2004.

Klose, D., "Chamavi," *BNP*, Vol. III, Leiden: Brill, 2002, cols. 185–86.

Koch, T., *Comicorum Atticorum Fragmenta*, Leipzig: B. G. Teubner, 1888.

Koestermann, E., *Cornelius Tacitus* Annalen, Vol. 2, Heidelberg: Carl Winter, 1965.

König, I., *Origo Constantini: Anonymus Valesianus*, Teil 1, Trier: Trierer historische Forschungen, 1987.

Körner, C., "Usurpers under Gallienus," *De Imperatoribus Romanis* (1999), http://luc.edu/www.roman-emperors/galusurp.htm.

Krumbacher, K., *Geschichte der byzantinischen Litteratur*, 2 vols., Reprint of 1897 ed., New York: Burt Franklin, 1970.

Laniado, A., "Un fragment peu connu de Pierre le Patrice," *Byzantinische Zeitschrift* 90 (1997), pp. 405–12.

Lee, A. D., "Treaty-making in Late Antiquity," *War and Peace in Ancient and Medieval History*, ed. P. de Souza and J. France, Cambridge: Cambridge University Press, 2008, pp. 107–19

Levick, B., *Claudius*, New Haven, CT: Yale University Press, 1990.

Lightfoot, C. S., "Armenia and the Eastern Marches," *CAH*, 2nd ed., Vol. XII, Cambridge: Cambridge University Press, 2005, pp. 481–97.

Mai, A., *Scriptorum veterum nova collectio e Vaticanis codicibus edita*, Vol. II, Rome: Typiis Vaticanis, 1827.

Martolini, A., *L'*Anonymus post Dionem, *Pietro Patrizio e la* Leoquelle: *Uno studio sulle fonti post-Dionee dell'* Epitome *di Giovanni Zonara*, University of Rome "La Sapienza" Dissertation, 2008–2009.

Martolini, A., "I frammenti dell' *Anonymus post Dionem*/Pietro Patrizio nell' ambito della storiografia tardoantica e bizantina," *Dalla storiografia ellenistica alla storigrafia tardoantica: aspetti, problemi, prospettive*, ed. U. Roberto and L. Mecella, Rubbetino: Rubbetino Editore, 2010, pp. 209–37.

Martolini, A., "I frammenti *ES* 176, 177 e 178 di Pietro Patrizio su Aureliano," *Koinonia* 34 (2010), pp. 1–6.

Mazzarino, S., "*L'Anonymus post Dionem* e la '*Topica*' delle Guerre Romano-Persiane 242/4 d.C.–283/(4?) d.C.," *Atti del Convegno internazionale sul tema: La Persia nel Medioevo (Roma, 31 marzo–5 aprile 1970)*, Rome: Accademia nazionale dei Lincei, 1971, pp. 655–78.

McCormick, M., "Emperor and Court," *Late Antiquity: Empire and Successors, A.D. 424–600, CAH*, 2nd ed., Vol. XIV, Cambridge: Cambridge University Press, 2000, pp. 135–63.

McInerney, J., "Dexippos," *BNJ*, Leiden: Brill, 2008.

Mecella, L., *Dexippo di Atene: Testimonianze e Frammenti*, Rome: Edizioni Tored, 2013.

Millar, F., *The Roman Near East*, 31 B.C.–A.D. 337, Cambridge, MA: Harvard University Press, 1993.

Mommsen, T., *The Provinces of the Roman Empire from Caesar to Diocletian*, Vol. II, trans. W. P. Dickson, New York: Charles Scribner's Sons, 1887.

Mommsen, T., "Ueber die dem Cassius Dio beigelegten Theile der Planudischen und der Constantinischen Excerpte," *Hermes* VI (1872), pp. 82–91.

Murison, C. L., *Rebellion and Reconstruction: Galba to Domitian, An Historical Commentary on Cassius Dio's* Roman History *Books 64–67 (A.D. 68–96)*, Atlanta, GA: Scholars Press, 1999.

Nauck, A., *Tragicorum graecorum fragmenta*, Leipzig: B. G. Teubner, 1856.

Németh, A., *Imperial Systematization of the Past: Emperor Constantine VII and His Historical Excerpts*, Central European University Dissertation, Budapest, 2010.

Ochoa, J., *La transmisión de la* Historia *de Eunapio, Erytheia: Estudios y Textos* 1, Madrid: Asociación Cultural Hispano Helénica, 1990.

Oxford Classical Dictionary, ed. S. Hornblower and A. Spawforth, 3rd ed., Oxford: Oxford University Press, 1996.

Oxford Dictionary of Byzantium, ed. A. Kazhdan, 3 vols., Oxford: Oxford University Press, 1991.

Parke, H. W. and Wormell, D. E. W., *The Delphic Oracle*, Vol. I, Oxford: Blackwell, 1956.

Patzig, E., "Die römische Quellen des salmasischen Johannes Antiochenus. Mit einem Anhänge zur Textkritik der Scriptores Hist. Aug.," *Byzantinische Zeitschrift* 13 (1904), pp. 13–50.

Peachin, M., "The Office of the Memory," *Studien zur Geschichte der römischen Spätantike: Festgabe für Professor Johannes Straub*, Athens: Pelasgos-Verlag, 1989, pp. 168–208.

Peeters, P. Paul, "L'intervention politique de Constance II dans la Grande Arménie en 338," *Bulletin de l'Académie royale de Belgique, Classe des Lettres* 17 (1931), pp. 10–47.

Pelling, C., "The Triumviral Period," *CAH*, 2nd ed., Vol. X, Cambridge: Cambridge University Press, 1996, pp. 1–69.

Potter, D., *Prophecy and History in the Crisis of the Roman Empire: A Historical Commentary on the* Thirteenth Sibylline Oracle, Oxford: Oxford University Press, 1990.

Potter, D., *The Roman Empire at Bay*, 2nd ed., London and New York: Routledge, 2014.

Prosopographia Imperii Romani, Pars III, ed. P. de Rohden and H. Dessau, Berlin: G. Reimer, 1897.

Prosopographia Imperii Romani, ed. E. Groag, L. Peterson, A. Stein, and K. Wachtel, 8 parts, 2nd ed., Berlin and New York: Walter de Gruyter, 1933– .

The Prosopography of the Later Roman Empire, ed. A. H. M. Jones, J. R. Martindale, and J. Morris, Vol. I, Cambridge: Cambridge University Press, 1971.

The Prosopography of the Later Roman Empire, ed. J. R. Martindale, Vol. II, Cambridge: Cambridge University Press, 1980.

The Prosopography of the Later Roman Empire, ed. J. R. Martindale, Vol. III, Cambridge: Cambridge University Press, 1992.

Rapp, C., "Literary Culture under Justinian," *The Age of Justinian*, ed. M. Mass, Cambridge: Cambridge University Press, 2005, pp. 376–97.

Rees, R., "The Emperors' New Names: Diocletian Jovius and Maximian Herculius," in *Herakles and Hercules: Exploring a Graeco-Roman Divinity*, ed. L. Rawlings and H. Bowden, Swansea: The Classical Press of Wales, 2005, pp. 223–39.

Reinhold, M., *From Republic to Principate: An Historical Commentary on Cassius Dio's* Roman History *Books 49–52 (36–29 B.C.)*, Atlanta, GA: Scholars Press, 1988.

Rémy, B., "La carrière de Q. Aradius Rufinus Optatus Aelianus," *Historia* 25 (1976), pp. 458–77.

Rich, J., *Cassius Dio: The Augustan Settlement (Roman History 53–55.9)*, Warminster: Aris & Phillips, 1990.

Rostovtzeff, M., *The Social and Economic History of the Roman Empire*, 2nd ed., Oxford: Oxford University Press, 1957.

Sartre, M., "The Arabs and the Desert Peoples," *CAH*, 2nd ed., Vol. XII, Cambridge: Cambridge University Press, 2005, pp. 498–520.

Saunders, R., "Aurelian's 'Two' Iuthungian Wars," *Historia* 41 (1992), pp. 311–27.

Scardigli, B., "Menofilo e i Carpi," *Studia Historica* 16 (1998), pp. 173–78.

Schottky, M., "Artavasdes 1," *BNP*, Vol. II, Leiden: Brill, 2003, col. 55.

Schottky, M., "Artavasdes 6," *BNP* , Vol. II, Leiden: Brill, 2003, col. 56.

Schottky, M., "Artaxias 2," *BNP*, Vol. II, Leiden: Brill, 2003, col. 58.

Schottky, M., "Orodes 2," *BNP*, Vol. X, Leiden: Brill, 2007, cols. 236–37.

Schottky, M., "Phraates 4," *BNP*, Vol. XI, Leiden: Brill, 2007, col. 189.

Seager, R., *Tiberius*, Berkeley, CA: University of California Press, 1972.

Sotiriadis, G., *Zur Kritik des Johannes von Antiochia, Jahrbücher für classische Philologie, Supplementband* 16, Leipzig: B. G. Teubner, 1888, pp. 1–126.

Southern, P., *The Roman Empire from Severus to Constantine*, London and New York: Routledge, 2001.

Stoll, H. W., "Kanake (1)," W. H. Roscher, *Ausführliches Lexikon der griechischen und römischen Mythologie*, Vol. II.1, Leipzig: B. G. Teubner, 1890–1894, col. 946.

Syme, R., *Tacitus*, Vol. II, Oxford: Oxford University Press, 1958.

Tafażżolī, A. and Rajabzadeh, H., "*Dabīr*," *Enclyclopedia Iranica*, Vol. VI.5 (1993), pp. 534–39; updated online version at http://www.iranicaonline.org/articles/dabir-secretary-scribe.

Takács, S., "Cleopatra, Isis, and the Formation of Augustan Egypt," *Cleopatra: A Sphinx Revisited*, ed. M. Miles, Berkeley, CA: University of California Press, 2011, pp. 78–95.

Thompson, D. and Koenen, L., "Gallus as Triptolemos on the Tazza Farnese," *Bulletin of the American Society of Papyrologists* 21 (1984), pp. 111–56.

Tinnefeld, F., "Constantinus 9," *BNP*, Vol. III, Leiden: Brill, 2003, cols. 721–22.

Treadgold, W., *The Early Byzantine Historians*, Houndmills, Basingstoke, and New York: Palgrave Macmillan, 2007.

Treadgold, W., *The Middle Byzantine Historians*, Houndmills, Basingstoke, and New York: Palgrave Macmillan, 2013.

Wallinga, T., "The Date of Joannes Lydus' *De magistratibus*," *Revue internationale des droits de l'antiquité*, Series 3, 39 (1992), pp. 359–80.

Watson, A., *Aurelian and the Third Century*, London and New York: Routledge, 1999.

Will, W., "Antonius, M., I 19," *BNP*, Vol. I, Leiden: Brill, 2002, cols. 803–5.

Will, W., "Iunius Brutus, M., I 10," *BNP*, Vol. VI, Leiden: Brill, 2005, cols. 1094–95.

Wolfram, H., *History of the Goths*, trans. by T. Dunlop, Berkeley, CA: University of California Press, 1987.

INDEXES

CORRELATION OF FRAGMENT NUMBERS WITH MÜLLER *FHG*

FHG Fragment Numbers of Peter	Fragment Numbers in This Edition
F 1	F 2 and 5
F 2	F 22
F 3	F 43
F 4	F 113
F 5	F 114 and 115
F 6	F 125
F 7	F 127 and 128
F 8	F 170
F 9	F 173
F 10	F 175
F 11	F 176
F 12	F 191
F 13	F 201
F 14	F 202
F 15	F 207
F 16	F 213
F 17	F 214
F 18	F 215

FHG Fragment Numbers of the *Anon. Cont.*	Fragment Numbers in This Edition
F 1	F 171
F 2	F 172
F 3	F 174
F 4	F 177 and 178
F 5.1	F 179

FHG Fragment Numbers of the *Anon. Cont.*	Fragment Numbers in This Edition
F 5.2	F 180
F 5.3	F 181
F 6	F 182
F 7	F 183
F 8.1	F 184
F 8.2	F 185
F 9.1	F 186
F 9.2	F 187
F 9.3	F 188
F 9.4	F 189
F 10.1	F 190
F 10.2	F 192
F 10.3	F 193
F 10.4	F 194
F 10.5	F 195
F 10.6	F 196
F 11	F 197
F 12	F 198
F 13.1	F 199
F 13.2	F 200
F 13.3	F 203
F 13.4	F 204
F 13.5	F 205
F 13.6	F 206
F 14.1	F 208
F 14.2	F 209
F 14.3	F 210
F 15.1	F 211
F 15.2	F 212

LITERARY SOURCES

INSCRIPTIONS

MANUSCRIPTS

INDEX OF PEOPLE, GODS, AND PLACES